D0758752

The Disinherited Mind

Jede dumpfe Umkehr der Welt hat solche Enterbte,
denen das Frühere nicht und noch nicht das Nächste
    gehört.

[Each torpid turn of the world has such disinherited chil-
    dren,
to whom no longer what's been, and not yet what's com-
    ing, belongs.]

RILKE

Yet I felt no certainty about anything, demanding from
every single moment a new confirmation of my existence
. . . in truth, a disinherited son.

FRANZ KAFKA

ERICH HELLER

The Disinherited Mind

*Essays in Modern German
Literature and Thought*

BOWES & BOWES

LONDON

All rights reserved
ISBN 0 370 00211 3
Printed in Great Britain for
Bowes & Bowes (Publishers) Ltd.
9 Bow Street, London, WC2E 7AL
by Lowe & Brydone (Printers) Ltd.
London, NW10
First published 1952
Third edition 1971

ACKNOWLEDGMENTS

My thanks for permission to reprint previously published material are due to The Cambridge Journal, The Listener and The Times Literary Supplement. The Hogarth Press and Messrs. Secker & Warburg Ltd. have kindly allowed me to quote from English translations published by them; the former, from Rilke's *Duino Elegies,* translated by J. B. Leishman and Stephen Spender, from Rilke's *Sonnets to Orpheus* and Hölderlin's *Selected Poems,* both translated by J. B. Leishman; the latter, from Willa and Edwin Muir's renderings of Franz Kafka's *The Castle* and *The Great Wall of China.* In all these cases the use of mere fragments of translations has made it necessary for me to introduce occasional changes in order to get the precise emphasis required by my context. Thanks also are due to Messrs. Faber and Faber for permission to quote from T. S. Eliot's *Four Quartets.*

The number of friends, colleagues and pupils who, through conversations, questions and criticisms, have helped me in writing this book is too large for individual acknowledgments. They will easily recognize their share and, I hope, be sure of my gratitude. The debt, however, acknowledged by the dedication is truly immeasurable.

The essay "Rilke and Nietzsche" owes much to Professor Eudo C. Mason. Indeed, it was his book *Der Zopf des Münchhausen* and the ensuing correspondence with its author that gave the essay its direction. The knowledge that my conclusions would be different from his has not deterred this pre-eminent scholar and interpreter of Rilke from generously supplying me with much information and material. Even if he cannot accept all I have done with it, I should like him to accept the expression of my profound gratitude and of my respect for his convictions, which is unimpaired by disagreement.

Finally, I should like to thank my friends and colleagues, E. K. Bennett, of Gonville and Caius College, Cambridge, and R. J. Taylor, of University College, Swansea, for the great help they have given me at the proof-reading stage.

E. H.

CONTENTS

Anyone engaged in the study, teaching and criticism of literature as a University discipline is likely to become at some time or other aware of one fundamental problem raised by his own pursuits, of a difficulty that is all his own and is not, or at least not to the same extent, shared by his colleagues in other subjects. For however sincerely he may struggle against bias and prejudice in his own approach and appreciation, his work will still be very intimately related to his experiences in wider fields. It is true that his devotion to literature is capable of purging his affections of too narrowly subjective and emotional elements; yet his comprehension will remain largely determined by his own character, his spontaneous sympathies or antipathies, the happiness he has enjoyed or the disasters that have befallen him. And this, he will see, is no shortcoming of his own discipline, to be conquered in scientific campaigns or disguised by scientific masquerades, but is in fact its distinctive virtue. For the ultimate concern of his subject is neither facts nor classifications, neither patterns of cause and effect nor technical complexities. Of course, strict honesty in the face of facts and a certain mastery in dealing with their manifold interconnections are the indispensable qualifications of the literary scholar. In the end, however, he is concerned with the communication of a sense of quality rather than measurable quantity, and of meaning rather than explanation.

Thus he would be ill-advised to concentrate exclusively on those aspects of his discipline which allow the calm neutrality of what is indisputably factual and 'objective'. His business is, I think, not the avoidance of subjectivity, but its purification; not the shunning of what is disputable, but the cleansing and deepening of the dispute. As a teacher he is involved in a task which would appear impossible by the standards of the scientific laboratory: to teach what, strictly speaking, cannot be taught, but only 'caught', like a passion, a vice or a virtue. This 'impossibility' is the inspiration of his work. There are no methods that comprehend his subject; only methods, perhaps, that produce the intellectual pressure and temperature in which perception crystallizes into conviction and learning into a sense of value. Goethe tells of a Greek nobleman who was asked about the education of his children. 'Let them be instructed,' he said, 'in that which they will never be able to learn.'

The unifying theme of this book, then, is the sense of values as shown or embodied in the works of some modern German poets, writers and thinkers from Goethe to Kafka. Perhaps it would be more correct to say: the sense of the value of life. For I have stressed what appears to be one of the distinctive symptoms of modern literature and thought: the consciousness of life's increasing depreciation. If Thomas Aquinas saw the link between poets

B

and philosophers in their preoccupation with the marvellous, their modern successors seem united in the reverse; either they try systematically to strengthen, or desperately to ward off, the predominance of the prosaic. I deal with this problem in its most direct form in the essay 'Rilke and Nietzsche' (particularly in the discourses on the relation between thought, belief and poetry) and in the second section of the essay 'The World of Franz Kafka'.

I do not wish to suggest that the selections of this book can be justified on any other but personal grounds. Yet its choices are, I believe, representative enough to avoid the charge of arbitrariness. Arbitrary are merely its omissions. For I could have included, without losing sight of the central theme, many more names. In fact, I can hardly think of one major writer or thinker within this period of German literature whose works would not reflect the situation of mind and spirit which I have tried to describe within the limits of my choice. In a way it is even true to say that the silent centre of this book is Hölderlin; its theme and its hesitant hope are certainly contained in Hölderlin's lines:

Und nun denkt er zu ehren in Ernst die seeligen Götter,
  Wirklich und wahrhaft muss alles verkünden ihr Lob.

Aber wo sind sie? wo blühn die Bekannten, die Kronen
  des Festes?

Warum zeichnet, wie sonst, die Stirne des Mannes ein
  Gott nicht,
    Drückt den Stempel, wie sonst, nicht dem Getrof-
    fenen auf?
Oder er kam auch selbst und nahm des Menschen
  Gestalt an
    Und vollendet und schloss tröstend das himmlische
    Fest.

Aber Freund! wir kommen zu spät. Zwar leben die
  Götter,
    Aber über dem Haupt droben in anderer Welt.

Endlos wirken sie da und scheinens wenig zu achten,
  Ob wir leben, so sehr schonen die Himmlischen uns.

Denn nicht immer vermag ein schwaches Gefäss sie zu
    fassen,
  Nur zu Zeiten erträgt göttliche Fülle der Mensch.
Traum von ihnen ist drauf das Leben. Aber das Irrsal
  Hilft, wie Schlummer und stark machet die Noth und
    die Nacht.

                    Indessen dünket mir öfters
  Besser zu schlafen, wie so ohne Genossen zu seyn,
So zu harren und was zu thun indess und zu sagen,
  Weiss ich nicht und wozu Dichter in dürftiger Zeit?

Now will he strive in earnest to honour the dwellers in
    Heaven,
  Everything living must utter their praise, in word and
    in deed.

Where, though, where are they, the famous, those
    crowns of the banquet?

Why does a god no more inscribe the brow of a mortal,
  Setting his seal, as of old, on the victim chosen above?
Or he would come himself, assuming the shape of a
    mortal,
  Thus with solace and peace to crown the celestial
    feast.

But we, my friend, are too late. The gods, it is true, are
    living,
  Yet far above ourselves, away in a different world.
There they are endlessly active and seem but little re-
    gardful
  Whether we live or no, such is their tender concern,
Knowing that fragile vessels like us cannot always con-
    tain them,
  Only at times can man endure the abundance of
    gods.

Life thereafter is but to dream of them. Yet our wanderings
Help, like sleep, and anguish and night give strength.

Meanwhile, it seems to me often
Better to slumber than live without companions, like
this,
So to linger, and know not what to begin or to utter,
Or, in such spiritless times, why to be poet at all?

PREFACE
TO THE AMERICAN EDITION

This edition differs from the original version by including, as a kind of epilogue, "The Hazard of Modern
Poetry", a series of talks, printed as delivered, which were
first given on the B.B.C. Third Programme and repeated
as one of the Morris Gray Poetry Lectures at Harvard
University. They were published in *The Listener* and
again in the form of a booklet by Messrs. Bowes & Bowes,
London. It is by their kind permission that these talks are
now reprinted together with the book of which too they
are the original publishers.

"The Hazard of Modern Poetry", being in the nature of
a summing-up of the main themes of the book, repeats
some of its quotations and references. I can only hope
that the reader will find the repetitions more illuminating
than tiring. He will also find there an attempt to para-
phrase in English Rilke's poem *"Taube, die draussen
blieb,"* despairingly left without a translation in the essay
"Rilke and Nietzsche." The Postscript was written in the
place of individual replies to many a letter from kind,
puzzled and dissenting listeners and readers of the talks.
In so far as I have made literal use of their queries and
disagreements, I should like to acknowledge my thanks
to them.

For the convenience of the reader I have separated, throughout the book, footnotes (marked by asterisks) which have some bearing on the text from mere references to sources of quotations (marked by numbers). The latter, much more frequent than the first, are relegated to the Appendix and need not distract the reader's attention.

E. H.

PREFACE

TO THIS EDITION

This, the latest of a series of British and American editions, is, with one exception, a reprint of the text as it was published in America*. It differs from all previous editions by a new version, or rather extension, of the essay on Karl Kraus. I have joined with the original piece another essay on 'The Satirist in the Modern World' written for *The Times Literary Supplement*. It appeared there – anonymously, as it is the custom of the journal – on the front page of No. 2,675, dated May 8, 1953. This amalgamation I had carried out long before I knew that my contribution to the T.L.S. had also contributed to the poetry published by Hugh MacDiarmid (Dr. C. M. Grieve), the Scottish poet. His poem 'And above all, Karl Kraus' (from his cycle *In Memoriam James Joyce*) consists of 157 lines of which 149 lines are taken – with their identity substantially intact – from my essay. As this poem is contained in the Penguin Book *The Mid-Century English Poetry 1940-60, 1965 and 1968*, I feel I must at least mention this transformation of my essay into Hugh MacDiarmid's poetry in order to avoid the suspicion of plagiarism, an apparent hazard of modern prose.

E.H.

Northwestern University,
Evanston, Illinois,
September, 1970

* Meridian Books

GOETHE AND THE

IDEA OF SCIENTIFIC TRUTH

1

'1794—here at last was a year which I felt was going to compensate me by some diverting activities, some inspiration, some pleasure, for much that I had missed and suffered in the preceding years; and goodness knows I was badly in need of it.' This is how Goethe, in his *Annals*, begins his report on the year 1794. The modern reader can hardly fail to respond to Goethe's catalogue of grievances: the agitated restlessness of Europe; rumours of the approach of the enemy and of fussy aunts evacuated from more directly disturbed areas; the hasty selling of houses, the loss of friends through political partisanship; the clandestine distribution of French revolutionary manifestoes—'they even found their way to me,' Goethe exclaims, 'and this through people whom one

would never have suspected'; and above all the rule of
Robespierre, 'the terrors of which had so deprived the
world of any sense of joy that nobody felt like rejoicing
even at the downfall of the tyrant'. And in addition, the
distressing chaos, the obstreperous hollowness of the
German literary scene! Goethe had returned from Italy
with that vision of serenity and equipoise with which
he hoped he would conquer the national imagination,
which he had previously done so much to fill with unruly enthusiasm for suicidal lovers and rebellious knights
with fists of iron. But, alas, while the Master recuperated
in the sun of the South, the infection, the cold and the
fever, were spread by his disciples in the unregenerate
nordic climate. There was, for instance, that man Schiller, this 'vigorous but immature talent', as Goethe calls
him, whose drama *Die Räuber* 'disgusted me in the extreme', 'because he poured out over the country, in a
gushing, irresistible torrent, precisely those moral and
theatrical paradoxes which I had striven to eradicate
from my own work'. And there were more such offenders:
Heinse, for instance, whose *Ardinghello* was hateful to
Goethe because its author used his art for the purpose
of 'giving affected glamour to crass sensuality and abstruse modes of thought'. 'I was terrified,' Goethe continues, 'by the hubbub they caused in the country, and
by the applause with which the monstrous creations of
their fancy were received by wild undergraduates and
genteel ladies of the court alike.' 'Imagine the state I was
in! I had hoped to cultivate and to communicate the
purest ideas; and now I found myself squeezed tight between Ardinghello and Franz Moor.' 'It seemed as though
all my labours would be lost, all the things towards
which, and all the ways in which, I had educated myself would be abolished and frustrated.' Goethe's intense
dissatisfaction, his conviction of futility, culminates in the
wish to abandon 'the contemplation of the arts and the
practice of poetry altogether'—and we know that this was

more than the fleeting whim of a disgruntled Olympian
—'for there appeared to be no chance whatsoever to compete with those wild productions of disorganized genius'.

Yet Goethe's desolation was caused not merely by the
unseemly behaviour of the world around him; there was
an inner uncertainty too—an uncertainty which, in one
form or another, was to provide the rest of his life with a
deep dilemma, a source of inspiration as well as confusion, now raising his poetry and thought to those
heights to which only the force of tension could carry
them, now again trapping his genius in a tangle of in-
soluble contradictions. His doubts about the worth-while-
ness, indeed the possibility, of continuing his work as a
poet will recur, and the blame will not always fall on the
Robespierres of this world and other poets' successful
Robbers. Now, in the year 1794, the dilemma took this
form: 'The conflict which my scientific efforts had brought
into my life was as yet by no means resolved; for my
dealings with nature began to make claims on *all* my
inner faculties'.

Thus, for the time being, Goethe was divided within
himself, and out of harmony with nature; for his great
Nature did not take the slightest notice of the afflictions
of this year: 'The crops of the fields prospered magnificently, everything ripened a month too early, the fruit
of the trees grew to perfection; apricots and peaches,
melons and even chestnuts offered themselves in choice
profusion, and also among the years of exquisite vintage
1794 has its place'.

The exquisite vintage is reassuring; Goethe's anger at
Schiller's success in the theatre had nothing to do with
sour grapes; in any case, it seems certain that this year,
in which Nature was in so exuberant a mood, could not
possibly end for Goethe on a note of unrelieved gloom.
But it is a coincidence, as neatly ironical as the sweetest
apricots ripening in that summer of acrimonious discontent, that the light fell into Goethe's darkness through

the arrival in his life of the author of the repulsive *Robbers*: Friedrich Schiller. This is what Goethe's diary says: 'In the midst of all these oppressions and conflicts the suddenly developing friendship with Schiller gave more to me than I could have dared hope for; it ranks among the most precious gifts of fortune which my later years held in store for me'. The irony of fate is indeed profound, and deeper still than appears at first glance. For, as we have seen, Goethe's depression was partly due to his fear that his absorbing interest in scientific studies was feeding on his poetic resources; and now it is in a meeting of a society of natural scientists that the friendship begins with the man to whom four years later he was to express his gratitude for having cured the paralysis of his poetic genius. 'And this happy occasion came about through my work concerning the Metamorphosis of Plants.' After that meeting—it took place in Jena and some scientist lectured—Goethe and Schiller, leaving the room, happened to reach the door at the same time. 'A conversation ensued; he, Schiller, appeared to have taken an interest in the lecture, and remarked, very intelligently, perspicaciously and to me most agreeably, that such a dissecting manner of dealing with Nature could not possibly attract the layman. I replied that this manner may be uncanny even to the initiates, and that perhaps there was still the possibility of another method, one which would not tackle Nature by merely dissecting and particularizing, but show her at work and alive, *manifesting herself in her wholeness in every single part of her being.* He said he would like to learn more about this, though he did not conceal his doubts. He would not admit that all this emerged, as I insisted, *from experience itself.*'

In no time at all, it seems, their conversation had reached the crucial point. This is a dramatic climax in the history of German thought and letters: Goethe and Schiller, whose names will for ever mark the summit of literary achievement to which the genius of their nation, and probably of Europe, could rise in the second half of the eighteenth century, wandering through the streets of Jena, really in contact with each other for the first time. That it had not happened before—in spite of some previous chance meetings—was the outcome of strategy on the part of Goethe, who was determined to avoid the man from whom he was separated 'by more than the earth's diameter' and whom he found guilty not only of theatrical excess, but also of philosophical wrongheadedness. Schiller's essay *Anmut und Würde* (The Graceful and the Exalted) had displeased him by its Kantian abstractness, but above all by its antagonism to Nature, in which Goethe, significantly enough, saw hostility towards himself; 'and if it was *not* aimed at me, so much the worse!' But there they go, engrossed in what seems merely a discussion about the growth of vegetables, but is, in fact, about the human mind in its search after truth.

They arrive at Schiller's house and, still talking, Goethe enters. This is Goethe's account of the occasion: 'I explained to him with great vivacity the Metamorphosis of Plants and, with a few characteristic strokes of the pen, conjured up before his eyes a symbolical plant. He listened, and looked at it all with great interest and intelligence; but when I had ended, he shook his head saying: This has nothing to do with *experience*, it is an *idea*. I raised my eye-brows, somewhat annoyed. For he had put his finger on precisely the point which separated us. His argument from *Anmut und Würde* came to my mind; the old anger began to stir, but I constrained myself and replied: Well, so much the better; it means that I have ideas without knowing it, and can even *see them with my eyes*.' They carried on their discussion, with great polemical obstinacy on each side. Goethe reports that some of Schiller's sentences made him 'quite unhappy'; for instance, the following: 'How can one ever equate experience with ideas? For an idea is characterized precisely by the fact that experience can never be fully congruous to it.' And Goethe, in his account of the discussion, reflects that 'if he takes for an idea what to me is experience, then there must, after all, prevail some mediation, some relationship between the two'.[1]

At this point Goethe's account of his first conversation with Schiller breaks off. Owing to his new friendship, this year of troubles and tribulations ends, as he says, with a foretaste of spring. And, indeed, there will be flowers and colours; but also a theory of colours and much speculation about the objects of Nature. In the period to come Goethe was to write, if not his most popular, yet his profoundest poetry. The danger of inspiration drying up in later years, the fate of Wordsworth, is averted. The dilemma of which we have heard appears to be solved. There will be poetry *and* science— a science, it is true, radically at odds with the scientific temper of the age; a science doubtful and often unambiguously wrong in its results, but of immense importance for our understanding of the intellectual and spiritual situation of the age, and of the nature of poetic and scientific truth. Goethe's science has contributed nothing substantial to the scientific progress between his time and ours, and nothing whatsoever to the advancement of techniques for the mastery and exploitation of Nature; but he did, by his opposition to contemporary science, lay bare in his time, with remarkable precision, the very roots of that crisis and revolution in scientific method in which the twentieth-century scientist finds himself involved. In the history of science from Newton to Einstein, Goethe, the scientist, plays a Cinderella part, showing up the success and splendour of his rich relations, but also the potential *hubris* inherent in their pursuits. There may come a day when this Cinderella story will find the conclusion proper to such tales—but perhaps not before the new ecclesia of technology has had its consummate triumph by bringing to their explosive fusion the iciest mathematical abstractions and the hot appetite for power.

We left the first disputation between Goethe and Schiller where Goethe himself chose to leave it. Perhaps it was a wise break, for the next step would lead still deeper into the region of metaphysics, an area which is strictly out of bounds for the brave soldiers of the positivist age, and full of the unspeakable dreads and bogies which inhabit the nursery-tales told to the children of science. But it is, at the same time, the very workshop where that invisible mould is cast and re-cast from which all our organized intellectual activities take their shape. It may be rewarding to ignore the warnings and enter it for a while. First, however, it is advisable to look at that symbolical plant which Goethe had sketched out for Schiller, and which, in spite of Goethe's 'characteristic strokes of the pen', remained an 'idea' for that disciple of Immanuel Kant, even in the face of Goethe's assurance that he could see it with his eyes.

2

Palermo, April 17th, 1787—seven years before Goethe's first meeting with Schiller. This is what the chronicle of the *Italian Journey* says under that date:

'It is a real disaster for a man to be tempted by a host of conflicting demons. This morning I went to the Public Gardens, calmly and firmly determined to carry on with my poetic designs; yet in no time another ghost, which had secretly pursued me all these days, had caught hold of me. The many plants which elsewhere I used to see only in pots, and mostly under glass, grow here cheerfully under the open sky, and, living as they are really meant to live, reveal themselves to us with greater clarity. Confronted with so many new shapes, I was once more overcome by my old whimsical fascination: might I not discover among this crowd the *Urpflanze* (that original plant from which all others are derived)? After all, it must exist; how could I otherwise know that this shape and that are both plants if they were not all organized according to one principle?' And even then the cry of the distracted poet: 'My poetic intention had come to nothing. . . . Why are we modern people so open to distraction, why so easily provoked into pursuits which are bound to lead nowhere?'[2] Yet this particular diversion did seem to lead somewhere. Exactly a month later, on May 17th, 1787, he wrote from Naples to Herder: 'And then I must confide to you that I am very close to discovering the secret of the creation and organization of plants. Under this sky one is able to make the most beautiful observations. The crucial point from which everything else must needs spring, I have already established beyond doubt; the rest too I can see in outline; only a few points have still to be ascertained. The *Urpflanze* is to be the strangest creature in the world; Nature herself shall be jealous of it. After this model it will be possible to *invent* plants *ad infinitum*, which will all be consistent, that is, they *could* exist even if they have no actual existence; they would not be mere picturesque or poetic shadows or dreams, but would possess an *inner truth and necessity. And the same law will be applicable to everything alive.*'[3]

These enthusiastic outbursts seem to bode ill for the scientific work that was to be based on the discovery made in Italy. Yet, when three years later, in 1790, Goethe's *Metamorphosis of Plants* appeared, it was as quiet in tone, as systematic in approach, as painstaking in minute observation, as any classical scientific composition. Its central idea is that all the single parts which constitute a plant are derived from one original formation, and that all varieties of plants, beginning with those of the simplest organization and ascending to the most complex structures, are the result of a gradual metamorphosis or transformation, brought about by the *re-*

sponsiveness of the organism to the restrictions put upon it, or the advantages offered to it by the surrounding world, the soil, the weather, the insects. This responsiveness, however, is not a mere giving-in to external influences, it is rather like a creative conversation between within and without, a kind of dialectical education through which the individual form becomes in actuality what from the very beginning it had been potentially. For what is within and what is without are for Goethe merely poles of one and the same thing:

Natur hat weder Kern
Noch Schale,
Alles ist sie mit einemmale.[4]

[Nature has neither kernel nor shell; she is everything at once.]

Classifying the various types of metamorphosis as progressive, retrogressive and arbitrary, he starts with investigations into the manifold forms of the cotyledon, the seed-leaf of plants, and seeks to establish its development from shapelessness to shape, from something that looks, as it were, like nothing, to something that distinctly looks like a leaf; he observes a gradual increase of this embryonic leaf in the direction of 'leafishness', an ever clearer articulation, in which the slow emergence of greenness plays its part, until it becomes the full-grown leaf of the plant. It is this very leaf which in its turn is modified and diversified into sepal, petal, pistil and stamen; he shows us how, for instance in the carnation, sepals merge with petals, and how they can be met, in an effort to produce a full corolla, by an identical transformation of filament, anther and stigma. 'Everything is leaf,' is Goethe's final finding, but he is perfectly aware of the *verbal* embarrassments and misunderstandings

c

that such a theory must needs produce; he himself anticipated the objections which Helmholtz was later to
raise to this monistic simplification, showing the tauto-
logical character of Goethe's theory. Any definition of
that unique vegetable organ, Goethe's 'leaf', Helmholtz
says, which is to comprehend all other aspects of the
plant, would have to end up by stating that it is 'a lateral
appendix of the plant axle'—in fact, the same as the
flower itself. 'And in order to see that no Goethe was
needed.' [5]

Even if one grants that Goethe's theory is untenable,
Helmholtz's criticism makes no sense either, but only
shows how unbridgeable is the gulf between Goethe's
vision and what can be comprehended through the mental operations of modern science. The two never meet, and
polemic becomes an intellectual fidgeting about in strictly
separated and closed compartments. It is obvious that, if
Goethe says 'leaf', he does not mean a 'lateral appendix
of the plant axle'; he means, or rather sees before his
eyes, what is the Platonic idea of a plant in its simplest
and, in its perfect simplicity, most perfect form. Goethe
himself felt over and over again with naïve dismay and
painful poignancy how ill-served *his* science was by the
established methods of scientific exposition. His inquisi-
tive gaze was focused on a sphere of experience which
defies that logical analysis proper to the sphere of modern science, and whose language is fundamentally untranslatable into the logically respectable medium of
polite abstractions. This will be still more obvious when
we come to Goethe's campaigns in physics and to his
Thirty Years' War against Newton.

For the time being we can see Goethe desperately trying to straighten out the vicious circle of tautologies in
which, very much later, Helmholtz showed the 'scientific
fallacy' of his omnipresent leaf to move. In one of the
concluding paragraphs of his *Metamorphosis of Plants*
Goethe says: 'It is evident that we should need a general

word with which to denote that organism which is capable of transforming itself into such a variety of shapes, and against which we could set up all the phenomena into which it unfolds. For we can say just as well that a stamen is a contracted petal as we can say of the petal that it is a stamen in the state of expansion. . . .'[6] And among his posthumous notes there was found the following jotting: 'Leaf as a definite organism in the empirical sense, as a determinable organism in a higher sense'.[7] Add to this what he says about the *Urpflanze* in the *History of my Botanical Studies*, written during the last years of his life: 'As all these manifold forms of plants can be subsumed under one idea, it became increasingly clear to me that my intuition could be aided by a yet higher means—a possibility which hovered before my mind's eye in the concrete shape of an ideal *Urpflanze*. I followed up all the changing forms as they appeared to me, and at last, at the end of my journey, in Sicily, the *original identity* of all parts of the plant stood revealed before me'[8]—and Goethe's struggle to convey in scientific terms the intuitive nature of his vision emerges in all its pathetic beauty.

His difficulty is, in reverse, the same as that which obstructs the way of the modern physicist when he sets out to translate the findings of his science into the language of concrete images; then we are in no time in a Walt Disney world of colourful absurdities, watching the voids of infinitely finite space heaving and waving with nothing to heave and wave with, but providing in this odd manner the ideal medium for insubstantial substance to travel through with unimpeded speed; or we applaud the surprisingly clever devices by which our universe expands, where nobody would have expected anything to expand into; or we are entertained by the merry-go-rounds of tiny nonentities, performing from time to time the most unpredictable antics, for no obvious reason but just to exercise their own free will.

If one takes into account the underlying incongruity between Goethe's vision and the medium in which modern science operates, and, resulting from it, Goethe's own indecision as to the nature of the *Urpflanze*, now treated as though it were the pragmatical ancestor of all plants, and now again like their Platonic idea, then it is still more surprising to see how fruitful Goethe's biology was. He is one of the first to be fully conscious of the morphological problem in biological studies. It is the unsolved problem and the inspiration of all theories of evolution, concerned, as it is, with the living *form*, its genesis and transformation. 'To recognize living forms *as such*, to see in context their visible and tangible parts, to perceive them as manifestations of *something within*, and thus to master them, to a certain extent, in their *wholeness* through a concrete vision (*Anschauung*)': [9] this is how he introduces the purpose of his morphological studies. Their pursuit clearly presupposes more than an analysis of sensory preceptions. Goethe's morphology, with its insistence on the relevance of 'something within', was incommensurable with the scientific methods of his age; and Goethe knew it. 'How few,' he exclaims, 'draw their inspiration from what is visible to the mind alone!' 'He who concentrates his powers of understanding entirely on the particular and on those exact observations which can be analysed, tends to regard as a nuisance everything that, emerging from an idea, leads back to an idea.' [10] His biological interest is centred in that *inner* principle which determines the organization of living forms. Indeed, he is aware, as we have seen, of the perpetually modifying forces working from without, but remains fascinated by what he calls 'the self-revealed mystery' (*das offenbare Geheimnis*) which maintains the fundamental unity of the created shape, its idea, through all its variations and modifications.

Thus Goethe's biology has its somewhat puzzling place in as close a neighbourhood to Plato and Aristotle, on the one hand, as to Darwin on the other—just as through his literary output he divides the camps of critics by his mystifying kinship to both Homer and Stendhal. Hold beside one another the two following biological statements of his: 'What determines the living form is its innermost nucleus; the external elements modify its appearances' [11] and, at the other end of the scale, 'The more highly organized beings advance a few evolutionary stages, leaving behind their fellow-creatures,' [12] and you see his mind most busily occupied in a splendidly equipped half-way house of which, however, you cannot be quite sure whether it looks like the Academy of ancient Greece or the Cavendish Laboratory at Cambridge. It would be unwise to see the first utterance, with its emphasis on the decisive power of the innermost nucleus of an organism, as an ingenious anticipation of genes and chromosomes; it is, in fact, far nearer to Aristotle's entelechy than to modern genetics. And concerning the second quotation with its Darwinian ring (and it is only one out of many that could be quoted), the interpreters of Goethe's science are by no means united; those who see in Goethe's works nothing but the second coming of the spirit of antiquity suggest that he would have rejected Darwin's theory *in toto*; others, for whom Goethe is the first-born of modernity, claim him as one of the direct ancestors of the *Origin of Species*. It is more likely that Darwin's work would have attracted as well as repelled Goethe; attracted, because it supplied powerful evidence for Goethe's fondest belief in the fundamental oneness of all that lives, and above all in the uniformity prevailing within each type of living creature. It was with rhapsodic enthusiasm that in 1784 he had reported to Herder his first scientific triumph: the discovery of the *os intermaxillare* (the intermaxillary bone) in the human skull which finally showed the complete structural identity of all vertebrates, including human beings. The assumed absence in the human skeleton of this peculiar bone of contention had, in a generation of scientists afflicted by an unbelievable feebleness of spiritual convictions, been the last shred of proof that they had been created by God according to a very special anatomical design.

And yet, Goethe would also have been repelled by Darwin's theory. He would have seen in it yet another, and very decisive, step along that road which, he believed, would lead to spiritual perdition. No, Goethe was not afraid of the first chapter of Genesis being discredited as a set book by the Honours schools of geology, biology and anthropology; but he was terrified that experimental science in alliance with a mechanistic philosophy of nature, so successful in posing and answering questions about the 'How' of things, so prolific in establishing expected and unexpected *relationships between* this, that or the other, might finally abolish in the world all creative interest in *what* this, that or the other *are* and *mean*. For Darwin's theory was bound to feed the body of superstitious beliefs that had grown rampant ever since medieval scholasticism suffered its final defeat at the hands of Francis Bacon.

Willingly or unwillingly, Darwin had to give still greater force to that system of unsystematized, inarticulate metaphysical fallacies which one might term the Creed of the Ontological Invalidity; both in the sense that it dismisses *a priori* as invalid all ontological assertions, i.e. assertions about the nature and meaning of Being (as different from the laws governing the processes, connections and interconnections of the phenomenal world, of all that becomes, develops, evolves), as well as in the sense that it has made an incurable invalid of that faculty of the human intelligence which, grasping their relevance, is capable of responding positively to questions asked about *what* the world is. To such questions the modern intelligence is prone to respond with that mixture of shame, embarrassment, revulsion and arrogance which is the characteristic reaction of impotence to unfortunately unmanageable demands. This invalid has been left ever since in the nursing care of unhappy poets, dreamers or religious eccentrics if he was not satisfied with the treatment he received as an outpatient of the Church. Once man's ability to respond creatively to the ontological mystery had been stunted into something that produced merely an irritated state of mystification, he was left to the spiritual destructiveness of that battle raging within himself: between the conviction of being nothing in the vastness of the universe, and the natural urge which, prompted by the ungrace of self-assertion, persuades him of his all-importance. To be nothing and yet everything—this seeming paradox is the pride and the humility of the creature before a God of infinite power and infinite love; but it is the spiritual death suffered by man in the incessant struggle between arrogance and humiliation, in his exposure to the mighty lovelessness of a chance constellation of energy. It is this gloomy story that is told by modern literature from Nietzsche to Kafka, from Proust to Sartre, from Yeats to T. S. Eliot, from Dostoevsky—to his being banned by a government which has decreed that the ontological mystery is to be abolished.

This state of spiritual affairs accounts for Goethe's strange position in the history of modern science. He appointed himself a kind of emissary of Being in a territory of the human mind which had given itself up to the alluring mechanics of becoming, progressing, evolving and revolving. He too realized—and more profoundly than the world around him—that growth, transformation, metamorphosis, was the element of life. One of his greatest poems, *Selige Sehnsucht*, ends with the verse:

Und solang du das nicht hast,
Dieses: Stirb und Werde!
Bist du nur ein trüber Gast
Auf der dunklen Erde.[13]

meaning that we remain but dim shadows on a dark planet as long as we have not experienced within ourselves, not consummated through our being, many a death and many a resurrection. 'Die and rise again!' But this sequence of dying and becoming, of systole and diastole, of breathing in and breathing out, this polarity of life within man and outside him, is for Goethe not the rhythm of a motion prompted by external, and spiritually neutral, forces, directed towards an unknown destination in an as yet empty future, but is held together at every moving point and at every fleeting moment by a centre of stillness:

Und alles Drängen, alles Ringen
Ist ewige Ruh in Gott dem Herrn.[14]

[And all this struggle, whirl and stir is infinite peace in God.]

That man is related to the animal world (and to all that is alive) Goethe knew before Darwin; the theory that he is descended (if anything, *ascended*, Goethe would have said) from some sort of ape-like creature would have roused in him a technical interest, the same that he took in the colours with which the painter painted and the material in which the sculptor hewed. But beyond that he would, I think, have regarded it as the kind of knowledge not worth having. If it were not preposterous to add to the unmanageable quantity of things that Goethe has said, a few guesses about what he might have said, it would be very tempting to let one's imagination play on the possible responses which Darwin would have evoked in Goethe. It might bring out very clearly one of the most important aspects of Goethe's idea of truth. And as I have already been unguarded enough to say that he would have dismissed a great deal of the knowledge supplied by Darwin, not as incorrect, but as worthless, let me dwell a little on this apparently outrageous paradox. Paradox or not, there *is* a sense in which Darwin's theory, though it be perfectly correct, may yet be blatantly *untrue*. There is a very simple mystery behind this assertion, shocking to common sense only because common sense in each epoch consists in an astonishingly complex agglomeration of highly sophisticated half-truths. One such half-truth in which our common sense indulges (and much in our higher education is based on it, including its 'crisis') is the doctrine that any kind of knowledge, as long as it supplies us with correctly ascertained facts, is worth teaching and learning, and that the more such correct facts we accumulate, the nearer we come to Truth. We have become so democratic in our habits of thought that we are convinced that Truth is determined through a plebiscite of facts.

To all this Goethe's idea of Truth, including, to his own bewilderment and ours, 'scientific' truth, is in radical opposition. Nobody familiar with Goethe's writings can possibly overlook the deep-rooted antagonism of his genius to the mental habits predominant in his age; but neither must one ignore his occasional strains, embarrassments and confusions, caused by the simultaneous desire to realize to the full his citizenship in the contemporary world. Very often in Goethe's works—with the exception of his lyrical poetry—there comes a point where the innate tendency of his genius and his mundane wisdom get into each other's way, producing artistic discords. Take, for instance, his *Tasso*: here the emotional defeat of the poet is meant to carry the message that even poetical souls should heed the ways of the world; yet this defeat gives birth to such exquisite poetry, and the executive organs of the victorious world appear at times so unconvincing and even petty, that often, instead of being spontaneously persuaded by the instruction of wisdom, one longs to have a soul as sensitive, as alive and as innocently uncompromising as Tasso's. To be

Tasso, the poet, *and* Antonio, the worldling, was Goethe's consciously accepted programme. But how is the poet to remain in the world if the world becomes more unpoetic every day? How is one to keep spiritual communion with the Earth Spirit, and at the same time outphysic Newton? Only if Tasso was as much prepared to learn his lesson from Antonio as the Newtonians in their turn were prepared to listen to the poet. Undoubtedly, the world is made of harder stuff than the poetic imagination, and is altogether too dark a place to suit to perfection a soul asking from beginning to end, and with its very last words, for 'more light'; therefore leave the light alone in its unsynthetic whiteness, and the colours, the offspring of light and darkness.

Behind Goethe's scientific experiments and results, presented in a detached, sober and even laboriously pedantic fashion, one can discern clearly the strategic plan of a man engaged in a campaign for restoring the balance of power between analytical reason and creative imagination, between the 'merely concrete' and the 'idea'. For 'the better part of human nature' will always try 'to bestow upon the concrete the honour of the idea', as he wrote to Schiller (February 10th, 1798), and 'pursue its inalienable right . . . to penetrate to the point where idea and object are as much at one as they can possibly be' (February 14th, 1798). For him all things had an ideal character, not merely within an actual work of art, but also as potential subjects for a work of art. The anxiety that the world, in the course of its increasing analytical disruption, may approach the point where it would become poetically useless, and a barren place for the human affections to dwell in, informs Goethe's scientific motives and makes him persist in an activity which, for long periods, to the detriment of his poetic creativeness and to his own dismay, 'absorbs all my inner faculties'. William Blake, unknown to Goethe, but his brother-in-arms against Newton, found things easier. He was a medieval peasant compared with Goethe, who had so big a share in mundane sophistication. For Blake the inventor of modern physics was simply party to a conspiracy of spiritual sin, a mythological ambassador, the second person in the Trinity of Evil, flanked by Bacon and Locke. But then, Blake saw angels in pear-trees, Goethe only 'ideas'. For him it could not be enough to say that modern physics was wicked; it had to be proven wrong by experimental methods. Yet somewhere, behind all the scientific paraphernalia, he too denounces sin where he appears to expose, by sinning himself in a slightly modified fashion, the faultiness of a scientific theory.

But there is a dimension of experience where, on the other side of tricky philosophical speculation and rational argumentation, it becomes self-evident that what is not right cannot be true. It is the moment of comprehending what the indefinable good life is. Then there is no doubt that a man, given up to fascinations which exercise only those of his faculties which have the least bearing on what he is as a person, namely on his affections, his passions, his beliefs, his imagination—the least bearing, in fact, on the truth in which and by which he is a person —is merely digging away in the gulf between him and the good life. For Goethe all knowledge which cannot be assimilated in a concord of all the human faculties of understanding, heightening and cleansing them all in their mutual interplay, man's 'senses and reason, his imagination and his critical intelligence', as he puts it; all knowledge which will only cause a man 'to fret away his days in the narrowest and most joyless limitation' [15] is fundamentally worthless and undeserving of the name of truth. Can man, in this sense, assimilate, 'realize', his descent from the apes? Does he know better—not how he came to be, but what he *is*? Has the mathematical waving of a nondescript medium anything to do with the light and colour as man experiences them and as they affect him? These simple-minded questions carry the flavour of that simple mystery which, as I have said, was at the bottom of Goethe's conviction that there was neither grace nor truth in that type of science which he took so much unrewarded trouble to oppose.

3

Goethe's *Theory of Colours* which appeared in 1810 and of which he said one year before his death that it was as old as the world, is based—as all his scientific theories—on what he calls an *Urphänomen*, an idea so fundamental to the *quality* of a group of phenomena that the human mind is ill-advised to penetrate beyond it. It is that idea which, manifesting itself through the phenomena themselves, Goethe can, as he said to Schiller, see 'with his own eyes'. One step further, and we have lost sight of the world in which man *actually* lives, of everything that matters to him as a human being, of the sights, sounds, touches, smells, tastes, loves and hatreds—finding ourselves instead in an unrealizable infinity of potential abstractions. Thus the *Urphänomen* marks for Goethe the point where the observer is still in contact with what he observes, and beyond which the *real* relationship between a human being and an object of nature ceases, with the object no longer being what it is and the human mind establishing itself as a subjective tyrant: the physicist becomes the task-master of nature, collects experiences, hammers and screws them together and thus, by 'insulating the experiment from man, and attempting to get to know nature merely through artifices and instruments', engineers what Goethe calls 'the greatest disaster of modern physics'.[16] Goethe regards it as his own scientific mission to 'liberate the phenomena once and for all from the gloom of the empirico-mechanico-dogmatic torture chamber'.[17] After him, he hopes, scholars will refer to the Newtonian interlude in science as 'the pathology of experimental physics'.[18]

The *Urphänomen* underlying Goethe's *Theory of Colours* is the polarity between light and darkness. Light for him is the bright, white radiance of a sunny day, not that ray distilled by Newton, forced through the tiniest holes and tortured by complicated mechanisms. That white light should be a concoction of various colours is to Goethe 'a manifest absurdity'. It is not the colours which produce the white light, but the white light which produces the colours. 'Colours are the actions and sufferings of light',[19] he says, the result of its meeting with darkness. Thus darkness is not merely defined as the absence of light, it is a creative force in its own right. Darkness interferes with light through all the shades of opaqueness provided by various media. When Goethe, having studied for the first time, and misunderstood, Newton, looked through a prism he was taken aback by the fact that the white wall still appeared white. Colours appeared only where the whiteness of the wall came to an end at the frontier of something darker: the window-frame. Thus a demarcation line is necessary for colours to emerge, the frontier between light and darkness. There are only two fundamental colours, yellow and blue, yellow emerging at the point where light has to yield some of its territory to darkness, and blue where light makes its first tentative inroad into blackness. By intensification and mixing one obtains all the other colours; allow more and more darkness to intrude into yellow and you get orange and red, and give light a better chance in its combat with black, and violet and a bluish red appear. Mix the two elemental colours, yellow and blue, and you have green. Thus Goethe arrives at his colour-cycle where yellow and blue, red and violet, green and what he calls purple, face one another; they are complementary colours. It is all very delightful and very obvious: you need only look at the sun, setting behind the vapours of the evening; it turns yellow, orange, red as the opaqueness of the atmosphere increases; look at the smoke rising from the chimney of your neighbour's house; now it is a light bluish-grey colour, and now again almost black, according to the density of the opaque particles which it carries.

Though it is delightful and obvious, it is yet quite useless to the mathematical physicist. Less useless were Goethe's theories to the physiologist; for he was the first to treat seriously of the *active* role which the eye assumes in the creation of light- and colour-effects. The opening section of his work is devoted to what he calls 'physiological colours', as distinct from physical and chemical colours, and it is this section which inspired the work of Johannes Müller, the founder of the theory of specific sense-energies. Through him Goethe, ignored by the physicist, still plays his part in modern physiopsychology (and, of course, in aesthetics, an aspect of the problem of colours to which the last section of Goethe's work is devoted and which abounds, as one would expect, in the most penetrating observations about the emotional value of colour and colour-compositions—very similar in approach and results to the theorizing on the subject by Leonardo da Vinci, whose writings on colour seem to have been unknown to Goethe).

It may have become clear by now that Goethe's physics, though anti-Newtonian in motivation, is, in fact, not anti-mathematical, but, as it were, a-mathematical, which is as much as to say that it is not physics at all—at least, not in the now accepted sense of the word. Newton's and Goethe's theories never meet, except at some points of confusion on the part of Goethe. I have attempted to say something about the nature and motive of Goethe's opposition, his method and approach. Yet there is more to it, and it is this 'more' which is at the very centre of Goethe's idea of truth, of which we have already seen some facets. In order to approach that centre more closely, we have to risk that long postponed plunge into metaphysics which loomed darkly before us when we left Goethe and Schiller debating the question whether the *Urpflanze* was an 'idea' or something 'real'.

The preface to Goethe's *Theory of Colours* contains the following key-passage: 'It is the strangest claim in the world—raised sometimes, but never lived up to even by those who raise it—that one should present experiences without any theoretical link between them, and leave it to the reader, or the pupil, to form his own convictions. But the mere looking at a thing is of no use whatsoever. Looking at a thing gradually merges into contemplation, contemplation into thinking, thinking is establishing connections, and thus it is possible to say that every attentive glance which we cast on the world is an act of theorizing. This, however, ought to be done with consciousness, self-criticism, freedom, and, to use a daring word, with *irony*—yes, all these faculties are necessary if abstraction, which we dread, is to be rendered innocuous, and the result which we hope for is to emerge with as much liveliness as possible.' [20]

Goethe, with all his insistence on objectivity, concreteness of thought (*Gegenständlichkeit*), with his un-Kantian confusion—so exasperating to Schiller—of transcendence and immanence, idea and experience, with his repeated protestations that 'philosophy is not my métier', in this passage gives himself away as a profound philosopher. 'Theorizing' is inherent in all human experience, and the highest intellectual achievement, he says elsewhere, 'would be to comprehend that everything factual is already theory'.[21]

Now Goethe had no distinct historical interests, but his *History of the Theory of Colours* may well be the first history of scientific method. It is, though the student of Goethe is apt to avoid it carefully, in parts an astonishingly interesting book. Read with one's attention focused on certain problems, it exposes the naïve fallacy of the still predominant absolute belief in the pragmatic test. One knows, of course, how many scientific theories have, for very long periods of time, stood the test of experience until they had to be discarded owing to man's decision, not merely to make other experiments, but *to have different experiences*; one also knows how often, after having lain for whole epochs in the cosmic dustbin of untruth, a theory, in one form or another, has been fetched back in triumph. For more unsophisticated aesthetic demands the game of musical chairs in which, ever since Newton and Huygens, the corpuscles and waves of light have found themselves involved—until, by a blatant breach of the rules of the game, they simply sat down together on one seat—may be as entertaining as the outdated but certainly loftier delight of musical spheres. And has not Einstein shown that the whole quarrel between Rome and Galileo was merely the outcome of a scientific misunderstanding?

But it is not only this exuberant dance of scientific hypotheses which is revealed by Goethe's history of science. What, above all, emerges most clearly is the fact that every scientific theory is merely the surface rationalization of a metaphysical substratum of beliefs, conscious or unconscious, about the nature of the world. And it is these beliefs too, these models of reality constructed in human minds and souls, which live and prosper for vast stretches of history in perfect pragmatic integrity, and, to a remarkable extent, *create*, not find and accept, the shape of the external world. The totems and taboos of savages, the pyramids of Egypt, the Acropolis of Athens, the cathedral of Chartres *pragmatically* prove as much, or as little, of the ultimate nature of reality as any modern scientific experiment. It is indeed amazing how malleable the world is and how easily it models and remodels itself according to the inner vision of man, how readily it responds to his 'theorizing' ! Thus the most important advice which an educator can give to his pupils may easily be: Be careful how you interpret

the world; it *is* like that. One usually assumes that the
beliefs or unbeliefs of modern man originate in the scientific discoveries made in the seventeenth century; it may
be equally correct to say that the scientific discoveries
of the seventeenth century could not have been made
without the vision of reality, held by man, having previously undergone a radical change. There is perhaps a
direct line linking the minds of the Reformers of the sixteenth century, invoking the authority of the Bible against
the tradition of the Church, to the mind of Francis Bacon claiming the authority of nature against the tenets
of scholastic philosophy; from Luther's biblical pragmatism to Bacon's natural pragmatism, and from Rome
being discredited as the focus of Christendom to the
earth being dislodged from its central position in the
universe.

Goethe's *History of the Theory of Colours* gives us a
few chapters of this Odyssey of the human mind. 'The
history of the world must be rewritten from time to time,'
he says, 'not because many events of the past are being
rediscovered, but because new vistas are opening up,
new ways of looking at things, which show the past in
a different light.' [22] Of Bacon he says: 'In the second
half of the sixteenth century the emancipation of the
individual progresses. Everyone comfortably enjoys what
has been gained, and rushes through the liberated spaces;
the disinclination to acknowledge authority becomes
more and more marked, and as one has protested in religion, so one will protest, at all costs, in science, and at
last Bacon of Verulam dares to wipe out, as if with a
sponge, everything that had been inscribed upon the
tables of mankind.' [23] And in one of his diary jottings he
anticipates with remarkable precision what in our century Whitehead has called the Fallacy of Misplaced Concreteness, the fatal illusion of an age which accepts the
sketch of the model of reality that it has drawn itself, its
own theoretical presuppositions, as the concrete nature

D

of reality. Goethe says: 'Have thought about fiction and science. The disaster they cause comes from the need of reflective reason which creates, for its own use, a sort of image, but will afterwards set it up as true and concrete.' [24] Or again: 'However fully developed our nomenclature is, we must remember that it is only a nomenclature; that a word is merely a sign of syllables attached to a certain phenomenon. Thus it can never express Nature completely and ought to be regarded as mere equipment for our comfort.' [25]

But all this profound insight into the follies and fallacies of man thinking his way through the ages does not with Goethe, as it so easily could, lead to any historical relativization of the idea of truth. What saves him is what would save the authentically great artist and what would be shatteringly naïve on any other level but his: the faith in the intuitive, indeed visionary faculty of his genius. Of course, this faith never becomes pompously articulate. When Goethe speaks of it, he speaks with that irony which with him is a prerequisite of intellectual honesty—perhaps it hardly ever becomes conscious. But there is one occasion where, again with some irony, he seems to reach a final, and for him indeed very satisfactory, conclusion to that argument with Schiller, and through Schiller with Kant, which I quoted at the beginning. That Kant had absolutely denied to human intelligence the possibility of 'seeing ideas', of reaching the absolute lucidity of Plato's ἐπιστήμη, that the human understanding should be for ever imprisoned within the confines of that unhappy hunting-ground where the physical scientist is after his phenomenal game, had been a secret vexation to Goethe ever since he came into contact with that philosophy which satisfied the philosophical need of the modern mind, as Thomas Aquinas had satisfied that of the Middle Ages.

On the occasion of which I am speaking, he had once more struggled with Kant and underlined the following sentence in which the philosopher deals with the rational possibility of conceiving of a divine mind: 'We are able to think of an understanding which, not being discursive as ours, but intuitive, starts with a universal vision and descends from there to the particular, that is, from the One to the Many'. And Goethe notes: 'I suppose the author hints here at divine intuition; yet if it is possible for us (as Kant admits) to lift ourselves up to a higher region in the moral sphere, through faith in God, virtue and immortality, and draw nearer towards the supreme Being, then, perhaps, it may be the same in the intellectual sphere and we may, by our contemplation of incessantly creative Nature, become worthy of some intellectual participation in her creativeness. If, to begin with, I strove, unconsciously and merely prompted by an inner motive, to reach the *Urphänomen* and the secret of the type, and if I even succeeded in erecting on this basis a theory in accordance with Nature, then nothing shall prevent me from braving now what the old man of Königsberg himself calls the *Adventure of Reason*.' [26]

And so he braves it. To the end of his life he will fail, or refuse, to grasp completely what Schiller and Kant were about. The unfathomable, before which he too resigns himself, is yet revealed to him in the world of phenomena; not the Absolute itself, but the mirrored reflection of its majestic remoteness: 'Im farbigen Abglanz haben wir das Leben'. Absolute Truth and the Goethean Scientific Truth are not different in kind, merely in degrees of, as it were, absoluteness. Therefore by scientific truth Goethe never means the results, correct or incorrect, produced by what he denounces, implicitly and explicitly, as a strange aberration of the human mind, a rather perverse marriage between the crudest empiricism and the most abstruse mathematical abstractness. His science, like his poetry, is founded on the conviction—self-evident to him—that man, if only he exercises *all* his faculties of understanding, is, as he says, 'adequately equipped' [27] to know what he is meant to know about life, without having to put 'nature on the rack'; for there, he says, she remains silent.[28]

Truth is what man is meant to know—this is the centre of Goethe's intellectual existence. It is rather perturbing to the modern intelligence; where are the measures, it will ask, by which we can assess what is 'meant'? Goethe himself cannot define them. He merely feels that 'in natural sciences as much as in ethics we need a categorical imperative'. [29]

We have seen that his opposition to Newton springs from a moral impulse expressing itself in scientific language; yet it can, despite the strains imposed upon it by the incongruous situation, express itself in such language because both Goethe's ethical and scientific convictions are mere aspects of that faith which forms the core of his spiritual existence: the faith in a perfect correspondence between the inner nature of man and the structure of external reality, between the soul and the world. Hence there is for Goethe neither tragedy—for tragedy results from a fundamental misunderstanding between the human heart and the order of the world—nor modern physical science, which he sees but as the mind's strategy in its self-assertive campaign against Nature. It is in this sense that Goethe calls modern physics, rather startlingly, 'subjective'. To him it seems the outcome of an excessive emancipation of the subject from a totality of which it is a mere part, and therefore involved at every point in a manoeuvre of cosmic impiety. He resigns himself, as he says, on reaching the *Urphänomen*, that is, 'at the boundaries of humanity'; the mathematico-analytical scientist, on the other hand, appears to him imprisoned 'within the hypothetical limitations of an obstinately self-willed and narrow-minded individuality'.[30]

Goethe deems his own science 'objective' because it has its source in his belief in a pre-established equation between subject and object. In his *Theory of Colours* he praises the Ionian school for 'repeating again and again, with so much emphasis, that knowledge is only through the response of equal to equal', and he translates Plotinus' *Neque vero oculus unquam videret solem nisi factus solaris esset* into German verse:

Wär nicht das Auge sonnenhaft,
Wie könnten wir das Licht erblicken?
Lebt' nicht in uns des Gottes eigne Kraft,
Wie könnt uns Göttliches entzücken? [31]

[If the eye were not sun-like, how could we ever see light? And if God's own power did not dwell within us, how could we delight in things divine?]

To Eckermann he says (February 26th, 1824): 'If I had not carried, through anticipation, the world within myself, I would have remained blind with my eyes wide open, and all search and experience would have been nothing but a dead and vain effort'. Therefore, he says, Truth is 'a revelation emerging at the point where the inner world of man meets external reality. . . . It is a synthesis of world and mind, yielding the happiest assurance of the eternal harmony of existence' [32]; and again, 'there resides, in the objective world, an unknown law which corresponds to the unknown law within subjective experience', [33] and—though he used them himself—'when it comes to it, microscopes and telescopes merely confuse the pure human vision'. [34] Unknown and yet revealed—this is the nature of truth which Goethe seeks to make more and more his own by exercising his intuition, imagination *and* discursive intelligence, with freedom and irony.

It is only on those very few occasions when he seems to be persuaded that Kant is right after all, and that Schiller may have justly denied him the privilege of di-

rect intercourse with the ideas, that he seems to be prepared to leave science alone and resign himself to his
poetry. This he expresses in a little meditation (*Bedenken
und Ergebung*—Reflection and Resignation) in which he
gives a most exact précis of Kant's philosophy, stating in
conclusion that 'understanding cannot think together
what the senses convey to it in separation, and so the
conflict between perception and idea remains for ever
unresolved. Therefore we shall escape into the sphere of
poetry where we may hope to find some satisfaction.' [35]

It is this impulse (which Goethe hardly ever allows to
get the better of him), this emphasis on the superiority
of the inner vision as against a spiritually barren external
world, that ever since has dominated European poetry.
This trend became more and more conspicuous with
time, so that the Romantics whom Goethe rejected seem
almost Realists compared with the later excesses of inwardness perpetrated by the Symbolists. The great significance of Goethe in the history of the European mind
lies in the fact that he is the last great poet who lived
and worked in a continual effort to save the life of poetry
and the poetry of life. All his fundamental scientific
ideas are capable of expansion into pure poetic vision.
The Metamorphosis of Plants is the title not only of a
biological treatise, but also of a poem, and the *Theory
of Colours* extends into some of the best verses of his
later years. It is the same principle that informs his poetry as well as his science, his *Faust* and his *Theory of
Colours*: that 'all that is transient is but a symbol', and
'everything that exists is an analogy of existence itself'. [36]
Thus Goethe is not merely against Newton, but also
against the Romantics and against Beethoven; for it is
no more the artist's business to melt away the solid reality
of symbolic living forms in the hot paroxysms of the
inner life than it is the scientist's to tyrannize these symbols of eternity which surround our temporal existence
into the subjective abstractions of mathematical reason-

ing, for, Goethe asks, 'what is there exact in mathematics except its own exactitude?'[37]

At times he is convinced that his science is of far greater historical importance than his poetry. 'Two things are necessary for a man to make an epoch in the world,' he once said to Eckermann (May 2nd, 1824), 'first to have a good brain, and then to come into a big fortune. Napoleon inherited the French Revolution, Frederick the Great the Silesian War, Luther the obscurantism of the monks, and to my lot have fallen the errors of Newtonian physics. The present generation has, of course, no idea what I have achieved in this field; but future ages will confess that in my time I had come into no small fortune.' Perhaps he was not quite so wrong after all. Can one not discern a very marked echo of Goethe's voice in the following sentence of the physicist Heisenberg: 'The dangers threatening modern science cannot be averted by more and more experimenting, for our complicated experiments have no longer anything to do with nature in her own right, but with nature changed and transformed by our own cognitive activity'?[38]

It was Goethe's ambition to play in the history of thought the role of another Francis Bacon, insisting on not merely pragmatic, but what he understood to be objective dealings with Nature; or that of an Immanuel Kant of the Objective Reason. He said in a review of a scientific work: 'A man born and bred in the so-called exact sciences will, on the height of his analytical reason, not easily comprehend that there is also something like an exact concrete imagination.'[39] This exact concrete imagination is the glory of Goethe's poetry, and he knew that it was the great instrument of truth. 'Beauty,' he says, 'is the manifestation of secret laws of Nature which, were it not for their being revealed through beauty, would have remained unknown for ever.'[40] All searches, discoveries and inventions, thrust on a world which is through these very activities and achievements progressively alienated from that truth which resides in the imagination and in a precise vision rather than in abstract formulae of the fittingness, beauty and significance of things, would ultimately spend themselves, Goethe feared, in the vain and desperate fidgetings of the good intention to make Hell a better place to live in.

GOETHE AND THE

AVOIDANCE OF TRAGEDY

Wenn ein moderner Mensch . . . an einem so grossen Alten Fehler zu rügen hätte, so sollte es billig nicht anders geschehen als auf den Knien. [If a man of our time were to find fault with such a great man of the past, then, to be just, he should do so on his knees.]—Goethe to Eckermann, March 28th, 1827

1

In 1797, after a lapse of seven years following the publication of the *Fragment: Faust*, and more than twenty
years after the completion of the first draft of the dramatic poem, the *Urfaust*, Goethe announced in a letter
to Schiller (June 22nd) that, finding himself in a state
of acute unrest, he was preparing, as a kind of spiritual
sedative, to take up *Faust* once more and to retreat 'into
that world of symbols, ideas and mists' (June 24th). He
begged his friend 'to think it over in a sleepless night',
and to tell him what he would expect of the whole work
and, as it were, 'interpret, as a true prophet, his [Goethe's]
own dreams' (June 22nd). Goethe must have known
that he would arouse some uneasiness in Schiller's methodical mind when he added: 'As the various parts of the

poem can be treated in different modes if only they fall in with the spirit and the tone of the whole, and as, moreover, this creation is subjective in kind, I shall be able to work at it in odd free moments now and then'. Schiller's reply was as prompt as it was suggestive of misgivings. 'With all its poetic individualism,' he said, 'this play cannot escape the demand for symbolic significance. . . . The duality of human nature and the unsuccessful striving for a reconciliation in man between what is divine and what is physical—this is something one cannot lose sight of; and just because the story tends towards shrillness and formlessness one does not wish to be arrested within the subjéct itself, but to be guided by it towards ideas. In brief, the claims made upon *Faust* are at the same time philosophical and poetical, and in whatever direction you may turn, the very nature of the subject will impose upon you a philosophical treatment, and the imagination will have to put up with a period of employment in the service of an idea' (June 23rd).

It is, once again, the issue raised by *Naive und sentimentalische Dichtung*. In that essay, which had appeared in the preceding year, Schiller defended the workings of his own reflective genius against the overpowering spontaneity of Goethe's. This time, Schiller seems to imply, Goethe will have to leave behind the state of innocence, submitting himself to a more complex, more philosophically disciplined inspiration. If it appeared to Schiller that in *Werther*, in *Tasso*, a miraculously preserved innocence, a poetic imagination of almost terrifying integrity, had told the story of a world divided and coming to grief—as though the genius of the tree in Paradise had opened its mouth to announce to the world the news of the Fall—then the continuation of that record could only come from the creature that had eaten the apple. For the hero of *Faust* was no longer the kind of person that Werther was, or Egmont, or Tasso, or Iphigenie, who are all profoundly 'naïve'—the word to be understood with its German connotations. One might be tempted to apply to them Pascal's reflection that 'the heart has reasons of which the reason knows nothing', were it not for the fact that Pascal meant *reasons* of the heart (Hölderlin had them), tools of the highest *understanding* of the world, whereas Werther, Egmont, Tasso and even Iphigenie, live, with regard to the world, in a state of fundamental incomprehension, varying between the raptures of bliss ('himmelhoch jauchzend') when the heart, wholly immaculate, to use Iphigenie's phrase, enjoys itself, and the agonies of woe ('zu Tode betrübt') when the uncomprehended world interferes. *They do not know*—in the sense in which knowledge means the knowledge of good and evil; they live, not beyond, but before that fatal rift, and thus reflect an essential characteristic of their creator's genius and sensibility. Here is at least one of the roots of Goethe's uniqueness within the European tradition, a uniqueness revealed in achievement as well as in failure. This also accounts for the extremes of Goethe worship (mostly inside Germany) and Goethe rejection (mostly outside Germany, and by critics of the stature of, for instance, Irving Babbitt, Ortega y Gasset, George Santayana, T. S. Eliot).

Any criticism of Goethe requires the utmost tact. Not only is the man so immense—and nothing is more difficult in criticism than to keep alive at every moment that sense of proportion which the very difference in level between creativeness and critical judgment demands; criticism is, alas, an unaristocratic habit, easily tempted into a false intimacy, in praise and negation alike—but also so much of the perennial discussion about Goethe is so massively wrongheaded, and so passionate, that it has filled the atmosphere around him with an abundance of electrical charges, making it all too easy to produce short circuits. I am saying this because I wish to speak of a limitation in Goethe's range of awareness and of a defect in his sensibility, and because I believe, paradoxically enough, that this limitation lies in the very boundlessness of his genius, and the defect in the inexhaustible richness of his sensitivity. It would be preposterous to derive the standards for an assessment of Goethe's achievements from anywhere else but the great classics of European civilization. Yet it would be futile to seek a place for him in a pattern determined by Homer, or Sophocles, or Virgil, or Dante, or Shakespeare. His range is too wide, and his gifts too universal ever to find full realization in one type of work alone, and his genius too diffused ever to concentrate on a single exemplary, classical achievement; and while in scope he is too vast ever to represent the character of an age, the mode of his imagination, its susceptibilities and idiosyncrasies, partake, at the same time, too definitely of the unresolved problems of the late eighteenth century for him easily to be acknowledged as being for all times and all places. With regard to Goethe's position within his own nation, it is very revealing that it could be said with some justice—as it was said immediately after the Second World War by Karl Jaspers—'that we came face to face with experiences in which we had no inclination to read Goethe, but took up Shakespeare, or the Bible, or Aeschylus, if it was possible to read at all'.[1]

What was the nature of the experience in the face of which Goethe offered no help? It was the very kind of experience before which Goethe himself always proved helpless: the exposure to the manifestations of evil and sin. 'The mere attempt to write tragedy might be my undoing,'[2] he once said, and it was the truth—at least for the greatest part of his life. Among his dramas there are three dramatic poems which, more than any other dramas he wrote, established his fame: *Iphigenie*, *Tasso*, *Faust*. All of them are potential tragedies, indeed so much so that one may feel that the tragic conclusion could only be avoided at the price of complete artistic conclusiveness. They show a moving and yet unsatisfac-

tory reluctance of mind and imagination to accept the
rule of the road leading to the very centre of human destiny. This is not to imply that in that very centre there
dwells, inescapably, tragedy. But once a man is compelled to penetrate to that central point in all seriousness,
then there is only one region' left that stretches, for the
European, beyond tragedy. Beyond Hamlet and the rest
that is silence, there stands only Prospero:

> And my ending is despair,
> Unless I be reliev'd by prayer,
> Which pierces so that it assaults
> Mercy itself, and frees all faults.

And frees all faults; the German translation of this is:
Alle menschliche Gebrechen, which, we are told by
Goethe, are redeemed by 'pure humanity', of which
Iphigenie is the embodiment.

Anyone who has ever come under the spell of Goethe's
Iphigenie knows its power to persuade, to convince and
to move. There seems to be no doubt that it is poetically
true. But which aspect of poetic truth do we mean? The
same that applies to *Antigone* or *King Lear*? No, certainly not. *Iphigenie* is lyrically, but not dramatically
true, which is as much as to say that it has the truth of a
vision of what life and the world could be if they corresponded to what is best in a great and good soul. It is
dramatically not true because the objective world which
is the scene of the play is not real enough to offer serious
resistance to the realization of that vision. In other words,
there is no real evil in that world. All the evil inherent in
the mythological pattern taken over from the Greeks is
considerably reduced in stature so as to lose an essential
degree of reality. The reality of evil asserts itself poetically on only three occasions, which are scattered about
the play like three erratic blocks in the gentle groves of
human kindness: Iphigenie's story of the horrible deeds

perpetrated in her family, Orestes' account of the murder of his mother with the rage of madness that follows, and the *Parzenlied* (the song of the goddesses of Fate). For the rest—and it is all but the whole play—the inexorable hardness of the Greek myth is dissolved into the softer substance of the goodness of human nature.

From the opening monologue of the first act onwards we are sure that, unless the poem were to become grossly incongruous, Iphigenie could not seriously be asked to perform, or indeed seriously consider, human sacrifices, let alone the sacrifice of her own brother. And the much-discussed question of the 'cure' of Orestes reveals, through the very wording of the question as suggested by the play, the surprising shift of emphasis from what was once, and is again, the centre of the problem, to a more humane periphery. Cure? Of what? Of a temporary fit of madness? For surely there is no 'cure' for the murder of a mother. There is, for the Greeks, only the supreme sacrifice to atone for it, or else the direct intervention of the gods to lift the curse—which is, in spite of all the fundamental differences, nearer the Christian repentance and the forgiving grace than the administering of pure humanity. If the curse on the house of Tantalus and the deed of Orestes are to be taken as real—as real, say, as the murder committed by Macbeth—then Goethe's solution is not dramatically true. We simply have to discard the reality of curse and murder—and, indeed, this oblivion is granted to us by the lyrically soothing climate of Arcadian Tauris itself—we have to accept curse and murder as mythological names for a less spectacular kind of guilt, and finally allow a more vaguely general state of spiritual restlessness to assume the place of any articulate guilt if we are to remain convinced of the effectiveness of a purely human redemption.

Schiller's dramatic instinct sensed this defect of Goethe's Orestes; in criticizing him in terms of purely dramatic considerations, he yet pointed to the profounder issue when he wrote to Goethe (January 22nd, 1802): 'Orestes is the most doubtful figure of the drama. There is no Orestes without Furies; and when the cause of his condition does not strike the senses but lies hidden in his mind and emotions, his is too long and monotonous an agony—without an object. Here we are up against one of the limitations of modern drama as compared with ancient tragedy. I wish you could think of a remedy; but bearing in mind the economy of the play, I do not think it likely that you will; for you have indeed done everything that is possible without gods and spirits.'

I have said that the theme of *Iphigenie* would lend itself to, indeed invite, a tragic treatment. The reply that the play of Euripides, from whom the story is borrowed, is not a tragedy either would be beside the point, for it is too obvious that Goethe's heroine is a person totally different from Euripides' Iphigenia. Yet there is one Greek tragedy which, in situation and aspects of the main character, is related to Goethe's *Iphigenie*: the *Antigone* of Sophocles. In both plays it is a loving sister who has determined in her soul to abide by the divine law as it is given to her, and to remain, as Antigone says, 'imprisoned in the fear of the gods', and thus to defy all worldly power and the rules of common sense. In both plays the conflict involves death—or, at least, potentially death—not merely for the one who is so madly resolved, but for those whom she loves as well: in *Antigone* for Ismene, perhaps, the sister, and for Haemon, the lover, and in *Iphigenie* for Orestes, the brother, and Pylades, the friend. In the one play as much as in the other, the heroine is bound by bonds of gratitude to him whom she has decided to disobey; in both plays the king has provided a home for the child of a cursed race after her great tribulations. For Antigone as well as for Iphigenie it is not merely the wish for full moral realization of her

E

own character that inspires her deed, but the hope of redeeming the guilt of ancestors. Moreover, in both plays the king is finally moved to revoke his own law and to yie¹d to an overriding commandment. Thus it is through the contrast between Sophocles' *Antigone* and Goethe's *Iphigenie* (and not in comparison with the play of Euripides, where such problems never enter) that one can see most clearly the limitations of the Iphigenie faith.

These limitations might be artistically irrelevant were the play not such that its subject could not be dealt with on the level which Goethe set himself, without implicitly giving a comprehensive vision (a vision, not a discussion) of the ultimate nature of the moral problem involved. Also one cannot state these limitations by simply drawing attention to the tragic ending of *Antigone* and the happy solution of *Iphigenie*. But perhaps one can bring home the point that matters by saying that Iphigenie would not do what she does—or rather, would not be what she is—if her vision of life really comprehended the possibility of her having to put her brother to death; whereas Antigone, whether or not she is to die herself and bring death to others, *is* the realization of the truth that the triumph of divine law may involve at every point disaster in terms of human aspirations. In other words, there is in Goethe's *Iphigenie* an incongruity between the radicalism with which the moral problem is posed, and the certainly lovable gentleness of the spiritual nature that has to carry it. The *dramatic* flaw of Goethe's other great poetic drama, *Torquato Tasso*— lyrically as supremely successful as *Iphigenie*—is that the spiritual excitement of the hero is in excess of the moral facts of his situation, while in *Iphigenie* the moral situation outweighs the spiritual stature of the protagonist. It is because in the dramatic order of things natures like Iphigenie must not be made to encounter such situations (which could only crush them without affording them even the semblance of spiritual triumph) that, in this case, the moral problem is identical with the problem of dramatic integrity.

At the root of this problem there is not merely the time-honoured and, in this form, interminable antithesis between the belief in the fundamental goodness and the dogma of the essential corruption of the human heart. Not one of the characters of *Antigone* is 'bad'. If Creon were a wicked man there would still be catastrophe, but no tragedy. For both Greeks and Christians it is not in terms of morality that the moral problem can be solved. Once more, it is not the belief in man's readiness to be persuaded and moved into goodness that limits the spiritual scope of Goethe's *Iphigenie*. The uneasiness springs from a different question, which is, I think, implicitly answered by Goethe; the question: what would happen to the human spirit if all human goodness were of no avail on this earth, as happens to be the case in *Antigone?* Would the ending be despair then, or a faith beyond despair? The light and the beauty which emanate from Iphigenie have their source in her (or Goethe's) conviction that in the final reckoning such questions will not be asked. Yet as it happens, Iphigenie actually does ask the question. From the depth of her conflict she implores the gods that good should prevail on the shores of Tauris, that they should save her and thus *'save their image in her soul'.*[3] In other words, the image of the gods in Iphigenie's soul is such that it would be undone by catastrophe and her faith would crumble. But this is an extraneous and somewhat illegitimate consideration; it would be better to say that Iphigenie simply embodies the belief that the gods cannot fail her by contradicting her own convictions of what is good and necessary. Thus she stands for the impossibility of tragedy. Antigone, on the other hand, knowing that she is to die and lamenting her fate, asks on which right of the gods she might have trespassed. Why should she in her wretchedness still raise her eyes to the heavenly powers? 'My lot was godlessness received in exchange for piety. But if this is good before the gods then I shall suffer, and in suffering come to know my sin.'

If it can be said that Goethe's limitations have their origin in the apparently limitless scope of his genius, then what is meant is his *genius*, not his talents; on the contrary, he always used his talents to defend himself against his genius. In the deployment of his extrapoetic talents he often seems to insist stubbornly on a playfully cultivated mediocrity. This we can see at work in his unsophisticated taste for rather dull drawings, in his 'classical' preoccupation with the most uninspired examples of Roman sculpture, in his preferring Zelter's innocuous music to Beethoven's and, above all, in the all but philistine pedantry betrayed by his endless collecting, cataloguing, describing and displaying of all manner of objects, documents and instruments. People lacking in a sense of humour have often blamed Goethe for so irresponsibly scattering his interests and wasting his time. Their insatiable desire for still more and still greater poetry is sadly frustrated by the Herr Geheimrat's habits of painstaking theatrical management and time-squandering mineralogical meticulousness.

Yet there is, of course, in all seriousness something puzzling in those radical defensive manoeuvres of Goethe, and I think that only by understanding them as necessary defences can one hope to arrive at some comprehension of Goethe's genius. Only then may one see a little more clearly why his lyrical achievements should have been so truly incomparable, his embarrassment in the face of tragedy so conspicuous, the moral solutions offered by some of his works such anti-climaxes that Irving Babbitt could speak of them as 'sham solutions', and, incidentally, his science so aggressively anti-Newtonian. It may also help to explain why his greatest work, *Faust*, had to remain so ambiguous (and I mean an ambiguity falling short of the essential ambiguity of all great art, an ambiguity not in terms of unresolvable paradox, but of plain contradiction)—so ambiguous that throughout the message-ridden German nineteenth century it could, with the support of what were quite unambiguous quotations, be interpreted as the high-poetical celebration of restlessly active striving and of a freedom that resides in conquest; whereas now, with the ethos of 'action and aggrandizement deflated, and again with quite unequivocal support from the text, it can be shown to proclaim the hope in the inscrutable workings of divine grace which may descend upon the greatest sinner.

2

Critics have always tried to account in various ways for Goethe's more baffling waverings and uncertainties. Some say that at times he jeopardized his genius by occupying himself with the wrong things; others, that he allowed himself too easily to get entangled in the wrong emotions. Yet it is difficult to be convinced by the standards such critics apply in their assessments of what was 'right' for Goethe. Is it what Ortega y Gasset calls the 'realized *Existenz*' of Goethe the man? This might only have been attained by the sacrifice of Goethe the poet. Or is it the idea of contented equilibrium and psychological balance which Barker Fairley's *Study of Goethe* appears to put forward? But surely this therapeutic approach is most unbecoming for the literary critic, who would soon be out of his job if poets decided to accept for the conduct of their lives the rules of mental health. To say that Goethe was pathologically introspective in his youth is to say that we should be prepared to dispense with *Werther* and the original design of *Faust*; and to imply that Frau von Stein was bad for Goethe is equal to holding that it would have been just as well if

Goethe had not written *Iphigenie* or *Tasso* or *Erhabner Geist, du gabst mir, gabst mir alles* or *Warum gabst du uns die tiefen Blicke*. This kind of criticism implicitly pretends to possess the secret of an ideal pattern of creative life which, had it only been adopted by Goethe, would have made him into a still greater poet and a better and happier man.

The paradox of limitations caused by universality, with which Goethe confronts us, originates in a violent clash between the nature of Goethe's genius and his historical situation. In the spiritually barren climate of eighteenth- and nineteenth-century society, amidst that vanity fair of conflicting values and self-contradictory aspirations, a genius apparently so chaotic and yet so profoundly organized as that of Goethe's will easily seem to itself (and to others) to be something almost monstrous, demonic, extra-human—in fact, the spirit of *Nature* itself. And this is what, set up against the spiritual character of his age, Goethe's genius was. If Goethe is not a *European* classic, this is due to the fact that his society was lacking in a fundamentally accepted and generally valid spiritual mould in which alone a classic can be cast.

In spite of all the unavoidable cleavages, disharmonies, animosities and antagonisms which are the perennial lot of human beings and human societies, there is a possibility—and this possibility is called culture when it is realized—of a community of men living together, and maybe fighting one another, in a state of tacit agreement on what the nature and meaning of human existence really is. This unity will then show itself to be at work beyond, or beneath, or despite all differences of actually proclaimed beliefs and articulate opinions. Such must have been the society for which the performances of the tragedies of Aeschylus and Sophocles were national celebrations; such were wide stretches of what we rather vaguely call the Middle Ages; such were, to judge by

their artistic creations, the days of the Renaissance and of
Elizabeth. The age of Goethe, however, was not of this
kind. Its true representatives were the twin creatures of
spiritual chaos: rationalism and romanticism, the one ab-
horring, the other worshipping the irrational aspect of
man. In the absence of a genuine supranatural order
human beings were thrown back on their purely naturalistic resources, with analytical sceptical reason on the
one hand, and disorganized emotions on the other. Pascal's reasons of the heart degenerated into sheer emotion-
alism, which was mistaken for spirituality, and Plato's
reason of understanding into the crudest empiricism,
which prided itself upon its 'realistic' outlook. In vain
had Kant fought his lonely battle. Those who came after
him, the great philosophers of the age of Goethe, who, of
course, felt and knew the disaster that had befallen the
spirit, raised their arbitrary, 'exciting', 'interesting' metaphysical towers above the heads of a society that had
become Babel in its mutual incomprehension.

Into such a situation there was born a genius who,
more than any other of his time (with the possible exception of Blake), seemed to have been sent to fill with
precious life whatever order of the spirit, whatever tradition he may have found upon his arrival—as Sophocles
had done with the religious tradition of Greece, and
Dante with the scholastic order of the Middle Ages. But,
alas, 'the day was so absurd and confused', as Goethe
himself put it in his last letter to Wilhelm von Humboldt,[4] and his genius, being a perpetual source of light
to the world, had itself to grope in darkness. What, I
think, is correct in Ortega y Gasset's and—in some measure—Karl Jaspers' thesis of Goethe's *Existenz* having remained unfulfilled is the fact that his own genius was an
unending puzzle to him. For the very nature of this
genius deprived Goethe of that particular kind of historical sense, that intuitive grasp of the historical char-

acter of his age and his own position in it, which Schiller
had and, above all, Hölderlin, who wrote:

> . . . *Indessen dünket mir öfters*
> *Besser zu schlafen, wie so ohne Genossen zu seyn,*
> *So zu harren und was zu thun indess und zu sagen,*
> *Weiss ich nicht und wozu Dichter in dürftiger Zeit?* [5]

> . . . Meanwhile, it seems to me often,
> Better to slumber than live without companions, like
>   this,
> So to linger, and know not what to begin or to utter,
> Or, in such spiritless times, why to be poet at all?

Goethe too knew that question, and there were periods
in his life when he actually did answer it in the negative
and all but behaved accordingly. But for him the question was not an historical one; not 'why to be poet at all
in spiritless times', but solely whether he himself *was* a
poet. True, he once wrote (and just when he was about
to resume his work on *Faust*): 'We are compelled to
step out of our century if we wish to work according to
our convictions' (to Schiller, November 25th, 1797); but
such statements are extremely rare. Unaware of the
deeper historical perspective of his situation, he merely
perceived through his own agonies and through his spontaneous hostility towards almost all and everything that
represented the spiritual character of his century—its
rationalism, its romanticism, its unnatural hysterias, its
cold empiricism, its idealistic philosophies, its tempestuous music—that there was a gulf fixed between what he
himself was in his inmost being and the world in which
he lived as a citizen. Yet, unlike Hölderlin, he would not
allow his genius to burden and destroy him with the
historical mission of poetic prophet-martyr. He continually tried to 'do the duty of the day' by seeking a compromise between opposition and collaboration. Within

his genius (which is never the whole man) he was un-divided, in the sense in which a genuine pattern of nature and spirit fused, or any vital religious and cultural order, is undivided; but in the absence of any such valid order of human life outside himself he came to identify the in-ner order, inherent in his genius, with the spirit of nature itself.

'Unnatural,' in the mouth of Goethe, was one of the strongest invectives. 'Diese verdammte Unnatur!' he ex-claimed, faced with the productions of Kleist, and Kleist was judged. Thus pantheism, God in nature, became his natural religion, and Spinoza his chosen prophet. 'This philosopher,' he wrote in a letter to Jacobi (June 9th, 1785), 'does not prove the being of God; God is being. And if others, because of this, blame him as an atheist, then I feel like praising him as *theissimum*, indeed *chris-tianissimum*.' In the same letter, however, he confesses, in a rather touchingly ingenuous fashion, that he had never read systematically what the philosopher wrote (if he had, there is reason to think that he would occasion-ally have felt rather sadly disappointed): 'My way of living and thinking does not permit it. But whenever I cast a glance into his books, I believe I understand him, that is, he never seems to be self-contradictory, and I can derive from him something that affects my own feelings and doings in a very salutary manner.' How amazingly self-assured was Goethe's conviction that he represented, as it were, nature in her own right! And what a wonder-ful intimacy with all the disguises of the godhead is dis-played in the following lines (from a very much later letter to Jacobi, January 6th, 1813): 'With all the mani-fold facets of my being, one way of thinking is not suffi-cient for me; as a poet and artist I am a polytheist, but a pantheist as a student of Nature, and either belief I hold with equal determination. And if I need a divinity for my personal being, my moral existence—well, this need too is promptly catered for.'

Goethe, having to express the whole order of spirit and nature through his own genius, was limited in the performance of such an impossible duty by the absence of anything corresponding to that order within the society to which he belonged. Goethe's genius is miraculously 'natural' and 'uncivilized', in the sense that he has no support from a society civilized in the mould of the spirit that was his. And this is why, as a member of this society which had so little use for his genius, he could be so amazingly 'civilized', often to the point of cold formality and embarrassed stiffness, and even to the point of saying that he would rather commit an act of injustice than tolerate disorder. And this is also why his genius seems so boundless and its limitations, at the same time, so striking; for within his own contemporary situation such genius as his hovers perpetually on the precarious dividing-line between greatness and excess. (His counterpart, in the sphere of political genius, was Napoleon.) In the absence of a tradition to feed and educate his genius, the umbilical cord between it and nature was, as Goethe himself once put it, never severed.

Schiller, while admiring this fascinating spectacle of an undivided poetic nature, yet ceaselessly strained to play the part of midwife. In the letters about *Faust*, and still more in the correspondence about *Wilhelm Meister*, he makes the ever-renewed and ever-frustrated attempt to civilize, educate and discipline what seemed to him a too luxurious production of genius. Yet he was bound to fail, in spite of the fact that he had a profounder understanding of Goethe than anyone else. In one of the very first letters he wrote to him (August 23rd, 1794) he said that if Goethe had been born a Greek or in any other civilization where he would have been surrounded by 'an exquisite nature and an ideal art,' his struggle 'would have been shortened or even been superfluous'. At least in the creation of certain types of work—*Faust* and *Wilhelm Meister* for instance—Goethe, he thought, ought to resign himself to the rigours of a more philosophical discipline. It was no good. Ideas were not embodied in the society of his time, and in the abstract terms of philosophical speculation Goethe had no use for them. He had to *see* and feel them; but when he did see and feel them they became so real to him that he was even surprised that to others they appeared to be mere 'ideas'.

The impression that Goethe's genius is 'wholly nature' is partly due to an optical illusion caused by the refraction in the medium of a 'spiritless time' where the spiritual had ceased to be incarnate, having evaporated into vague abstractions. The anaemic and artificial civilization of his day drove Goethe again and again into a realm where the 'real thing' could be found. This is why Italy was such a revelation to Goethe. There, set up against a clearer sky and the memory of a clearer realization of the human destiny, he found a vision of life in which nature and humanity were merged in a 'natural civilization'.

It would be inadequate to the point of idiocy to approach Goethe in a moralizing fashion; but there is no reason why one should not see that, with such a predominance of nature within him and such a lack of civilized tradition around him, he had to fail when faced with the tragic or religious aspect of the moral problem as it is inherent in the very plots of both *Iphigenie* and *Faust*. No human being can come to grips with such a problem unaided by tradition and traditional teaching. As it happened, within the 'tradition' of Goethe's day it was precisely this problem that had been deformed and dwarfed beyond recognition. The practical, 'lived' side of it was indeed, after all is said (and said with great affection) about Fräulein von Klettenberg and other beautiful souls, too pietistically mediocre ever really to mean anything to Goethe; and its philosophical side too speculative, abstract and metaphysical not to be discarded by Goethe's passion for 'reality'. In the spiritual climate of the eighteenth and the beginning of the nineteenth centuries the terror of a man's exposure to the need for ultimate moral or religious decisions could not be creatively grasped, either on the level of Greek tragedy or on that of undiluted Christianity, or indeed even on the level of that unique encounter of both which took place in the Elizabethan drama. And Goethe was of his age in failing to grasp it in either of these spheres.

We have seen what happened in his dealings with a classically tragic subject; how he missed the meaning of the cross of Christianity is best illustrated by that passage from *Wilhelm Meisters Wanderjahre* where he 'draws a veil over this suffering' just because he 'reveres it so deeply', and because he 'regards it as a damnable insolence to expose the agonies of the saint to the sun which had hidden its face when an infamous world obtruded upon it this sight'.[7] (It happened to be Weimar where an American commandant very wisely decreed that Hitler's electorate in what was once Goethe's city were to be shown the horrors of Buchenwald concentration camp.) And summing up the meaning of *Hamlet*, Goethe defines it as the tragedy of a man who was too weak to carry the burden of his mission. Stating the problem in terms of strength and weakness, he once more fails to be impressed by the moral aspect of *Hamlet* and the all-pervasive, all-corroding power of evil, the 'morbid' preoccupation of Elizabethan tragedy. For to be able to perceive and creatively to articulate this problem, that is, to form a vision of it rather than to discuss it, presupposes a theology underlying, however dispersedly, the picture of reality that an age possesses; and this is something different from a philosophy of nature and from even the highest human wisdom. Goethe's genius soared gloriously above the flat expanses of contemporary religious sentimentality and mediocre morality, in triumphant opposition to all puritan gloom, moral suspicion and tearful piety, asserting that life, whatever it be, is good and beautiful: 'wie es auch sei, das Leben, es ist gut', and

Ihr glücklichen Augen,
Was je ihr gesehn,
Es sei wie es wolle,
Es war doch so schön ! [8]

It is this finality in his assertion of life that makes it possible to claim for Goethe the position of the greatest
lyrical genius of Europe. But though it is *his* final assertion, it is not ultimate. It indeed transcends all sorrows
of Werther, Tasso and Ottilie, and endless conflicts most
deeply felt and suffered. But would it transcend, one
wonders, tragedy fully realized? And only there is the
place of an ultimate 'Es ist gut'.

3

Under such auspices what was to become of a dramatic
plot in which a man enters into a contract with the Devil,
signing away, on certain conditions, the fate of his soul?
What was to become of *Faust*? One may well ask. It took
Goethe, all in all, sixty years to decide, or rather to decide that he would not quite decide. Certain things, however, the play decided for him. For instance, that it
would, being Goethe's, become a lyrical masterpiece.
There is no greater and no more varied lyrical poetry to
be found within the German language. And more: *Faust*
became a pageant of the human spirit on its voyage
throughout the ages. An extraordinary wealth of mythological creatures, Teutonic, Greek, Christian, populate
the scene, all testifying to their creator's inexhaustible
imaginative power. And still more: the hero of the play
was to become the representative of a whole epoch of
history, its lust for knowledge, for power over nature, its
intellectual and emotional instability, its terrible failure
in love, humility and patience. And still more: the first
part of the play, dominated by what is usually called the
Gretchen tragedy, was to bring out most movingly the

undoing, by the Faustian manoeuvres, of what was left in the world of simplicity of heart, devotion of love and innocence of feeling. This part of what is, after all, called the tragedy of Faust, developed by its own momentum into a poetic and dramatic achievement so immaculate that it will, I think, for ever hold its place by the side of what is great in the literature of the world—and this precisely because in its design it is not, in the traditional sense, tragic but lyrical. It is what might have become of the play *Hamlet* if Ophelia and not the Prince of Denmark were to be its protagonist. In other words, Goethe may have succeeded in creating a new genre: sentimental tragedy, or the tragedy of human *feelings*: Werther, Gretchen, Ottilie. What he could not write was the tragedy of the human *spirit*. It is here that the tragedy of Faust fails and becomes illegitimately ambiguous, because there is for Goethe in the last analysis no specifically *human* spirit. It is fundamentally at one with the spirit of nature. Hence it is He, the Spirit of Nature, or the Spirit of Earth, not God or the Devil, who holds in his hands the final decision over Faust's bliss or damnation. Had He, when He appeared to Faust in the first scene of the play, not rejected him, neither God in Heaven nor the Devil in Hell would have had a chance. And one of the only two scenes in which Faust really regrets that he has committed himself to his satanic company is the great monologue *Wald und Höhle*:

Erhabner Geist, du gabst mir, gabst mir alles . . .[9]

Oh thou great Spirit, thou has given me all . . .

when it appears that this Spirit did not crush him after all.

There are in this vast display of demons great and small only two that affect Faust demonically; certainly not God, who is a jovial old gentleman, enlightened and

rather commonplace in some of his utterances ('Ein guter
Mensch, in seinem dunklen Drange, Ist sich des rechten
Weges wohl bewusst', which really means not more than
that a good man will not altogether go astray; a conviction
not so difficult to hold that it would need a divinity to
persuade one), and certainly not Mephistopheles, a Vol-
tairean spirit, with whom Faust is from the very beginning on terms of great familiarity. Goethe himself, in a
conversation with Eckermann (March 2nd, 1831), has
denied him all demonic properties: 'He is altogether too
negative,' he said, and has explicitly stated in the play
itself that he is of lesser rank than the Spirit of Earth.[10]
But the two which teach Faust what a real demon is
are the Earth Spirit and the Mothers, the innermost spirits of nature and life. They represent the demonic element in Goethe's genius. It is in union with this element
that Faust seeks his happiness from beginning to end,
or *almost* to the very end, and not in the realization of
a specifically human spirit. And Faust has been in contact
with those demons before Mephistopheles enters the
scene. This contact means black magic, and Faust is a
magician when the curtain rises. It is this that reduces
the *dramatic* stature of Mephistopheles to all but nil, and
not the rather naïve consideration that Goethe has fore-
stalled all dramatic tension in this respect by making, in
the Prologue, the Lord himself, a sure winner, as it were,
party to the wager. All that Mephistopheles can do for
Faust is to give him a hand in a job of which he already
knows the essential tricks of the trade. And throughout
the play the Devil performs hardly any magical feats
with which one would not willingly credit the magician
himself who had already succeeded in establishing contact with the very spirit of life.

All this would be rather irrelevant if it were not at
the centre of the essential ambiguity of *Faust*—the most
striking outcome of Goethe's avoidance of tragedy. What
does Faust *really* expect of Mephistopheles? Still more

magic? No; but contentment, rest, peace; to be able to say to the moment: 'Verweile doch, du bist so schön'.[11] [Stay, thou art so fair.] In other words, life is good. True, this is preceded by Faust's contemptuous identification of such a state with self-complacency. But it is the words themselves, not what leads up to them, which become the condition of the wager. And their poetic truth gives the lie to the preamble. They are made of the same stuff as 'Es sei, wie es wolle, Es war doch so schön!' And this the devil is to provide? The very same devil whom Faust, a few scenes later, when he has found temporary peace in the company of the Spirit of Nature, knows to be the spirit responsible for

> *So tauml' ich von Begierde zu Genuss*
> *Und im Genuss verschmacht' ich nach Begierde* [12]

Thus I tumble from desire to fulfilment
And in fulfilment I crave for more desire

for ever destroying that very peace which communion with the Spirit of Nature gives him. With the Devil defined as the spirit of negation and unrest, this becomes indeed a very strange condition meaning in fact that the Devil is to have Faust if Faust ever escapes the Devil.

What, on the other hand, is the condition of the wager between the Lord and Mephistopheles?

> *Zieh diesen Geist von seinem Urquell ab* [13]

Drag this spirit away from the very source of his life

The Lord, that is, challenges Mephistopheles to alienate Faust from the springs of life, to uproot him. If he succeeds, Faust will be his. This sounds more like 'Deprive him of all peace, if indeed you can' than 'Make him contented with the moment'. And in the end, when Faust,

anticipating this peace and contentment, blinded by anxiety, deluded into the belief that the great work of colo-
nization has begun while, in actual fact, the busy noise
is merely the sound of shovels digging his own grave,
utters the fatal words, in the face of a vision so totally
unconvincing in its meagre guilt-burdened town-and-
country-planning bliss that one cannot but agree with
Mephistopheles that it is the emptiest moment of his
life, then the Devil is cheated of his apparently well-de-
served prey by the feeble trick of a future tense ['Im
Vorgefühl von solchem hohen Glück'],[14] and by the intervention of divine grace called down upon him by the
only human love Faust ever received and experienced.

How is this? Faust has indeed promised that he would
content himself, even anticipated the enjoyment of peace
['Geniess' ich jetzt . . .'] [15] in his vision of the contented future. He has satisfied the Devil who has never
been found wanting in the shrewd judgment of any situation, and is, having faithfully renounced his programme
of eternal striving, carried into Heaven in reward for his
determination to strive eternally:

Wer immer strebend sich bemüht,
Den können wir erlösen.[16]

It is the struggling, striving man
Whom we are free to save.

What is at the root of such confusion, which has indeed defeated four generations of interpreters of *Faust*,
and, if we are to trust Eckermann's report, Goethe's own
faculties as a commentator? It would be tempting to
relegate it to the place where many an impenetrable
mystery is stored, were it not for the persistent suspicion
that we are faced here not so much with a genuine poetic
paradox as with a plain contradiction. It is the inevitable
contradiction of the undedicated mind and heart. In
Faust's world there are no real loyalties to be realized

F

and no real commitments to be broken. Both his eternal striving and his desire for peace are merely the extreme stations of his mind and heart in their never-ending voyage of self-exploration. His 'tragedy' is that he is incapable of tragedy. For tragedy presupposes the belief in an external order of things which is indeed incomplete without the conformity of the human soul, but would be still more defective without the soul's freedom to violate it. Yet Faust's dilemma is different. His 'two souls' are merely the one soul divided in itself because it knows of no independent external reality to which it is related as a free agent. Faust is in every essential respect Goethe's *alter ego*, the embodiment of that part of his self which remained unprotected by his apparently fondest trust and belief: that he belonged to Nature as her most precious possession. Faust, outside this zone of safety, is therefore torn between the belief in a world to which, strive as he may, he has no access whatever, and the belief in himself as the creator of his own world. Thus the spiritual extremes of his existence are not guilt and atonement, but despair and titanism. It is a situation unresolvable in tragedy.

Nature is fundamentally innocent, and Goethe's genius is in communion with Nature. Hence there can be, for Goethe, no catharsis, only metamorphosis. It is never with the spirit of a transcendent God or with the spirit of Man that Goethe's potentially tragic heroes are reunited after their dramatic crises. When the crisis is over, they are at one again with the spirit of Nature. They are not purified in a tragic sense, not raised above their guilt through atonement, but enter, as it were, a biologically, not morally, new phase of life, healed by oblivion and restored to strength through the sleep of the just. This is what happens to Orestes, and what happens to Faust at the beginning of Part II. Both put down their cup of Lethe and burst into magnificent praises of Nature. But such, clearly, could not have been the conclusion of Faust. He had to be saved or damned, for Heaven and Hell had become involved by virtue of the legendary pattern. But it is *only* by virtue of the legendary pattern that they have become involved at all. For the world of Faust is only just Christian enough to have room for purgatory. It is a purgatory suspended between two half unreal spheres. Hence 'Mephistopheles must only half win his wager', and Faust be 'only half guilty', as Goethe himself put it in a letter which looks forward to the play's 'most serene conclusion' when 'the old Lord may exercise his privilege of mercy'.[17]

What is Faust's sin? Restlessness of spirit. What is Faust's salvation? Restlessness of spirit. The confusion lies in a perpetual criss-crossing of restless strivings of different qualities: the striving for peace, and the striving for sensation; or, to put it differently, and in terms of the quality of the contentment sought, the striving for that peace that passeth all understanding, and the striving for a state of calm, an 'enough' which is merely a state of emotional exhaustion. What the heavenly powers mean by that striving which carries its own salvation must surely be different from the striving the goal of which Faust hopes to achieve with the help of black magic and the Devil. Yet these two kinds of striving perpetually get into each other's way throughout the poem, and the entanglement is at its worst in the crucial last scene of Faust's life when his desire for doing good and for the realization of his humanity within its decreed limits is inextricably bound up with the delusion and madness of titanism. Of these two strivings the one desires the attainment of the superman, the alchemist heightening of all human faculties, whereas the other aims at renunciation and resignation to the simple state of man. The first is the native element of Goethe's genius, the second the longing of Goethe's moral existence.

Könnt' ich Magie von meinem Pfad entfernen,
Die Zaubersprüche ganz und gar verlernen,
Stünd ich, Natur, vor dir ein Mann allein,
Da wär's der Mühe wert, ein Mensch zu sein.[18]

[Could I forget my sorcery, and ban my magic, stand, stripped of it utterly, oh Nature, face to face with thee, it would be worth while then to be a man.]

This outcry of Faust's, towards the end of the play when he is visited by *Sorge*—and this is the second place where Faust is prepared to renounce the Devil—reveals perhaps Goethe's deepest secret. To cut the umbilical cord joining him with Nature and her magic power, not to remain what he once called 'a magic oyster over which there pass mysterious waves',[19] to be face to face with Nature and escape the fate of Proteus—this only would be human happiness. Over and over again he sought deliverance from his genius in work, in the practical jobs of everyday life, through Wilhelm Meister's, through Faust's solution, and so desperately that as a man of fifty he confessed to Schiller (January 6th, 1798) that he owed it to him if he had learned to 'look at the manysidedness of my own inner being with more justice. . . . *You* have made me a poet again which I had all but ceased to be.' Such was the nature of his genius and the character of his age that the spirit could only live at the expense of life, and life only at the expense of the spirit. Thus the meaning of creative genius as well as the meaning of doing the sober work of the day, inwardness as well as action, had to remain puzzles to each other, anonymous, undefined strangers. They never met in a common dedication and could not be at peace with each other because they knew no will other than their own. And at such distance from 'la sua volontate è nostra pace' neither divine comedy nor human tragedy can be written.

It was impossible for Goethe to accept this situation,

and impossible, by the very nature of things, to solve it. Hence his perpetual oscillation between the precarious magic of the inner communion with the deep where the Earth Spirit dwells, and the moral determination to reconcile himself to the cruder demands made on human existence by society, with the emphasis of approval shifting to and fro between the two: Egmont and Oranien, Tasso and Antonio, Prometheus and *Grenzen der Menschheit*, elective affinities and legal bonds. Was harmony ever to be achieved? The answer may be found in the ambiguity of *Faust*.

BURCKHARDT AND NIETZSCHE

1

When in 1495 Raphael was apprenticed to Pietro Perugino at Perugia, this city was one of the many Renaissance centres of political strife, moral outrage and ruthless violence. Matarazzo, the chronicler of the Perugia of that time, relates in some detail the story of the two rival families, the Oddi and the Baglioni, interlocked in a deadly struggle for the possession of the city. The Baglioni had been victorious and remained for some time the overlords of the Republic. The Oddi and their soldiers lived as exiles in the valley between Perugia and Assisi, being attacked by, and counter-attacking, the Baglioni in a perpetual war which devastated the rich Umbrian land, turned the peasants into beggars or robbers, and the vineyards into jungles where wolves fed on the dead of the battles. One day, however, the soldiers of the Oddi succeeded in taking Perugia by storm. Coming up from the valley, they overwhelmed the defenders at the city gates and reached the piazza. But there, in front of the cathedral, they were defeated by Astorre Baglione. The contemporary reporter describes the daring feat of courage and martial skill that Astorre performed; at the last moment and against superior numbers, he threw himself into the battle, sitting upright on his horse, with a falcon on his helmet and with his golden armour glittering in the sun. He looked and acted, Matarazzo says, like the God of War himself.

Jacob Burckhardt, in his *The Culture of the Renaissance in Italy*, draws freely on such sources, and, in this particular case, reflects whether it is not the hero of this episode whom we can see in Raphael's early paintings of St. George and St. Michael; adding that in the figure of the celestial rider in the Heliodorus fresco Astorre Baglione has found his final glorification.

Again, using Matarazzo as his source, Burckhardt tells the story of Atalanta, the beautiful mother of Grifone Baglione, who was for some time ruling prince of Perugia. He had fought his way to power against rival members of his own family. His mother Atalanta was on the side of his enemies. On her son's victory she cursed him and fled from the city. But Grifone's rule was shortlived. He was soon overpowered by his rivals and mortally wounded. When Atalanta heard he was dying, she returned with her daughter-in-law. At the approach of the two ladies, the tumultuous crowd on the piazza parted, both sides fearing the wrath of the bereaved mother. She, however, went straight to her son, and, far from contemplating further violence, implored him to forgive those who had dealt the deadly blow. After he had thus renounced the spirit of revenge, he died with the blessings of his mother. Then the two women left the city again, and the crowd, partisans of both camps, knelt down and wept as they crossed the piazza in their blood-stained garments. It was for this Atalanta that Raphael later painted his *Deposizione*. Thus, Burckhardt writes, 'her own suffering was laid at the feet of the most sublime and sacred agony of a mother'. After all this the cathedral of Perugia, which had stood in the midst of these many scenes of felony and murder, was washed with wine and consecrated anew.[1]

Anecdotes of this kind occur frequently in Jacob Burckhardt's book on the Renaissance, which was first published in Basle in 1860, when its author had reached the age of forty-two. Are they, the historian of to-day may ask, worthy of a self-respecting scholar? Have they not the romantic flavour of a fanciful dramatization rather than the authentic ring of precise recording? What is the value of a source like Matarazzo's chronicles? Was he not a partisan himself, bent upon building up a heroic reputation for the Baglioni, and, at the same time, a story-teller determined to entertain and edify his public rather than to instruct it?

We may, in the context of such queries, note that, when he began his university education in Basle as a student of theology, Jacob Burckhardt soon developed a very sceptical attitude towards his subject. He was the son of a Protestant minister of the Church, and it was his father's—and originally his own—wish that he should become a clergyman himself. Soon, however, he decided to give up theology because the rationalist Bible criticism of his teacher de Wette had undermined his faith in orthodox beliefs. 'De Wette's system,' he wrote in a letter to a friend, 'grows before my eyes to colossal dimensions; one *must* follow him, nothing else is possible; but, alas, every day there disappears under his hands a fragment of the traditional teaching of the Church. To-day I have finally discovered that he regards the birth of Christ as a myth—and I with him. It was with a shudder that I thought of a number of reasons why it all but had to be like this. . . . ' [2] Did this critical passion leave him during his subsequent training as a historian? And, after all, this history of the Renaissance was published by a pupil of Ranke's—Ranke whom he always respected, though without much affection, and in whose seminar he had learned how to handle sources and be critical of them. Are we not, therefore, entitled to expect something more sophisticated than heroic tales from this Professor of History, holding a chair in the University of Basle?

Before raising such questions we may first ask ourselves: what is the picture produced in our minds by these unverified, and probably unverifiable, anecdotes? It is composed of intense evil and sublime beauty, of hatred and charity, of degradation and purification, of the unscrupulousness that inflicts pain, and the reverence felt for suffering, of sin, contrition and atonement. Indeed, the source from which it springs is not chosen for the sake of factual exactitude. Its authority is of a different nature. It has for Burckhardt the authenticity of the mind, imagination and spirit of the Renaissance, and if it yields a negligible *quantity* of reliable facts, it nevertheless reveals something more important to him: the *quality* of the life of the period, or as he would have called it, the *Geist* of the epoch. To reproduce this is the concern of what he calls History of Culture as distinct from Political History. If he is to recapture the quality of life lived by a certain age, the historian must bring to his study not only industry, intelligence and honesty, but also something of the sensibility and intuition of the artist. History of Culture has a critical method of its own, still more difficult to acquire than the ordinary techniques of critical investigation. In fact, it is not a technique at all, but rather creative sympathy. If we do not possess this we are perpetually misled by the egocentricity of our intellectual concepts; for we are prone to overrate the power as well as the range of application of our abstract thinking. Notions, for instance, like 'freedom' and 'slavery'; 'tolerance' and 'intolerance'; 'tyranny,' 'aristocracy', 'democracy'; 'belief' and 'superstition', which we believe we are using objectively, applying them to certain observed phenomena, are, in fact, value-judgments charged with all the sentiments and resentments of our contemporary perception of human affairs. The very sound in our ears of the word 'slavery' may render our imagination impotent in its dealings with the particular quality of Greek civilization, and the emotional charge contained in the term 'freedom of thought' or, indeed, 'objectivity' itself, may practically blot out all our understanding of the quality of the knowledge and wisdom of a medieval sage. Yet there is a possible scale of human achievement on which a wretched feudal drudge may appear to approach the degree marking absolute freedom, and the constitutionally free citizen of a free republic the state of absolute slavery.

To come back to Burckhardt's Renaissance scenes: who can, as long as he remains within his restricted moral senses, assess the spiritual power present in a society and ready to be spent on the transformation of a ruthless prince into the Raphael picture of a warrior of Heaven, and of a cunning and power-seeking woman into a *mater dolorosa*? And when it comes to our contemporary debates, we might become considerably more economical and subtle in drawing historical parallels and comparisons, if we were inspired by only one spark of what Burckhardt meant by historical understanding. We might not have to risk in every attempt at, for instance, appreciating the spiritual life and character of the Middle Ages, the release of cataracts of moralizing recriminations about religious wars, crusades, inquisitions and other pestilences.

Indeed, Burckhardt, like his teacher Ranke, is convinced of the fundamental importance of original sources and warns his pupils against text-books, digests and interpretations, not because he upholds the superstition of perfect objectivity emerging like the vision of a god from the assiduity of the source collector, but because he believes that the activity of the imagination can be stimulated as well as purified by an ever-renewed contact with the documents which reproduce the impact made by an event in human history upon particular minds. Such a mind—and here the method of the historian of a culture differs from that of the political or economic historian—may be a naïve chronicler like Matarazzo or, indeed, an inspired painter like Raphael. Did they report or paint what *really* happened? Of course not, if 'real' is to denote the pure abstract of an event, which is, in fact, no event whatsoever. For something that happens becomes an event only when it is mentally and emotionally perceived and registered. Matarazzo, therefore, in all his naïvety, and Raphael, with all the transforming power of his art, are both sources for the historian of a culture, who is, as Burckhardt once put it in his unphilosophical manner, as much concerned with 'represented history' as with what 'literally happened', forgetting that nothing happens literally—unless we are determined to make our own perception the criterion of the perception of truth itself, and to say that what *really* happens is precisely what we would have noticed had we been on the spot. Thus it is with some justification that Burckhardt maintains, in a neat over-statement, that for the history of culture the facts to be assessed are identical with the sources. Claiming for his method *primum gradum certitudinis*,[3] he upholds in defiance of the fact-worshippers that even records of things that have not happened at all may be important by virtue of the typical mode of their distortions and misinterpretations. Of Aeneas Silvius he says in his *Renaissance*: 'One may distrust the testimony of that man completely, and yet one would have to admit that there are not many other men in whose minds the picture of the age and its intellectual culture is reflected with such perception and liveliness.' [4]

The idea, however, of arriving at any positive certainty by accumulating more and more sources until that point of completeness is reached at which we may, in Bury's words, 'grasp the complete development of humanity', is, of course, dismissed by Burckhardt as a chimaera. The very attempt, he holds, would interfere with any comprehensiveness of vision. Pedantry to him is one of the most cunning enemies of truth, luring the search into the dusty lumber rooms of the past where only mice may hope to find something to eat. Mind and imagination must needs choke in them, and Buckle, for instance, he says, owes his paralysis of the brain to his exclusive obsession with the Scottish sermons of the seventeenth and eighteenth centuries.[5] The very spiritual poverty of what Burckhardt calls his 'pretty century' drives many of its academic studies into some narrow recess of the past where the ideal of precision and completeness may hide from the adept the absence of true comprehension. It is in those holes of the mind that the indiscriminate and diffused suspicion is bred which tends to dismiss as vague generalizations *all* historical assessments based on a broader vision. For the modern mind, in some of its most vocal representatives, has yielded to the inferior magic of facts, numbers, statistics, and to that sort of empiricism which, in its passion for concreteness, paradoxically reduces experience to a purely abstract notion of measurable data, having cast aside the 'immeasurable wealth' of authentic experiences of the spirit and imagination. The specialization in trifles which results from such abstractions seeks its justification not only in the arithmetical deception that a thousand futilities add up to a large piece of significance, but also in the strange belief that the great issues have all been fully explored and the outstanding sources exhausted. For Burckhardt, however, it merely brings to light that waning sense of significance which he finds and deplores in his age, the crumbling of all central convictions and the spontaneous disinclination of mediocrity to expose itself to the impact of what is great. It may be, he says, 'that there is still hidden in Thucydides a fact of capital importance which somebody will note in a hundred years time'.[6] For the present, Burckhardt maintains, 'a single source, happily chosen, can, as it were, do duty for a whole multitude of possible other sources, since he who is really determined to learn, that is, to become rich in spirit, can, by a simple function of his mind, discern and feel the general in the particular'.[7]

This is an echo from Goethe's world. For Goethe knew the difference in quality between a writer who, starting with preconceived ideas, assembles his particulars to fit the needs of his generalities, and a poet who 'discerns and feels' the universal in the particular phenomenon.[8] Like Stifter, with whom he has so much in common, Burckhardt felt himself to be one of 'Goethe's family'. As a young man he hoped he would become a poet—and he actually did publish a number of poems—and throughout his life history remained for him a poetic activity. 'As a historian,' he once wrote, 'I am lost where I cannot begin with *Anschauung*.'[9] It is a Goethean word and hardly translatable. Its connotations are visual, and it means the mental process by which we spontaneously grasp, through observation aided by intuition, a thing in its wholeness. Goethe uses it as the opposite of analysis, the mental approach which he feared would establish itself as the dominant habit of an age fascinated by Newtonian physics, only to destroy all culture of the intellect. Sometimes Burckhardt even felt it to be a nuisance that the historian, in presenting his historical narrative, was bound by the chronological order compelling him to tell one thing after the other, when the true order 'could only be represented as a picture'.[10] With such a mind it is not surprising that he agrees with Aristotle and Schopenhauer in claiming for poetry and art a higher rank in the hierarchy of understanding and knowledge than history could ever hold. In those lecture notes which he prepared in the years 1868–71, posthumously published by Jacob Oeri in 1905 under the title of *Weltgeschichtliche Betrachtungen* (Reflections on World History), he states in a fashion leaving no doubt about the degree of his certainty: 'The rivalry between history and poetry has been finally settled by Schopenhauer. Poetry achieves more for our knowledge of the truth about mankind; even Aristotle said: "Poetry is more philosophical and profound than history", and this is true because the faculty which gives birth to poetry is intrinsically of a higher order than that of the greatest historian; further, the end to which it is created is much more sublime than that of history. . . . Hence history finds in poetry not only one of its most important, but also one of its purest and finest sources.' [11]

Saying this, Burckhardt refers to a number of specified passages from Schopenhauer's *World as Will and Idea*: they contain almost all that is needed for an understanding of Burckhardt's philosophy. Has he, then, a philosophy? He has no 'philosophy of *history*'; indeed, it is repugnant to him if by this forbidding term there is to be understood what dominated the philosophical and historical scene in his time: the attempt to transform history into philosophy and, indeed, into theology. In other words, Burckhardt hates the philosophy of Hegel. This fundamentally irreverent intimacy with Providence, this 'bold and insolent anticipation of a world plan',[12] as he calls it, is not for him. All the introductory remarks to his *Reflections on World History* are directed against Hegel. 'Our task in this course,' he writes, 'consists in linking a series of historical observations and findings to an all but arbitrarily chosen line of thought and then again to another one.' [13] Further: 'Above all, we shall not give any philosophy of history'.[14] And a few lines later, so as to leave no doubt what has prompted this renuncia-

G

tion of all philosophy of history, the name of Hegel is introduced: 'Hegel . . . tells us that the only idea which is "given" in philosophy is the simple idea of reason, the idea that the world is rationally ordered: hence the history of the world is a rational process, and the conclusion yielded by world history *must* be that it was the rational, inevitable march of the world Spirit. . . . Hegel speaks also of the "purpose of eternal wisdom", and calls his study a theodicy by virtue of its recognition of the positive in which the negative (in popular parlance, evil) vanishes, subjected and overcome. He develops the fundamental idea that history is the record of the process by which mind becomes aware of its own significance; according to him, there is progress towards freedom. In the East only one man was free, in classical antiquity only a few, while modern times have set all men free. Thus we find him putting forward the doctrine of perfectibility, that is, our old familiar friend called progress.' [15]

But in spite of his disclaiming it, Burckhardt has, of course, a philosophy; that is, he thinks philosophically about history. He has, however, no system which could be expounded apart from, and beyond, his historical and philosophical thinking. His metaphysical beliefs and fundamental thoughts, therefore, have to be perceived through his reflections about things. Yet there is one philosopher in whom he finds the dispersed elements of his own thought crystallized into a definite system. It is Schopenhauer, whom Burckhardt in conversations with Nietzsche called 'our philosopher'.[16] The introduction to his *Reflections on World History* is in part a précis of what Schopenhauer has to say about the subject and, above all, about Hegel's hypostasis of history. 'The Hegelians,' Schopenhauer says, 'who regard the philosophy of history as the aim of all philosophy, ought to be taught some Plato, who indefatigably repeats that the object of philosophy lies in the unchangeable and in what lasts, and not in the things which are now like this, and now again like that. All those who postulate such constructions about the world in motion, or, as they call it, history, have not grasped the fundamental truth of philosophy: that, philosophically speaking, what *really* is is the same at all times. . . . The fools, however, believe that it will develop and one day arrive. . . . Thus they regard the whirling world as they perceive it as the ultimate reality, and see its final meaning in a meagre bliss on earth which, even if cultivated evermore by man and favoured by fate, will remain a hollow, deceptive, fickle and sorry thing of which nothing essentially better can ever come through either constitutions, or legal codes, or steam engines, or telegraphs. Those philosophers and glorifiers of history are therefore realistic simpletons, optimists and eudaemonists, which is to say, mediocre fellows and obstinate philistines and, in addition, bad Christians. . . . A real philosophy of history ought to bear in mind what for ever *is* and never *develops*. It can, indeed, not consist in raising the temporal aims of man to the rank of absolutes, and furthermore, in constructing in an artificial and fanciful manner man's progress; but it ought to be based upon the insight that, in all those endless variations and turmoils, we have before us merely the one creature, *essentially* identical and unchangeable, busying itself with the very same things to-day, and yesterday, and forever. . . . . This identity, preserved through all changes, is founded on the fundamental qualities of human hearts and brains, many bad, few good. . . . For someone bringing philosophical intentions to history, the study of Herodotus is sufficient. There he will find everything that has gone into the making of all subsequent world history: the activities, afflictions and fortunes of the human race. . . .' [17]

Schopenhauer's philosophy pervades the whole work of Jacob Burckhardt, and letter after letter shows how deeply he was in agreement with it. For instance, in the

Introduction to his *Reflections* he says: 'Our point of departure is the one and only thing which lasts in history and is its only possible centre: man, this suffering, striving and active being, as he is and was and will be for ever. . . . The philosophers of history see the past in opposition and as a preliminary to us as the more developed; *we* shall study what is *recurrent, constant* and typical as echoing in us and to be understood by us.' [18]

In this context Burckhardt, as though casually, makes a remark which strikes at the very centre of what can, after all, be called his philosophy of history. Man, he had previously asserted, not a Hegelian *Weltgeist*, is the centre of history. Is this to be taken as the declaration of a humanistic creed, pure and simple? In a sense, it is— in as far as it draws a definite line between the study of the *historical* aspect of human life and all theology. But while he definitely attacks the Hegelian brand of *secularized* theology, he acknowledges, without accepting it for himself, the particular justification of a genuinely religious interpretation of history, the great model of which he sees in Augustine's *De Civitate Dei*.[19] It is, however, none of his business. He is concerned with man, he says, and not with God. Is he, therefore, simply a humanist? We might be allowed to assume this more lightheartedly were it not for the remark which I have hinted at, and which concludes the paragraph that allots to man the central position in Burckhardt's studies. It says: 'Hence our study will, in a sense, be pathological in kind'. In other words: the perpetual agent of human affairs is a pathological creature, the Fall the beginning of history, original sin its driving force and redemption its end. Although this may sound very much like a surreptitious opening of the theological floodgates, it is, in fact, implied by Burckhardt when he regards the study of history as an essay in pathology.

He may have lost his faith in Christianity, very much as 'our philosopher' Schopenhauer had lost it; he may have abandoned the belief that the offer of redemption reached man in the shape of an historical event and was rejected by a creature bent on the *continuation* of his history. But, again like Schopenhauer, he accepts an *order of things* identical with that accepted by the Christian believer. It is the only order of things in which the religion of Christ can make sense; and if it is the *true* order of things, it is, at the same time, a profoundly *senseless* pattern *without* the religion of Christ. To look upon man, as Schopenhauer and Burckhardt did, as the fallen creature, on sin and evil as constituent and ineradicable factors in human history, on human affairs as pathological, without believing in the reality, existence, possibility and indeed the definite offer of spiritual health, must needs create a profound spiritual predicament. A tougher form of humanism than that of Burckhardt, a humanism coupled with rationalism, knows nothing of such difficulties. But it is astonishing how few people can really and truly attain to such toughness. Those who believe they can do without metaphysics are usually only those who cannot do with metaphysics, indulging instead in sentimentality and other secret betrayals of *ratio*, and in the kind of metaphysics which escapes being diagnosed as such merely by virtue of its diffuseness and conventional respectability; as, for instance, the metaphysics of equating scientific discoveries with the discovery of Truth, or the metaphysics of perfectibility and progress. For the rest the predicament persists; and it did, throughout their lives, persist for men like Schopenhauer and Burckhardt. They bore it nobly, and with a strength of spirit and character which is rare among human beings. They represent the true aristocracy of the nineteenth century. Within the German language writers like Stifter, Grillparzer, Mörike, Gottfried Keller, are of their kin. They are few indeed; and to all of them one could, in some measure, apply Nietzsche's words describing Schopenhauer in the image of Dürer's *Knight with*

Death and Devil, that man in armour 'who bravely travels along his path of horror, unperturbed by his terrible companions, and yet without hope'.[20]

Set up against such stoicism, those Germans who, in the nineteenth century, cried out their despair, appear somewhat obtrusive and vulgar. But who is able to judge whether in them—and I am thinking of men like Kleist, Büchner, Nietzsche himself—the sense of spiritual loss had not penetrated deeper? However this may be, it certainly was not met with the same inner resources of natural strength and tradition which saved Schopenhauer and Burckhardt.

2

Nietzsche, who, for a short time, was Burckhardt's very much younger professorial colleague in the University of Basle, once described him in a letter as 'that elderly, highly original man, given, not to distorting truth, but to passing it over in silence'.[21] He goes on to say that he deeply enjoys listening to Burckhardt's lectures 'with their profound thoughts and their strangely abrupt breaks and twists as soon as they touch the danger point'. Passing over the truth in silence, sudden twists as soon as the matter approaches a critical point: Nietzsche appears to imply that Burckhardt is in fact more of a rebel than he is inclined to show, and more profoundly desperate about the intellectual and spiritual situation of the age than his professorial equilibrium would betray. Indeed, Nietzsche was convinced to the very end of his conscious life that Burckhardt knew the desperate truth which he believed himself to have discovered and exposed, and that the resigned serenity of Burckhardt's life in Basle was a mask put on for the sake of self-defence. Again and again, from the depths of his loneliness, Nietzsche begged Burckhardt's understanding and sympathy. He was probably mistaken. The core of Burck-

hardt's being was not affected by his pessimism. There
was no need for him to attempt, in the manner of Nietzsche, any metamorphosis of spiritual gloom into Dionysian ecstasy. He knew, as certainly as Nietzsche, that the
civilization of Europe which he loved was doomed. To
one of his German friends, who placed high hopes in the
pre-1848 revolutionary and nationalist movement, he
wrote—to quote only one example out of a very great
number of similar statements: 'None of you has any idea
yet what a people is and how easily it deteriorates into
a barbarous mob. You do not know yet what a tyrannical
rule is to be set up over the spirit. . . . We may all
perish; but I for one shall choose the cause for which I
am going to perish: the culture of old Europe.' [22]

Burckhardt could not bear with Nietzsche's iconoclast
philosophizing. He had lost his religious faith, but, unlike Nietzsche, the loss was registered by the intelligence
alone. The 'shudder' with which, as a young student, he
discovered that he did not believe in the recorded circumstances of the birth of Christ did not disturb the core
of his being. 'Religions,' he said in his *Reflections on
World History,* 'are the expression of the eternal and
indestructible metaphysical need of human nature.' [23]
This he accepted as a self-evident and empirical truth—
in the same way in which it was accepted by Schopenhauer, who in his *World as Will and Idea* called man the
animal metaphysicum, in a chapter entitled 'About the
Metaphysical Need of Man'. And believing, as he did, in
a fundamental correspondence in the world between
needs and possibilities of satisfaction, Burckhardt could
not share Nietzsche's suspicion that man—the diseased
animal, for Nietzsche—was an eternally cheated misfit
within a universe catering, on the whole, for the natural
needs of its creatures. Should man alone have been
cursed with an everlasting appetite, to feed which all the
Heavens may be ransacked without result? Nietzsche
did believe this; and his Superman was the child of his

fancy, miraculously feeding on barren fields and finally conquering the metaphysical hunger itself. Burckhardt, on the other hand, was of a more robust spiritual nature and more firmly rooted in the Christian tradition of Europe. He continued to eat the bread and drink the wine, and called them by the names of culture and tradition. Religious crisis he regarded as only one more historical variation and change embedded in the spiritual *continuum* without which history would have meant nothing to him. To Burckhardt, therefore, Nietzsche's nihilism must have appeared monstrous, and yet it must have set in motion those elements of despair which were inherent in his own philosophy. The all but inhuman coldness with which he responded—or rather did not respond—to Nietzsche's entreaties for a word of encouragement can hardly be accounted for in any other way. We are reminded of Goethe's forbidding aloofness in his dealings with men of whom he sensed that too close a contact with them might endanger the subtle balance which he had achieved, because they embodied the *alter ego* of his own being, the *ego* of despair.

Nietzsche, however, remained convinced of Burckhardt's 'mask'. One of his notebook jottings from the years 1875–76 says: 'Those who are restrained, like Jacob Burckhardt, out of desperation',[24] and there is little doubt who is in his mind when in *Beyond Good and Evil* he remarks: 'There are "scholarly men" who make use of scholarship because it gives them a classically serene façade, and because scholarship suggests the conclusion that the man is superficial:—they *wish* that people should arrive at a wrong conclusion about them'. In the same context Nietzsche also speaks of 'buffoonery' as another possible disguise of 'desperate, all too certain knowledge'.[25] Clearly, he meant himself, referring to his own display of paradoxical formulations, witty extravagances, provocative exaggerations. The two supposed masks of despair, Burckhardt's scholarship and his own 'buffoonery', are mentioned once more: in the last letter Nietzsche wrote to Burckhardt after the catastrophe, foreseen by Burckhardt, had happened, and clinical insanity had descended upon him. It is one of the most extraordinary and most revealing documents ever composed by a madman, which begins with the words: 'Dear Herr Professor, when it comes to it I too would very much prefer a professorial chair in Basle to being God; but I did not dare to go as far in my private egoism as to refrain for its sake from the creation of the world', and in which the writer refers to himself as 'being condemned to entertain the next eternity with bad witticisms'.[26]

There were two men in Nietzsche's life whom intellectually he had abandoned, but whom he continued to love, respect and admire: Schopenhauer and Burckhardt. With regard to all others—and he was alone at the end— he identified their unwillingness to follow him intellectually with weakness of character, and discarded them. But to Burckhardt, about whose rejection of his own philosophizing he was left in no uncertainty, he submitted, as it were, his resignation in what are the only lucid words in an otherwise deranged note, written two days before the letter just quoted: 'Now you are our great—our greatest teacher'.[27]

In the case of Burckhardt, Nietzsche's love survived even humiliation. What then did, in so commanding a manner, hold Nietzsche's affection for Schopenhauer and Burckhardt? Undoubtedly what Goethe had praised in Schopenhauer: intellectual honesty. And something else as well: the spiritual vitality which enabled them to live on, and to remain sane in spite of their profound pessimism. This is precisely the same strength which the young Nietzsche, in his *Birth of Tragedy*, discerned in the Greeks, and which he passionately and lyrically exalted—so passionately and lyrically, indeed, that the work was, of course, rejected by the sound scholars of his day. Despair, reconciled to life through beauty: this is Nietzsche's interpretation of the Greek view of the world. It is identical with the view of Greek antiquity which pervades the pages of Burckhardt's *History of Greek Culture,* another of his lecture courses posthumously published between 1898 and 1902. Obviously, he had read his younger colleague's book on the *Birth of Tragedy.* Burckhardt, too, is attacking the conventional enthusiasts of classicism, who look upon ancient Greece as a prolonged jamboree of sunburned optimists and philosophizing athletes, and gives to tragic pessimism the central position in the picture he draws of their culture.

It is this tragic pessimism which, in the beginning of their acquaintance, Burckhardt and Nietzsche had in common. But Nietzsche soon went further, and the very way he went reveals—much to Burckhardt's horror—the precariousness of the position they had held in common. Nietzsche was more deeply wounded by the loss of positive religious convictions than Burckhardt, which is as much as to say that his nature was more in need of an articulate religious faith. The aesthetic comfort offered by the contemplation of the human tragedy was, in the long run, not sufficient to counteract Nietzsche's despair. For Burckhardt history, or rather the history of culture, was the medium of such selfless contemplation. Had his talents allowed him to become an artist, it would have been so much the better for him; as it was, the history of culture had to take the place of poetry. Here at least he could contemplate the *manifestations* of art. For it is the work of art (and with it, to a certain degree, culture itself) through which, according to Schopenhauer, man escapes from the drudgery of the Will and leaves behind the fetters of selfhood. Thus it testifies to man's share in a creative intelligence beyond the purely historical realm, the realm of original sin. Therefore, Burckhardt believes that it is in the sphere of culture that human contemplation can perceive that spiritual *continuum* which he believes gives meaning to all history. For the performance of this task, he maintains, 'the human mind is well equipped', for it represents 'the power of interpreting all things in an ideal sense. . . . Our spirit must transmute into a possession the remembrance of its passage through the ages of the world. What was once joy and sorrow must now become understanding. . . . Therewith the saying *Historia vitae magistra* assumes a higher yet a humbler meaning. We wish knowledge to make us, not shrewder (for next time) but wiser (for ever).' And finally: 'Contemplation, however, is not only the right and the duty of the historian; it is also a supreme need. It is our freedom in the very awareness of universal bondage and in the stream of necessities.' [28]

This is the nucleus of Burckhardt's view of history. It is, at the same time, the application of Schopenhauer's metaphysics to historical studies. It also contains Burckhardt's idea of the historian's objectivity, which for him does not consist in the seemingly simple and practically impossible device of suspending moral judgment or, indeed, any other judgment in the face of a phenomenon, merely because it happens to be historical. The evil which Burckhardt perceives in history—and he perceives more evil in it than good—he freely calls by its name; as freely as he calls beauty beautiful and ugliness ugly. 'From the fact, however,' he says in *Reflections on World History*, 'that good may come from evil, and from disaster relative happiness, it does not follow that evil and disaster are not what they are.' [29] *Values*, for him, are as real as facts and happenings. In this he remains with Schopenhauer a Platonic idealist, despising what he calls 'the frivolous pretence of objectivity' which, instead of achieving what it aims at, merely loses itself in a welter of relativities. By the objectivity of true contemplation he means the conquest of the self-will, the philosophical activity *kat'-exochen*. Its goal is certainly not the abolition of judgment, be it aesthetic or moral, but its purification.

There was a time when Nietzsche was prepared to

remain at rest here with Burckhardt. And indeed, we hardly know of any better resting-place. It is certainly good enough to deserve our most exacting efforts in defending it against the onrush of those noisily activist forces which, in the disguise and with the persuasion of social moralism, are undermining it from all sides. Burckhardt, in letters to his friends, called all 'these great achievements' in politics, industry and social organization which are demanded from us at the cost of all peace for contemplation 'thoroughly mediocre, and a nuisance because of the ever-increasing bother of "earnest work"'. He speaks of the 'frightful spiritual nullity' of 'radicalism',[30] of those 'odious windbags of progressive optimism', and fears that 'the conditions of Europe may overnight deteriorate into a kind of gangrene with all truly conservative forces suddenly dying away'.[31] In his critique of the age Nietzsche, consistently enough, was with him. At what point, then, did they part company?

It was, I would suggest, over a religious and moral issue.

The kinship between Schopenhauer's (and therefore Burckhardt's) philosophy of contemplation and Eastern forms of religion has often been emphasized. Yet we have, I think, little understanding of the nature of some aspects of Eastern quietism. What we really appreciate of it we judge by the tradition of European mysticism. The reward of this kind of mystical contemplation is the contact established with the divinity. Thus it is not practised for its own sake, but for the sake of this highest reward, which, as the highest reward, stands in no need of further justification. Schopenhauer's idea of contemplation also knows of some reward; but its reward is, or at least appears to be, the purest aesthetic experience. If life on this earth is sin and self-willed deception, if the misery of it by far outweighs the rare moments of happiness, if it is altogether the continuous and futile drudgery of a fallen creature—and this is, I believe, a faithful summing-up of Schopenhauer's and Burckhardt's views—then, surely, the desire to emancipate oneself from it, and seek reward in the sublimity of a self-detached vision, not of God but, for Burckhardt, of *history*, must needs provoke dissatisfaction and moral suspicion in a man to whom life on this earth is agony, precisely because he cannot attain to a vision of God.

This is where the roots of Nietzsche's catastrophic plight lie, and the deepest cause of his final breaking-away from his 'great educator' Schopenhauer and his 'great teacher' Burckhardt. With God 'being dead' for him he could find no lasting spiritual satisfaction in the pure contemplation of a creation deserted by its creator. If history, the dwelling-place of sin and evil, had thus lost its meaning, it had to be abolished; if the fallen creature had ceased to be redeemable, good and evil had to be transcended by the Superman; and the gloom of the Eternal Recurrence of a senseless world in motion (and not Burckhardt's spiritual *continuum*) was for him the only alternative to the Second Coming. Nietzsche, to the very end of insanity, spins out the thread of unbelief. In his very spiritual consistency there dwells the madness of desperation. Yet there was in him a mind nobler than the mind of those who, like Hegel's idealist and Marxian train, chose the other consistent alternative, seeking, and presumably finding, in the *historical* dimension of man's existence the promise of salvation, and in his mundane performances sufficient attraction for the *Weltgeist* to settle down among human beings, bringing with it the bliss of perfect harmony or, at least, a classless society.

Rare, however, are those who, on the highest level of spiritual awareness and in this hour of history, are blessed with the power to maintain the equipoise of suspense. Burckhardt was one of them. 'At every moment,' he wrote in a letter, 'I would be prepared to exchange my life for a never-having-been.' [32] He knew 'what beggars we mortals are at the gates of happiness',[33] but he was determined to 'die at peace with the world'. Yet his, on the surface, purely aesthetic faith was not the only source that sustained his soul. There was, though it remained inarticulate, much left in him of a faith which has a profounder reach. In his *Reflections on World History*, contemplating the power and the success of evil (and power he regarded as for ever predominantly evil, and Napoleon he called a personified absurdity), he dismisses the comfort which the Hegelian assumption of a historical master-plan for the world may give. 'Every successful wickedness,' he says, 'is, to say the least of it, a scandal,' and he adds: 'The only lesson to be derived from the successful misdeeds of the strong is to hold life here and now in no higher esteem than it deserves.'[34] And once, concluding one of his lectures about Greek art with some reflections on the sadness expressed in the faces of the marble images of Greek gods, he made the Vatican Hermes say: 'You are astonished that I am so sad, I, one of the Olympians living in perpetual bliss and immortal joy? Indeed, we possessed everything: glory, heavenly beauty, eternal youth, everlasting pleasure, and yet we were not happy. . . . We lived only for ourselves and inflicted suffering on all others. . . . We were not good, and hence we had to perish.'[35] This is not the language of a rhapsodist of beauty. It rather sounds like an echo of the voice of Jacob Burckhardt *senior,* Vicar of the Minster of Basle.

NIETZSCHE AND GOETHE

1

In 1817 Goethe published in *Kunst und Altertum* a little essay entitled 'Epochs of the Spirit, based on Hermann's newest records'.[1] Inspired by the book *De Mythologia Graecorum Antiquissimorum* of the Leipzig scholar Gottfried Hermann, this sketch, anticipating in its modest way the method of Spengler's historical morphology, speaks of four major phases in the history of man. These 'four epochs of the human spirit', 'profoundly contemplated', as Goethe claims, 'and fittingly named', he calls the Ages of Poetry, Theology, Philosophy and Prose. They are preceded, according to his account, by a state which does not even qualify for a name. It is the chaos before the beginning and before the Word—although even then a few favoured spirits might rise above the

H

speechless dark, crudely meditating the uncreated universe and uttering raucous sounds to express their confused astonishment. Theirs is an apparently barren state of mind which nevertheless holds the seeds of observation and philosophy, of giving nature names, and thus of poetry. From these inarticulate mutterings emerges the first Age proper, the Age of Poetry, in which man projects his tender familiarity with himself, his desires and fears, satisfactions and discontents, on to the things which surround him. It is a time of popular myth and poetical fancy; the soul overconfidently and lightheartedly frees itself of the cumbersome abstruseness of the primeval stage. The spirits of myth and poetry wield their undivided power over the community which is, as Goethe says, distinguished by a sensuousness at once free, serious, noble and enhanced by the imagination.

Soon, however, man finds himself, perhaps by force of external circumstances, thrown into new perplexities. The world ceases to be his castle, in which the mind and the imagination dwell comfortably between walls covered with allegorical tapestries, and appears once more inadequately understood and mastered. The poetically comprehending creature is again beset by apprehension, the idyllic order threatened by a multitude of demons demanding to be placated in their wildness, reverenced in their incalculable dominion, and conquered no longer by pretty fancies but only through a more energetic activity of the spirit. Gone is the graceful intimacy of the Age of Poetry, and Mystery is reinstated. It is to this epoch that ultimately God is revealed, with the fear and terror of the primeval phase purified into love and awe. We may call it, says Goethe, the Age of the Holy, or the Age of Theology, or the Age of Reason in its highest sense.

Again, it cannot last. For Reason will insist on reasoning and ultimately, as a conqueror often does with the object of his conquests, destroy what it is reasoning about. Analysing what eludes analysis, systematizing what defies the system, it will in the end deceive itself by pretending that the vainly besieged mystery does not exist. At this point the Age of the Holy gives way to the Age of Philosophy, or, to use a more familiar term, to enlightenment and finally rationalism. We cannot, says Goethe, but acknowledge the noble and intelligent endeavour of this epoch; yet while it may suit some talented individuals, it cannot satisfy whole peoples. The Prosaic Age is bound to follow. The all too radical attempt of the Age of Philosophy at a 'humanization' and rationalization of the mysterious ends in a perverted miracle. The mystery, cheated of its rightful place, goes underground, reverting to its primeval, unholy and barbarous stage. The human spirit, agitated by historical catastrophes, leaps backward over all hurdles which the guidance of reason has erected, clinging here and there to remnants of tradition, scattered residues of many incompatible beliefs, then plunges headlong into pools of insipid mythologies, bringing to the top the muddy poetry of the depths and proclaiming it as the creed of the age.

No longer are there teachers who teach with calm and reason, but merely men sowing grain and weeds in random profusion. No centre holds the human world together and men must lose their bearings; for countless individuals step forth as leaders, preaching their perfect foolishness as the acme of wisdom. In such an age every belief turns into blasphemy, and the proclamation of mysteries into sacrilege. Elements, once evolving naturally one from the other, are now interlocked in perpetual strife. It is the return of the tohu-bohu; yet a chaos not fertile as the first, but so deadening that not even God could create from it a world worthy of Himself.

It is surprising that a peaceful Leipzig scholar, whose attitude Nietzsche once described as the typically *sächsisch* combination of humanism and religious rationalism,[2]

should have been the begetter of such a rare flight of
Goethe's historical imagination, culminating in a precise
vision of the apocalypse through which we are living.
But although the condensed precision of this seemingly
casual prophecy is unique in Goethe's writings, shadows
of things to come fall on many a page of his mature work.
In the guarded and fortified stillness of *Wilhelm Meisters
Wanderjahre* (the work that occupied him at the same
time) echoes can be discerned of subterranean rum-
blings, menacing with future eruptions a society whose
exposures and dangers are acknowledged by the very
didactic passion of this extraordinary work—a work which
struck Nietzsche, in one of his more irreverent moods, as
a mixture of 'the most beautiful things in the world' and
'the most ridiculous triflings'.[3] Indeed, a certain paral-
lelism is obvious between the three epochs of the spirit
and the three stations in Wilhelm Meister's pilgrimage
which fill the first book of the novel, so that the monastic
sphere of St. Joseph the Second is informed with all the
ingredients of the Age of the Holy, with elements of the
Age of Poetry lingering on, while the estate of Hersilie's
uncle clearly represents the Age of Philosophy, with no
picture tolerated in the eighteenth-century portrait gal-
lery that 'might point even remotely towards religion,
tradition, mythology, legend or fable'.[4] And there is
finally Makarie's ancient castle, looking so fresh and
new—'as though builders and masons had only just de-
parted'[5]—where Goethe's, not Newton's, physics are pursued, a science whose calculations reveal, rather than
disturb, the harmony between man's intuitive and rational natures, showing him, not as the ruthlessly dominating, but as 'the spiritually integrating part'[6] of the
universe. This castle of Makarie's stands like a fortress,
built in Goethe's imagination, to ward off, as their most
positive alternative, the horrors of the Prosaic Age.

Furthermore, in that masterpiece of ambiguity, *Faust*,
the clash between the holy simplicity of the Gretchen

world and the reason of the philosopher, aided by the
prose of the Devil, determines not only the tragedy of
Part I, but finds expression also in Part II. Indeed, if we
sought in Goethe's works for the most poignant poetic
dramatization of the defeat of the holy at the hands of
prosaic engineering, we should have to call on the faithful old couple in their little house on the hill, sacrificed
to the planning of the future bliss of millions:

BAUCIS *Menschenopfer mussten bluten,*
   Nachts erscholl des Jammers Qual;
   Meerab flossen Feuergluten,
   Morgens war es ein Kanal.
   Gottlos ist er, ihn gelüstet
   Unsre Hütte, unser Hain;
   Wie er sich als Nachbar brüstet,
   Soll man untertänig sein.

PHILEMON *Hat er uns doch angeboten*
   Schönes Gut im neuen Land!

BAUCIS *Traue nicht dem Wasserboden,*
   Halt auf deiner Höhe stand!

PHILEMON *Lasst uns zur Kapelle treten,*
   Letzten Sonnenblick zu schaun!
   Lasst uns läuten, knien, beten,
   Und dem alten Gott vertraun! [7]

[Human sacrifices had to bleed, the night resounded
with cries of anguish; floods of fire poured into the sea,
in the morning it was a canal. Godless he is, lusting
after our cottage, our grove; boastful neighbour that
he is, he demands obedience.—Yet he has offered us a
pretty estate in the new country!—Do not trust the
watery soil, hold out on your height!—Let us go to
our chapel, catch the sun's last radiance, ring the bells,
and kneel and pray, and put our trust in God.]

What, in the Prosaic Age, is to become of poetry itself,
its activity and its enjoyment? How will this very poem

Faust be received? Goethe asks, five days before his death, in his last letter to Wilhelm von Humboldt. 'The absurdity and confusion of the day is such,' he writes, 'as to convince me that the honest and prolonged labour with which I have built this strange edifice will be but ill rewarded; it will be cast up by the sea as fragments of a wreck, and for some time to come will be buried under the barren dunes of the age. Confused gospels, begetting confused deeds, are abroad in the world, and my business is to enhance and purify what is mine and what has remained with me, as you, my worthy friend, also contrive to do up there in your castle.' [8]

In other words, the Prosaic Age is upon us, with its disenchantment of myth and poetry, and its 'mystification' of reason itself. It will—to use Goethe's words— 'drag into the vulgar light of day the ancient heritage of a noble past, and destroy not only the capacity for profound feeling and the beliefs of peoples and priests, but even that belief of reason which divines meaningful coherence behind strangeness and seeming disorder'. [9]

It is, then, the destruction, or rather the mutilation and deformation, of something which Goethe, perhaps for want of a better word, calls 'belief', which is one of the symptoms, or one of the causes, of the repulsiveness of the Prosaic Age. As soon as the notion of belief enters into our reflections about Goethe, we have to move with the utmost wariness; for Goethe, of course, was no believer in any doctrinal sense. On the other hand, we need not be too prudish and may take courage from the fact that Goethe, at about the same time, uses the word again in a very much more contaminated neighbourhood: namely, in connection with the Old Testament. Meditating on the desert adventures of the Israelites, he says, in his 'Notes and Discourses concerning the *West-östlicher Divan*': 'The one and only real and profound theme of the world and of human history—a theme to which all others are subordinate—remains the conflict between belief and unbelief. All epochs dominated by belief in whatever shape have a radiance and bliss of their own, and bear fruit for their people as well as for posterity. All epochs over which unbelief in whatever form maintains its miserable victory, even if they boast and shine for a while with false splendour, are ignored by posterity because nobody likes to drudge his life out over sterile things.' [10]

Paradoxically enough, what follows leaves no doubt that Goethe, indulging at this point in a rather ruthless sort of Bible criticism, does not mean the belief of the strict believer in the Old Testament. What, then, does he mean? For clearly, this belief can be no trifling matter; it makes and unmakes epochs by its very coming and going; it gives the Age of the Holy its holiness and in parting abandons the next to its prosaic fate; and its struggle with unbelief is proclaimed as the only theme of genuine historical relevance.

The question of what he meant by 'belief' would have drawn from Goethe different answers at different times, all equally veiled, ironical—and irritated. For the question touches upon a sphere which Goethe held to be reserved for the initiates—'Sagt es niemand, nur den Weisen, Weil die Menge gleich verhöhnet'. Thus it is impossible to state his beliefs in any doctrinal manner, particularly if one wishes to avoid a discussion of that sublime menace besetting all studies of Goethe: pantheism. For there is no creed to be elicited from Goethe's writings. Put together systematically as articulate opinions, his convictions would appear very inconsistent and at times self-contradictory. Yet it is neither his opinions nor their inconsistencies that matter in this context. What matters is the level on which his convictions are formed, or the pressure of spiritual energy by which they are sustained; and the quality and direction of his beliefs are most clearly revealed through Goethe's critique of his age. For there is little doubt that the mature Goethe would have put his contemporary world, in spite of occasional outbursts of Panama Canal optimism, into a rather shadowy place on his map of the world's historical epochs, at some removes, in any case, from the Age of Poetry and the Age of the Holy, and considerably nearer those grey stretches where history writes its most atrocious prose passages. And he would certainly not have discovered in it many glimpses of that radiance which emanates from 'epochs of belief'.

It would be easy enough to deny the historical accuracy of Goethe's scheme of epochs; but perhaps still easier to show that our seemingly most effective refutation would simply be due to our use of a different code of selection and emphasis in ordering the mass of historical raw material. Goethe's—and Nietzsche's—judgments on their contemporary world are undoubtedly what it is the fashion to denounce as 'wild generalizations'. But then, this is the same vice in which the prophets of the Old Testament indulged. Perhaps the Israel of their time was, in fact, a very much better community than their indignation suggests. But if we reached this conclusion, and even if it were based on the greatest profusion of historical evidence, our findings would ultimately reflect, not a higher degree of 'objective knowledge', but our allegiance to values which the prophets would have denounced as false. And as this mental and moral situation is the precise cause of their indignation, it is we who are under judgment—a position which is generally not regarded as favourable to the forming of unbiased views. Also, I think, our case against the justice of the judges must be aggravated by the fact that their prophecy has come true. The Temple was destroyed.

What the mature Goethe means by belief has this in common with the prophets—that for him too it is the active realization of certain *values* in the lives of men. And our question turns on the nature of these values, a question which, as Nietzsche knew, 'is more *funda-*

mental than the question of the certainty [of knowledge]: the latter becomes serious only if the question of values is answered'.[11] Goethe would have accepted this, although it stands as a key-phrase within a body of thought which at first sight is worlds apart from the world of Goethe. And Goethe actually did accept it, if not in the radical spirit in which Nietzsche proposed it, nor, of course, with the same intensity of desperate doubt about the worth of knowledge. His opposition to Newton, for instance, is ultimately based not on a conviction of his own *scientific* superiority, but on his commitment to values which he believed were threatened by man's adopting an exclusively mathematical-analytical method in his dealings with nature. Elsewhere in this book I have attempted to show how Goethe confuses the issue in his scientific writings; but outside the laboratory, as it were, he makes this abundantly clear, as, for instance, in the words which Wilhelm Meister, here no longer a disciple of life but the expositor of Goethe's own wisdom, addresses to the astronomer: 'I can well understand that it must please you, sages of the sky, to bring the immense universe gradually as close to your eyes as I saw that planet just now. But allow me to say . . . that these instruments, with which we aid our senses, have a morally detrimental effect on man. . . . For what he thus perceives with his senses is out of keeping with his inner faculty of discernment; it would need a culture, as high as only exceptional people can possess, in order to harmonize, to a certain extent, the inner truth with the inappropriate vision from without. . . .'[12]

2

'There must have been a time when the religious, aesthetic and moral perceptions were at one.'[13] This is not, though it could be, a sentence from the context of Goethe's 'epochs of the spirit', but one of Nietzsche's posthumous notes from the time of his *Transvaluation of Values*. It is so much a Goethean thought that it seems to have been expanded into the following reflection about Goethe in *Götzen-Dämmerung*, one of the last works of Nietzsche:

> Goethe—in a grandiose attempt to get beyond the eighteenth century through the naturalness of the Renaissance, a kind of self-conquest on the part of that century—had within himself its strongest instincts: its sentimentality, its nature-idolatry, its anti-historical bias, its idealism, lack of realism and revolutionary spirit (which is only one form of the lack of realism). He called in the help of history, of natural science, of antiquity, even of Spinoza, and, above all, of practical activity; he surrounded himself with closed horizons; he did not desert life, but placed himself at its centre and took as much as possible upon himself, above himself, into himself. What he aimed at was *totality*; *he fought against the sundering of reason, sensuality, feeling, will . . .* ; he disciplined himself into wholeness, he *created* himself . . . Goethe was, in the midst of an unrealistic age, a *convinced realist.* . . . He envisaged man as strong, highly civilized, skilled in all skills of the body, holding himself in check, having respect for himself as a creature who may be allowed to taste the whole width and wealth of naturalness, who is strong enough for this kind of freedom; who is tolerant, not from weakness but from strength, -because he knows how to use to his advantage what would destroy an average character. . . .[14]

Although things of this kind have been said so often in later appraisals of Goethe that they have come to smack of the commonplace, in the context of Nietzsche's *Transvaluation of Values* they have a profundity of their own, and receive in the concluding words of this passage, so far withheld, a surprising twist which we shall, a little later, allow to shock us. For the time being we should like to reflect on the identification in this passage of Goethe's realism with his antagonism to the severance of reason, sensuality, feeling and will; or, in Nietzsche's previous formula, on Goethe's roots in an imaginary period in which religious, aesthetic and moral perceptions were at one—a unity so disastrously destroyed in the Prosaic Age.

The term 'realism' had a definite meaning, as the opposite to nominalism, at a time when metaphysical disputes enjoyed the advantages of as rigid a discipline as is nowadays accorded to scientific research. But, of course, this was before the word became used as a coin of uncertain value in that nineteenth-century bazaar of ideas where other counters too, such as transcendentalism, idealism, empiricism, materialism, positivism, bought a few frills of the mind. Thus Goethe's 'realism', fallen among the philistines, assumed so often the meagre meaning of 'down to earth', or 'practical', or 'you will learn, my boy'. Or else, as the name of a literary genre, 'realism' was to provide a convenient common denominator for all writers who harness the exuberance of their imaginations to the austere task of calling a spade a spade.

Clearly, this is not what Nietzsche means in speaking of the realist Goethe. What, I think, he does mean I should like to illustrate with the help of three Goethe aphorisms which were first printed together in the same number of *Kunst und Altertum* (V, 3, of the year 1826). The first reads as follows: 'It is now about twenty years since the whole race of Germans began to "transcend". Should they ever wake up to this fact, they will look very odd to themselves.' [15] The second, famous enough, is: 'In a true symbol the particular represents the universal, not as a dream or shadow, but as the living and instantaneous revelation of the unfathomable'.[16] The third is at first rather obscure: 'All that is ideal will ultimately, once it is claimed by the real, consume it, and itself. As paper money consumes the silver and itself.' [17] There is, not merely by virtue of their sequence in print, an intimate connection between these three aphorisms. The first, of course, ridicules the German *Transzendentalphilosophie* of Goethe's time; the second provides the happiest condensation of Goethe's own idea of the relationship between the transcendent and the immanent, the 'ideal' and the 'real'; the third is the epigrammatic abbreviation of the prophecy of the Prosaic Age, this time seen as the destructive, nihilistic outcome of the tearing apart of the real and the ideal sphere.

It is a very long story which these three aphorisms succeed in cutting short, and it would be an invidious business indeed to restore it to its original length. But perhaps a few meditations are permissible.

Goethe's hostility towards all forms of transcendental philosophy has certainly no affinities whatever with a very much later philosophical offensive against the transcendent, waged under the name of positivism—a campaign with which Nietzsche is often associated by his more simple-minded interpreters. On the contrary, Goethe's ill feelings against the transcendentalists sprang from the same source which sustained his energetic attacks on the kind of positivism he believed to be inherent in Newtonian physics. He regarded both transcendentalists and positivists (of whom he had the idea, if not the name) as the systematizers of a perception of reality which to him appeared absurd, indeed as that very 'absurdity and confusion of the day' which he denounced at so late an hour of his life to Wilhelm von Humboldt. What both these tendencies of the mind—superficially so inimical to each other—have in common is a passion for abstraction. And it is in abstraction that Goethe saw the fatal loophole through which reason could escape into an illusory freedom from its commitments to what is of the senses, of feeling, of the will. He dreaded this eman-cipation of reason, whether exercised in adventures of transcendental speculation, or in the mathematical calcu-lus which creates, despite its apparent empiricism, the phenomena to be fitted into its abstract order.

Either method of emancipating reason from the totality of the human person appeared to Goethe as the denial of his vision of man, the negation of the values to which he was committed, the heresy *kat'exochen*. He sincerely believed that this way lay catastrophe.

In the pursuits of transcendentalism he discerned the danger that reason, doped with transcendental ambition, would construct a world too big in its anaemic hugeness for man to live and love in, distracting him at every point from—as Wilhelm Meister puts it—'attending with spon-taneous care to the duty of the day, examining the purity of your hearts and the stability of your minds. . . . Only then will you find the right attitude towards the sub-lime; for it is to the sublime that we dedicate ourselves in all manner of activities and in a spirit of awe. . . .' [18] In a spirit of awe; not of that spiritual conceit of which he suspected the architects of the transcendental Towers of Babel to be possessed.

If in transcendentalism human reason was perverted in the direction of the abstruse, in scientific positivism, so it seemed to Goethe, it was led astray in yet another way: in turning the universe into a plaything for mathematics and the wilful assertiveness of experimentation, reason once more placed the world out of the reach of true human comprehension. For the truth of human com-prehension resides for Goethe in that balanced vision in which the religious, the aesthetic and the moral percep-tions are at one. Only through their concord the world stands revealed as the proper home of man, appearing neither too great for his insignificance, nor too small for his greatness; neither too fantastic for his reason, nor too prosaic for his imagination; neither too unwieldy for his will, nor too unlovable for his affection. In a very profound sense of that word, *propriety* is for Goethe the criterion of truth. This is why Nietzsche admired him as the last of the great aristocratic minds of Europe.[19] For there is indeed something plebeian at work in all other standards of truth which have become, articulately or not, the fashion in modern intellectual activities: elements of either self-abasement or rational conceit, of excessive curiosity, of psychological tactlessness, and a sniggering suspicion of the absence of meaning in anything that evades definition or experimental proof, and above all a disregard for those intangible qualities that make the world a noble habitation.

Goethe's scientific labours were directed and sustained by his intuitive certainty that knowledge can only be true as long as it is not in excess of man's feelings. The problem involved is, of course, an old one, at least as old as modern science itself, and was first lived and struggled through by that extraordinary man in whom the mind of a mathematician clashed with the mind of a mystic—Pascal. His endless concern was with reason and that reason of which reason knows nothing: the reason of the heart; with the *esprit de géométrie* and the *esprit de finesse*. Since then the question and conflict, in innumerable variations, have never ceased to vex some of the finest minds of Europe. In Goethe's case, however, it can hardly be called a problem. For he had no serious doubts about the worthlessness of the *esprit de géométrie*. And where its achievements were beyond dispute, beyond even the negative certainty of Goethe, the utmost homage he was prepared to pay to them was the suggestion that a soul rich with intuition could reach at least as far as the newest telescopes. In the peculiar household of Makarie, the astronomer's business is simply to spot the stars which the lady of the house, harbouring all the galaxies in her breast, has seen in her dreams; an astronomical job not very much superior to that of the digger who digs for the water that the diviner has divined.

But beyond such indulgence of a wayward sense of humour, Goethe is deeply convinced that man can only do justice to himself and to the world and its maker by creating from within an image of both himself and the world which does not clash with his idea of the deity. And Goethe's idea of the deity was given to him in that 'revealed mystery', that 'living and instantaneous revelation of the unfathomable', through the symbolic nature of the particular. From this symbolic nature of the particular, to be grasped only in the concerted receptivity of sense, mind, feeling and will, man was increasingly alienated through the excessive rationalism of both his physics and metaphysics.

The Germans were indeed to look odd to themselves once they woke up to their real status after all the transcending had been done: as odd, one might add, as the scientist, confronted with the all but demonic unmanageability of the results of his analytical radicalism. For what is lost between the extremes of transcendence and analysis is the Goethean ideal of personality: a state of balance between what man *is* and what he *can do*. 'Man ought not to know more of a thing than he can creatively live up to.' Goethe might have said this. It was said by Nietzsche, reflecting on the sterility of philological studies, and comparing the quality of mind of his most learned colleagues with Goethe's meagre philological equipment; yet, he adds, 'he knew enough to wrestle fruitfully with antiquity!' [20] And elsewhere: 'Goethe's taste and ability ran parallel.' [21] This is a posthumous note from the time of the dithyrambus *Richard Wagner in Bayreuth*. Even then he knew what was to become violent polemic in later years: that this could not be said of Richard Wagner. And with the words 'the presumptuous' the remark on Goethe leads on to an observation about Richard Wagner's histrionic character.

Indeed, Nietzsche knew who Goethe was. There is the instruction of Goethe in his turning away from Wagner, the Goethean knowledge that it is the discrepancy between human substance and human virtuosity, between what a man is and what he can do, which is a dominant feature of the Prosaic Age. The Age of Talent may be an alternative name for it. The symptoms are displayed by art and life alike. Life is frightened out of its highly enlightened wits by the return of ancient nightmares: the tales of the sorcerer's apprentice, of dwarfs with magic powers. The promise of Heaven for the poor in spirit is understood to mean that, on earth at least, they should be educated into clever people able to manipulate and let loose the technical installations of Hell. And in art, there are sounds most skilfully organized, furies expressed in the most virtuoso fashion, and proud of signifying nothing. Whole systems of aesthetics are evolved to justify this state of affairs. A world emptied of meaning seeks to escape from the infinite boredom of its meaninglessness by the magic of words without flesh, and forms without content. And, indeed, the attempt to distil poetry from the things or ideas that form our 'real' world would be in vain. Poetry, we are told, is enchantment, and all things and thoughts have been robbed of their charm in the bright daylight robbery of utility and abstraction. Yet for Goethe things and thoughts shared that luminous concreteness which is the quality of a world with all its dimensions intact. Remember what he called 'thinking' in a passage of his *Second Sojourn in Rome*, where he describes his impression of Raphael's 'Transfigurazione': 'The kindred spirits among us were confirmed in their convictions,' he writes; 'Raphael, they said to one another, is distinguished by the rightness of his thinking.' And thus he interprets the two levels of being, represented in that painting: 'How can one sever what is above from what is below? The two are one;

below there is suffering and neediness, and above active mercy, the one reflecting upon the other in mutual interchange. Is it then, to express the meaning of this painting in a different way, at all possible to separate from the real its ideal relevance?' [22]

In the 'Buch Hafis' of the *West-östlicher Divan*, the section which has the motto:

> *Sei das Wort die Braut genannt,*
> *Bräutigam der Geist;*
> *Diese Hochzeit hat gekannt,*
> *Wer Hafisen preist.*[23]

[Let the word be named the bride, and the spirit the bridegroom; he who sings in praise of Hafis has known this wedlock.]

the poet, addressing himself to Hafis, proclaims his faith in a world marked with the imprint of the divine features and sings its praise in defiance of all negation, hindrance, robbery, that words and things endure at the hands of the detractors and abstractors:

> *Und so gleich ich dir vollkommen,*
> *Der ich unsrer heil'gen Bücher*
> *Herrlich Bild an mich genommen,*
> *Wie auf jenes Tuch der Tücher*
> *Sich des Herren Bildnis drückte,*
> *Mich in stiller Brust erquickte,*
> *Trotz Verneinung, Hindrung, Raubens,*
> *Mit dem heitern Bild des Glaubens.* [24]

[And so I am your perfect likeness, I who have taken on myself the glorious image of our sacred books: as on that cloth of cloths there was imprinted the countenance of the Lord, so, within my quiet heart, was I

I

refreshed, despite negation, hindrance, robbery, by the serene image of faith.]

This, then, is Goethe's belief, or his answer to the problem which is 'more fundamental than the question of the certainty of knowledge': the problem of values. The answer lies in Goethe's realism as understood by Nietzsche. It is the *realism of the symbol*; not of the obscure symbol thrown up by the collective unconscious of the symbolists, invading the husks of dead memories with dreamt and undreamt-of significances; nor of the symbol which refers to abstractions, in the manner of an allegory: the kind of symbol which the young philologist Nietzsche in a preparatory note for *The Birth of Tragedy* regarded as the sign of a dying art because it introduced, furtively and in flimsy disguise, abstract notions—but the symbol in its original meaning, defined by Nietzsche in the same note, in a strikingly Goethe-like manner, as 'the language of the universal'.[25] This realism of the symbol is the common property of all great art. It does not strain after an ideal sphere which may redeem the prosaic unworthiness of this world (as Schiller's art does), nor does it seek deliverance from the terror of truth in the healing unreality of the 'schöner Schein' (as Nietzsche sometimes believed), nor does it self-consciously call on dreams and nightmares pleasantly or unpleasantly to ruffle the boring smoothness of life's surface. It describes; and in describing it opens our eyes to what really is. And what really is is not a dream or shadow, nor the meaningless agony of the Will, nor the abstractions of Reason, but the living revelation of the unfathomable. Yet why should the unfathomable be beautiful? Because it can only be comprehended by the unfathomable, and the only truly unfathomable faculty of man is love. Thus the realism of the symbol becomes the artistic vindication of the reality of a lovable world. 'That something like Spinoza's *amor dei* could be experienced again!' [26] This is a note which

Nietzsche, during his most radical Anti-Christ period, made about Goethe.

3

At this point we had better return to that passage in Nietzsche's *Götzen-Dämmerung* from which, in quoting it before, we left out the concluding words. After he has called Goethe a 'convinced realist in the midst of an unrealistic age', Nietzsche continues: 'Such a mind, having attained to real freedom, lives at the very centre of all things with a joyful and confident acceptance of fate, lives in the faith that only the particular in its separateness is objectionable, and that in the wholeness of life everything is affirmed in its holiness—*he no longer denies.* . . . There is no higher faith than this: I have baptized it in the name of Dionysus.'[27]

This is very beautiful and true, and shocking only because of Dionysus so suddenly entering an apparently Apolline scene. Goethe, no doubt, would have been baffled by the choice of this godfather, and might have asked for some less inebriating deity to be his spiritual support—Apollo, perhaps, or even Eros. Yet it is precisely this invocation of Dionysus, forced upon Nietzsche (and not only upon him) by his determination to accept and affirm life, which is our theme; and we should lose track of it if we allowed ourselves to be persuaded that it was, as it were, Apollo's child's play for Goethe to persevere in affirmation, or simply due to his superbly fortunate temperament and genius. And our theme would equally be abandoned if we succeeded in no more than showing that the iconoclast Nietzsche surrounded the picture of Goethe with nothing but admiring marginal notes—significant though even this would be. Goethe would not be the author of Faust and Mephistopheles had he not known—and at times with terrible intimacy— the spirit of denial, of

. . . Was ist daran zu lesen?
Es ist so gut, als wär' es nicht gewesen,
Und treibt sich doch im Kreis, als wenn es wäre.
Ich liebte mir dafür das Ewig-Leere.[28]

[What can one make of it? It is as good as though it had never been. . . . And yet it rushes round in circles, as if it had some real existence. I should prefer instead eternal emptiness],

with its anticipatory echoes of Nietzsche's Eternal Recurrence of a positivistically self-contained world without any opening into meaning and sense. Indeed, he was only too familiar with the temptation of calling on magical powers to endow a drably disenchanted life with the poignancy of consuming beauty:

Und sollt' ich nicht, sehnsüchtigster Gewalt,
In's Leben ziehn die einzigste Gestalt.[29]

[And shall I not, with all the might of my craving, succeed in bringing to life the uniquely beautiful shape?]

This desire, even if realized only for that one fatal moment of ultimate satisfaction, is Faust's very challenge to the Devil. But the challenge is withdrawn at the end, and the *very desire for magical transformation identified with the act of blaspheming and cursing life:*

Könnt' ich Magie von meinem Pfad entfernen,
Die Zaubersprüche ganz und gar verlernen,
Stünd ich, Natur, vor dir ein Mann allein,
Da wär's der Mühe wert, ein Mensch zu sein.
Das war ich sonst, eh' ich's im Düstern suchte,
Mit Frevelwort mich und die Welt verfluchte.[30]

[Could I forget my sorcery, and ban my magic, stand,
stripped of it utterly, oh Nature, face to face with thee,
it would be worth while then to be a man. I was one
once, before I searched in the sinister sphere, thus
blasphemously cursing the world and myself.]

This rejection of magic is, of course, not merely a
poetical and secularized version of the traditional theological disapproval of that activity. Nor has it anything
in common with the conventional idea of piety. It
simply reflects Goethe's final acceptance of life as it is—
only that Goethe's vision of what is affirms the *reality* of
much that in the consciousness of the Prosaic Age is not.
Goethe is exemplary in his courage to trust in the
absolute reliability of that experiment which, in its utter
'subjectivity', is not merely one of many possible, but the
experience of life itself. And at least half of his experiment yields results dismissed by the Prosaic Age with
frowning vagueness as 'emotional' or 'mystical':

Sie haben dich, heiliger Hafis,
Die mystische Zunge genannt,
Und haben, die Wortgelehrten,
Den Wert des Worts nicht erkannt.

Mystisch heissest du ihnen,
Weil sie Närrisches bei dir denken,
Und ihren unlautern Wein
In deinem Namen verschenken.

Du aber bist mystisch rein,
Weil sie dich nicht verstehn.
Der du, ohne fromm zu sein, selig bist!
Das wollen sie dir nicht zugestehn.[31]

[They have called you, Saint Hafis, the mystical tongue;
but they, the scribes, have not recognized the mean-

ing of the word. To them you are mystical because you
inspire foolish thoughts in them, and because they
pour out their impure wine in your name. Indeed, you
are mystical, but only because they do not understand
you, you who are blessed without being pious. And
this they will not allow you.]

This is the poem 'Offenbar Geheimnis' from the *West-
östlicher Divan*. Nietzsche could have written it. It is
Goethe's most light-hearted assertion of the oneness of
the two spheres, of the revelation of the unfathomable in the reality of the symbol, and of the holiness
and blessedness which is the quality of being *really*
alive.

The 'ideal' aspect of life, abandoned by transcendentalists and positivists alike to some limbo of ideality, was
so inescapably real to Goethe that he was convinced it
would one day avenge itself on the age that has banished it from its 'reality'. This brings us to the last of the
three aphorisms from *Maximen und Reflexionen* which
we have selected to epitomize stages on the precarious
journey of the European mind. It is the aphorism which
follows immediately upon the definition of the symbol
from which this discussion has so far taken its bearings
and which it leaves now with one of the last jottings
among the posthumously published notes of Nietzsche:
'The interpreters of poets do not understand that the
poet has both: the reality and the symbol. Thus he has
the first and the second sense of a totality.' [32] This last
aphorism reads, once more: 'All that is ideal will ultimately, once it is claimed by the real, consume it, and
itself. As paper money consumes the silver and itself.'
And this is exactly what has happened within the fifty
years of the Prosaic Age, between Goethe's death and
Nietzsche's *Zarathustra*. Goethe's realism, on its profoundest level, was driven to despair. And Nietzsche, in
order to transform this despair into affirmation, had to

call in so un-Goethean a spirit as that of Dionysus. The comparison between the god of Goethe's *amor dei* and Nietzsche's love of Dionysus yields the measure by which we can assess the distance the Prosaic Age has travelled from Goethe's time to Nietzsche's, or the depth to which it has sunk. For with all the radical, and indeed obvious, differences between Goethe and Nietzsche—differences of character, genius, temperament, modes of thought and expression—they nevertheless meet in their concern for, and their vision of, the proper state of man. Nietzsche is the outraged believer of Goethe's beliefs, the scandalized and scandalizing upholder of Goethe's values, fighting out within his own soul the battle between belief and unbelief, accepting for himself the fates of the tortured martyrs of either side, and the role of the adjudicator of victories and defeats.

It is not only Nietzsche's consistent admiration that bears witness to his kinship with Goethe. There is no *internal* evidence either to refute the intellectual sincerity of Nietzsche's repeated assertions that there could not be any by-passing of Goethe when it came to tracing his own intellectual ancestry; and although the names he quotes on the occasions of such stock-taking vary, Goethe is invariably included. In the second volume of *Menschliches, Allzumenschliches,* he writes: 'I too have been in the underworld, like Odysseus, and shall be again and again; and not only rams have I sacrificed, but I have not spared my own blood. There are four pairs that have never denied themselves to me when I made my sacrifices: Epicurus and Montaigne, Goethe and Spinoza, Plato and Rousseau, Pascal and Schopenhauer. It is with these that I must come to terms again, each time after a long stretch of lonely wanderings; by them I want to be proved right or wrong, to them I want to listen when they prove one another right or wrong. Whatever I say, conclude, think out for myself and others, it is on those eight that my eyes are fixed.

. . .' [33] In another place, among the many notes from the time of *Zarathustra*, Goethe is again one of his ancestors, this time together with Heraclitus and Spinoza.[34] And in one of his own posthumously published critical comments on the writings of his early period, Goethe is thanked for having freed him from the pessimistic tyranny of Schopenhauer and Wagner: 'Now antiquity dawned upon me, and Goethe's insight into the nature of great art, and *now* I gained that *simplicity* of vision to see what human existence *really* is; I had the antidote to make sure that it did not turn into poisoning pessimism.' [35]

In *Menschliches, Allzumenschliches*, in one of the loveliest passages ever written on the *moral* task and function of literature (and, indeed, there is not much loveliness to be found in the repertoire of writers on this austere subject), the imprint of Goethe's genius is recognizable in every phrase: 'The works of such poets'— poets, that is, whose vision of man is exemplary—'would be distinguished by the fact that they appear immune from the glow and blast of the *passions*. The fatal touch of the wrong note, the pleasure taken in smashing the whole instrument on which the music of humanity has been played, the scornful laughter and the gnashing of teeth, and all that is tragic and comic in the old conventional sense, would be felt in the vicinity of this new art as an awkward archaic crudeness and a distortion of the image of man. Strength, goodness, gentleness, purity, and that innate and spontaneous sense of measure and balance shown in persons and their actions, . . . a clear sky reflected on faces and events, knowledge and art at one; the mind without arrogance and jealousy dwelling together with the soul, drawing from the opposites of life the grace of seriousness, not the impatience of conflict:— all this would make the background of gold against which to set up the real portrait of man, the picture of his increasing nobleness.' [36]

This, quite consistently, is written by the same Nietz-sche who, in listing the best books in German prose, re-served no place for either the tumultuous Kleist or the brilliant Heine or any of the Romantics, but chose, apart from Goethe and Goethe's Conversations with Ecker-mann, as the only works which deserve to be read again and again: Lichtenberg's Aphorisms, the first book of Jung-Stilling's Autobiography, Adalbert Stifter's *Nach-sommer* and Gottfried Keller's *Leute von Seldwyla* ('and this is likely to remain all there is, for some time to come').[37] But is it, one wonders, written by the same Nietzsche who has appealed to what is most immature in the popular imagination of his country, and largely antagonized that of the West, by 'philosophizing with a hammer', proclaiming himself dynamite, preaching the advent of the Superman? How is one to reconcile this violent mind with that Nietzsche whom we have ob-served painting, against a background of gold, the Goe-thean picture of man 'immune from the glow and blast of the passions'?

Throughout Nietzsche's life, and not merely from a certain point onward, his acclamations of Goethe, the dominant voice indeed, are yet interspersed with mis-givings. These are invariably concerned with the Goethe-Winckelmann idea of Greek antiquity and with Goethe's 'purely epic genius', which, according to Nietzsche, ren-dered him incapable of facing the problem of tragedy. He might have added, as a source of anxiety, the nature of Goethe's opposition to modern science.

As early as 1870, while he was writing his *Birth of Tragedy*, Nietzsche enters in his notebook the following remark: 'With Goethe, in accordance with his epic na-ture, poetry is the remedy, protecting him from full knowledge; with tragic natures art is the remedy, lib-erating them from knowledge'.[38] All that Nietzsche ever said in criticism of Goethe is contained in this observa-tion of the young philologist. Seven to eight years later, at the time of *Menschliches, Allzumenschliches*, it is applied to Goethe's reaction to Kleist: 'What Goethe felt at coming into contact with him was his sense of tragedy. Goethe turned his back on it; for tragedy represents the incurable aspect of nature. He himself was conciliatory and curable.'[39] At the same time, after some rather unfortunate gibes about 'the tragic problem' of *Faust*, Nietzsche exclaims: 'Is this really the greatest German "tragic idea", as the rumour goes among Germans?'[40]

These criticisms, clearly, are not determined by purely aesthetic considerations. Nietzsche was utterly incapable of dividing up his thought into any such neat academical departments. He once said: 'I have at all times written with my whole body and my whole life. I do not know what purely intellectual problems are.'[41] And again: 'You know these things by way of thinking, yet your thought is not your experience but the reverberation of the experience of others: as your room trembles when a car passes. I am sitting in that car, and often am the car itself.'[42] Thus Nietzsche's criticism of Goethe can be seen as part and parcel of his total strategy: the strategy of despair. Towards the end of his conscious life Nietzsche was convinced that the culture of Europe was doomed; that an eclipse of all traditional values was at hand, and that modern European man, this pampered child of the optimistically rational eighteenth century, would needs go astray in a wilderness without path or guidance. He quoted Pascal, who said that without the Christian belief we shall become to ourselves what nature and history will become to us—a monster and a chaos. We, he adds, shall make this prophecy come true.[43] The sections of his *Will to Power* which are concerned with the coming of European nihilism read like a vast elaboration of that dictum of Pascal's as well as of Goethe's prophecy of the Prosaic Age. Nietzsche believed that its approach was *inevitable*. But the paradox,

which is the very life of true prophecy, also sustained—
until madness possessed him—the prophet Nietzsche; that
prophetic paradox within which historical inevitability
is defeated through an act of spiritual conquest: 'God
has decided to destroy the Temple. In the name of God,
rescue the Temple from the wrath of God.' This is the
paradox of every true prophet.

What was inevitable, according to Nietzsche's prophecy, was the coming of nihilism. The conqueror, more
powerful than fate itself, was the Dionysian spirit, the
spirit that ruled Greek tragedy. The Dionysus of Greek
tragedy transformed the despair at the fate of man into
the bliss of ultimate acceptance, thus transcending the
very thing it accepted. There is an amazing consistency
running right through Nietzsche's wild contradictions.
The young philologist and philosopher had, in the *Birth
of Tragedy*, celebrated the god of ecstasy, redeeming
the spectacle of man's ultimate failure in the rapturously accepted wholeness of life in which there is nothing but ultimate succeeding. The writer of the *Will to
Power*, seventeen years later, demanded from European
man that he should perform the very same drama on the
stage of the world and, caught in the doom of his historical fate, transcend it through the act of tragic affirmation.

For him who believed he had recognized this, *Faust*
could no longer stand as the 'tragedy of knowledge', 'die
Tragödie der Erkenntnis'. 'Really? I laugh at Faust.' [44]
Salvation was no longer to be had from the 'Ewig-
Weibliche'. This was still merely comfort, a religious
illusion hiding the mercilessness from above against
which not man, in his weak and fallen state, will assert
himself, but only the creature graced with the grace of
Dionysus: the Superman. As far as man is concerned, no
chorus mysticus concludes Nietzsche's 'tragedy of knowledge', but Mephistopheles:

> *Kein Weg! Ins Unbetretene,*
> *Nicht zu Betretende; ein Weg ans Unerbetene,*
> *Nicht zu Erbittende. Bist du bereit?—*
> *Nicht Schlösser sind, nicht Riegel wegzuschieben,*
> *Von Einsamkeiten wirst umhergetrieben.*
> *Hast du Begriff von Öd' und Einsamkeit?*
>
> *Nichts wirst du sehen in ewig leerer Ferne.*
> *Den Schritt nicht hören, den du tust,*
> *Nichts Festes finden, wo du ruhst.*[45]

[No way! Towards untrodden ground, where none may tread; a way towards the unprayed-for, beyond all prayer. Are you prepared? There are no locks, no bolts to thrust aside; you will be driven hither and thither by hosts of loneliness. Do you know what void and loneliness mean? . . . You will see nothing in that distance of eternal emptiness, you will not hear your own step, you will find nothing solid for your rest.]

In those voids, the first sound that will be heard again, indeed be met by the resonance of a transfigured world, will be the voice of the Superman. He will find the firmest of all footholds precisely where man loses the ground under his feet.

To insist on the Mephistophelean prospect, and yet not to despair, and yet to glorify, indeed to transfigure existence—this is the goal of Nietzsche's desperate strategy. He was determined to go to the very end of the positivist disillusionment, shed skin after skin of comforting beliefs, destroy every fortress manned by protective gods, in fact, to banish the last vestiges of 'magic' which still save man from the final exposure to his tragedy—and *then* bring to life once more Goethe's vision of the glorious integrity of all things. Until this was done, even the nearest German approximation to Dionysian acceptance, even Goethe, would fail us. For he had an inclination to play truant when life was teaching its most desperate lessons—and indeed it was about to teach them to Europe. At the approach of the terror of ultimate knowledge, Goethe withdrew into the healing darkness of the unconscious, trusting to intuition that it would restore the brightness of day in the created work of art. But Nietzsche dreamt—and dreamt in vain—of an artist of the future who would reach in his art that turning-point where the highest degree of consciousness and self-consciousness transforms itself into a new spontaneity, primitivity and innocence—[46] just as he strove to realize the utmost of nihilistic despair to arrive at a new faith, and mobilized all forces of negation to defeat all denial. In one of the last paragraphs of *The Will to Power* he says: 'To have paced out the whole circumference of modern consciousness, to have explored every one of its recesses—this is my ambition, my torture, and my bliss. Really to overcome pessimism—; and as a result, *ein Goethischer Blick voll Liebe und gutem Willen.*' [47]

The desperate *experimentum crucis* failed desperately. Nietzsche's tragic failure is spiritual impatience. He was a Faustian, after all, in his deep-rooted belief that in the beginning was the deed. But it is certainly not in the end, and this increases the probability that it was not in the beginning either. He saw the end and took the initiative. Even the words suggest that this is incongruous. He had before him a world without faith or hope or love; and how much he was of the nineteenth century in attempting to create from his own impatience that trinity of spiritual survival which is 'all in the waiting'! Out of the goodness of his heart he believed

. . . such is the infection of the time,
That, for the health and physic of our right,
We cannot deal but with the very hand
Of stern injustice and confused wrong.

But such war-like preparations have a habit of producing the precise state in which the 'paper money consumes the silver and itself'. Nietzsche, with an intellectual courage, penetration and impatience which have no equal in the nineteenth century, made himself, with the most splendid invocations, the claimant of the ideal on behalf of the real; but in his time and place, already so hopelessly exposed, he merely succeeded in vindicating Goethe's prophecy that this will be the point at which the severed spheres consume each other.

RILKE AND NIETZSCHE

WITH A DISCOURSE ON

THOUGHT, BELIEF AND POETRY

1

'We came to speak of *Tasso,* and of the *idea* which
Goethe sought to represent in it,' reports Eckermann
under the date of May 6th, 1827. '*Idea?*' said Goethe—
'not that I know of!—I had the *life* of Tasso before me,
and my own life, and by jumbling up two such peculiar
figures . . . the picture of *Tasso* took shape within me.
. . . The Germans are really peculiar people!—They
make life more difficult for themselves than is necessary
by seeking everywhere, and putting into everything,
their profound thoughts and ideas.—Why not for once
have the courage *to give yourselves up to impressions,*
to allow yourselves to be amused, moved, edified, indeed
taught and roused to something great; but don't believe
all the time that everything must be vain if it is not

K

some abstract thought or idea. . . . A poetic creation is the better for being incommensurable and rationally incomprehensible.' A little later in the same year (July 5th, 1827), talking about inconsistencies in his treatment of the Helena scene in *Faust II*, Goethe says: 'I only wonder what the German critics will think of it. Will they have the freedom and courage to ignore the inconsistencies? The French will be hampered by their reason and fail to recognize that imagination has to abide by laws of its own which reason neither can nor should comprehend. The imagination would hardly be worth bothering about, if it did not create things which will for ever remain problematical to reason. This is the difference between poetry and prose. In prose, reason is and may and should be at home.'

For once Mr. T. S. Eliot seems to agree with Goethe, of whom generally he thinks rather unkindly. In his essay on 'Shakespeare and the Stoicism of Seneca'[1] he says about Shakespeare and his philosophical interpreters very much the same that Goethe said about his *Tasso* and the German critics. Mr. Eliot quotes someone who wrote that 'we possess a great deal of evidence as to what Shakespeare thought of military glory and martial events'. 'Do we?' asks Mr. Eliot, rather in the manner of Goethe's 'Not that I know of!', sure of the applause of anyone with even the slightest insight into the activities in a poet's workshop. For, indeed, what we possess of evidence goes to show conclusively that Shakespeare's imagination comprehended with the greatest precision every shade of difference between what, for instance, Anthony thought and felt about the significance of military events, both before and after he fell in love with Cleopatra, or what military glory meant to such varied characters as, say, Henry V, Ajax or Thersites. In fact, the politeness of good High Table manners, with everyone ready to see everyone's point of view except his own, is, on the highest level of imaginative achievement, the cardinal virtue of the dramatic writer; and the wider the scope of his imagination, the less evidence will he leave behind to show what he himself thought about this or that controversial issue. Having dwelt in so many divided minds and believed so many conflicting beliefs, he is likely to be slow in fulfilling the first commandment of all enlightened education: to form his own opinions. He may, alas, even begin *and* end by not knowing what he himself believes, or not believing what he himself knows.

So far, then, Mr. Eliot's 'Do we?' justly commands that general consent which rhetorical questions take for granted. Yet some of it may be withdrawn when Mr. Eliot continues 'Or rather, did Shakespeare think anything at all? He was occupied with turning human actions into poetry' [2]—in precisely the same way, that is, in which Goethe, without concerning himself with ideas, made poetry out of Tasso's life and his own. Again, very much in keeping with Goethe's notorious dictum that all his works form part of a great confession, but with a striking shift of emphasis from earlier meditations on the subject in the essay 'Tradition and the Individual Talent',[3] Mr. Eliot now maintains that 'every poet starts from his own emotions' and that 'Shakespeare, too, was occupied with the struggle—which alone constitutes life for a poet —to transmute his personal and private agonies into something rich and strange, something universal and impersonal'.[4] And in discussing whether the poet necessarily believes in such theories, theologies or philosophies as he may borrow for his poetic purposes—whether Dante actually believed in the theological system of Thomas Aquinas which he so magnificently used in the *Divina Commedia*, or whether Shakespeare, in poetically paraphrasing their thought, agreed with such thinkers as Machiavelli or Montaigne or Seneca—Mr. Eliot comes to a conclusion that seems to elaborate a Goethean image:

'The poet makes poetry, the metaphysician makes metaphysics, the bee makes honey, the spider secretes a filament; you can hardly say that any of these agents believes: he merely does'.[5] It is Goethe's Tasso who dismisses the advice that he should take a holiday from writing poetry, by exclaiming: Bid the silkworm stop spinning!

Clearly it all amounts to this: by drawing a parallel between Nietzsche, whose principal claim is to be a *thinker*, and Rilke, whose reputation rests on his *poetry*, the critic seems to commit the original sin of literary criticism. Yet I should be on safe ground if I now proceeded to show how Rilke used one or other of Nietzsche's ideas and, believing them or not, transformed them into poetry, as Goethe presumably drew on Spinoza, or Shakespeare on Seneca, Montaigne, and Machiavelli. This would be a literary exercise, respectable and time-honoured, and on this occasion promising high entertainment as it is a *chercher la femme* that lurks behind the 'and' connecting Rilke and Nietzsche: Frau Lou Andreas-Salomé, who played a not inconsiderable part in Nietzsche's life and certainly a very considerable one in Rilke's. The exercise would be still more rewarding if I could produce authentic records of conversations about Nietzsche which, of course, must have taken place between Lou and Rilke; or unearth a copy of *Also sprach Zarathustra* annotated in Rilke's hand. I might then go on to show what has happened to Nietzsche's thought in the process of its transmutation into Rilke's poetry, for, as Mr. Eliot says, the poet 'is not necessarily interested in the thought itself' but merely in expressing 'the emotional equivalent of thought'. But, as it is precisely this theory of the relation between thought, belief and poetry which I should like to challenge, I am obliged to follow a different course, with the strictly scholarly road being barred in any case by the remarkable scarcity of first-hand material. I am not even convinced that a full publication of the correspondence between Rilke and Lou will yield much useful information; for on the whole Rilke was in the habit of suppressing any more elaborate acknowledgment of his intellectual debts because he too believed that their assimilation and transformation in the unique medium of his art was the only thing that mattered.

2

The writings of the young Rilke show Nietzsche neither assimilated nor transformed, but rather imitated and sometimes vulgarized. In *Der Apostel* (1896),[6] *Ewald Tragy*,[7] and *Christus-Visionen* (1896–1897),[8] the effects of Nietzsche's hammering and dynamiting are unmistakable; yet there is not the slightest trace of the depth and complexity of Nietzsche's thought and feeling. When, early in 1897, in Munich, he met Lou Andreas-Salomé he must have still been in this 'Wie er sich räuspert und wie er spuckt' stage of his Nietzsche-fascination. We do not know whether he had read her book on Nietzsche, which was published in 1894,[9] and is, with all its inadequacies, profundity itself compared to the Nietzschean gesticulating of *Der Apostel* or *Ewald Tragy*. But even if Rilke did read it, the document he produced in the following spring and summer (1898), largely in Italy and entirely for Lou's eyes—his so-called *Tuscan Diary* [10]—is still quite innocently Young-Nietzschean in its rapturous vision of the Artist-Superman. Yet in retrospect the reader of the *Tuscan Diary* can clearly discern in it almost all the threads that were to go into the rich texture of *Duino Elegies* and *Sonnets to Orpheus,* so very much more intimately related to Nietzsche (as I shall hope to show) than all the Superman sound and fury lavishly displayed in Rilke's early writings. However, the year of the *Tuscan*

Diary marks the point at which, to my knowledge, all relevant direct references to Nietzsche, or obvious borrowings from him, end. Up to 1904 the name of Nietzsche casually appears now and then in articles or letters, and sometimes, though very rarely, a faint echo of the earlier crude instrumentation of Nietzsche *motifs* can be heard, but certainly in no manner to command attention. Yet although the Zarathustra *opinions* and *gestures* vanish from Rilke's writings, the kinship between his own and Nietzsche's *ideas* and *inner attitudes* is steadily deepening, and is nowhere profounder than in *Duino Elegies* and *Sonnets to Orpheus*, so dramatically released at Castle Muzot as near the end of the poet's life as 1922.

We must not be deceived by appearances; there are, at first sight, as many striking differences between Rilke and Nietzsche as definite similarities. They were both uprooted and homeless. 'Wer jetzt kein Haus hat, baut sich keines mehr,' writes the one, and the other: 'Weh dem, der keine Heimat hat!' They were lonely among men, driven by inner compulsion to shun all binding human relationships for the sake of an uninhibited indulgence of their one consuming passion: namely, to use Mr. Eliot's words about the poet in general, 'to transmute their personal and private agonies into something rich and strange, something universal and impersonal.' In their abhorrence of the democratic vulgarity of their times, they were both anxious to establish their own aristocratic descent. These are not mere biographical accidents. They have the same significance as their common dedication to a belief in everything that has never been uttered before, and to the adventure of willing what nobody has ever dared to will:

Ich glaube an alles noch nie Gesagte.
Ich will meine frömmsten Gefühle befrein.
Was noch keiner zu wollen wagte,
wird mir einmal unwillkürlich sein.[11]

[I believe in everything that has never been said before. My most dedicated feelings I desire to set free, and one day there shall come to me spontaneously that which nobody has ever dared to will.]

These verses of Rilke's spring from the very centre of Zarathustra's message. And, to the point of a near-identity of images conveying the conquest of loneliness, the harmonizing of inner conflict in the feast of reconciliation, of the One becoming Two through the arrival of the divine guest, Rilke's lines

Wer seines Lebens viele Widersinne
versöhnt und dankbar in ein Sinnbild fasst,
der drängt
die Lärmenden aus dem Palast,
wird anders festlich, und du bist der Gast,
den er an sanften Abenden empfängt.

Du bist der Zweite seiner Einsamkeit,
die ruhige Mitte seinen Monologen;
und jeder Kreis, um dich gezogen,
spannt ihm den Zirkel aus der Zeit.[12]

[He who succeeds in reconciling the many contradictions of his life, holding them all together in a symbol, pushes the noisy crowd from the palace and will be festive in a different sense, receiving you as his guest on mild evenings.

Then you will be the Other of his loneliness, the still centre of his monologues; and every circle drawn around you takes his compasses right outside time.]

sound like the *adagio* treatment of a theme which gets rather out of hand in the *fortissimo* passage of Nietzsche's finale:

um Mittag war's, da wurde Eins zu zwei. . . .
Nun feiern wir, vereinten Siegs gewiss,
    das Fest der Feste:
Freund Zarathustra kam, der Gast der Gäste!
Nun lacht die Welt, der grause Vorhang riss,
die Hochzeit kam für Licht und Finsternis. . . .[13]

[It was at midday when One became Two. . . . Together now and sure of our triumph, we celebrate the
feast of feasts: friend Zarathustra has arrived, the
guest of guests! The world is overjoyed, the weird
curtain is torn apart, the wedding day has come for
light and darkness.]

It is on evenings, calm and gentle, when the great
Other of Rilke's loneliness comes to his only disciple
who, in all his gentleness, has already managed to drive
the noisy crowd from the temple. Zarathustra, on the
other hand, arrives in the glaring midday hour. Midday
and evening—this example will have to stand for the most
striking difference, obvious throughout their works, between Rilke and Nietzsche. Nietzsche's tone is imperial.
He has received the great commandment, has once faced
his God, and henceforward he will speak out. Rilke's
orders are of a more cumulative nature. His head is bent
in the attitude of one who listens intently to 'das
Wehende', the continual lesson formed out of stillness.
But is this necessarily a difference in substance? Not if
the whispered news amounts in the end to the same as
the revelation which Nietzsche receives with the dramatic
incisiveness of the thunderbolt. Some, however, believe
that it is altogether other news, and are, I think, misled
by their belief; for they do not seem to know that one
theme may be sustained through many variations, and
one soul preserve its identity through many a season; and
while Nietzsche and Rilke may merely be two moods of

the same heart, they are often held to be possessed by fundamentally different certainties. It may be difficult to see the one garden for its very varied flowers. But only if we are inclined to take the transports produced by night-scented stock for a distinct spiritual initiation shall we be convinced of the profound difference between Rilke's religion and Zarathustra's, proclaimed in the proudest of daylights with 'the crown of roses on the prophet's brow'. Yet we should perhaps remember that St. Paul served with prophetic zeal the same God whom others loved in humbler dedications. We shall come to see Rilke as the St. Francis of the Will to Power.

This assertion will seem extravagant only to those who are victims of the popular misapprehension which suggests that the Will to Power is a kind of moral teaching sanctioning violence and ruthlessness, and not the profound metaphysical inspiration which in fact it is, comprehending, or at least attempting to comprehend, the real meaning behind the representative beliefs and unbeliefs, activities and philosophies of Europe in war and peace throughout its more recent history. Rilke may be to Nietzsche what Orpheus is to Dionysus; and Rilke's Orpheus and Nietzsche's Dionysus are brother deities, by virtue of that peculiar adjustment to more modern attitudes of the soul which was forced upon Greek mythology by the spiritual need and hunger of modernity. But before we establish this equation, we shall have to attend to what else they have in common.

They are both initiates in the alchemy of loneliness and suffering. Rilke as well as Nietzsche discovers the fountainhead of joy in the very heart of the land of sorrow. Happiness for them is not, as it was for Schopenhauer, in the absence of pain; it is the fruit of so radical an acceptance of suffering that abundant delight springs from its very affirmation. For the denial of pain means the denial of existence. Existence is pain, and joy lies not in non-existence, as Schopenhauer would have it, but in its tragic transfiguration. This is the theme of Nietzsche's *Birth of Tragedy* as well as of *Zarathustra* and of *The Will to Power,* where it is treated with ever growing assurance by a man, it is well to remember, who wrote to a friend: 'The terrible and all but incessant torture of my life makes me thirst for the end. . . . As far as agony and renunciation are concerned, my life during these last years is a match for that of any ascetic at any time. . . . Yet no pain has been able or shall be able to tempt me into giving false testimony about life as I recognize it.' [14] And this recognition is praise. From the darkest night of the soul rises Zarathustra's 'Trunkenes Lied', his Dionysian song of the deep suffering of the world, which is yet surpassed in depth by that rapture of delight which wills, not that the world with its pain should pass away, but that it should last for ever:

doch alle Lust will Ewigkeit –,
– will tiefe, tiefe Ewigkeit! –

an eternity not of joy (as Nietzsche is so often misunderstood to mean) but of the world *with* all its sorrow, transfigured in the act of willing it.

If we bear in mind what has been said about the difference in tone and gesture between Rilke and Nietzsche, there remains hardly a single element in Nietzsche's acceptance and transformation of suffering that could not also be found in Rilke. Indeed, the parallels appear to be exact. As early as his *Tuscan Diary* he writes: 'To think that I myself was once among those who suspect life and distrust its power. Now I would love it at all events. . . . Whatever of it is mine . . . I would love with tenderness, and would bring to ripeness within myself all possibilities that its possession offers to me.' [15] And much later, in the Tenth Elegy, we encounter what is an elegiac version of the theme of *The Birth of Tragedy*: Rilke's Klage, the embodiment of Lamentation, guiding

the dead youth through the country of her ancestors
with its mines of sorrow, until they reach the terminus
where Klage and youth must part, that gorge

wo es schimmert im Mondschein:
die Quelle der Freude. In Ehrfurcht
nennt sie, sagt: 'Bei den Menschen
*ist sie ein tragender Strom'.**

where it gleams in the moonlight:
the source of Joy. With awe
she names it, says 'Among men
it is a carrying stream'.

And not even an intonation alien to Nietzsche's, but
merely the presence of the Angels seems (and merely
seems) to render the beginning of Rilke's Tenth Elegy
unsuitable as an epitaph for Nietzsche:

Dass ich dereinst, an dem Ausgang der grimmigen
  Einsicht,
Jubel und Ruhm aufsinge zustimmenden Engeln.
Dass von den klargeschlagenen Hämmern des Herzens,
keiner versage an weichen, zweifelnden oder
reissenden Saiten.

Some day, emerging at last from the vision of terror,
may I burst into jubilant praise to assenting Angels.
May no one of the clear-struck keys of the heart
fail to respond through alighting on slack or doubtful
or rending strings!

* With a number of separate editions of *Duino Elegies* and
Sonnets to Orpheus available, I shall refer to these poems by
their numbers only. The translations are, with some modifications of my own, by J. B. Leishman and Stephen Spender
(*Duino Elegies,* London, 1948) and J. B. Leishman (*Sonnets
to Orpheus,* London, 1946).

Nietzsche, who for so long believed that he was a musician as well as a philosopher, once composed a 'Hymn to Life', the text of which is—strangest of biographical coincidences—by Lou Salomé. In *Ecce Homo* he says that he chose it because its last lines possess greatness; their meaning is that suffering is no argument against life: 'Hast du kein Glück mehr übrig mir zu geben, wohlan! noch hast du deine Pein. . . .'[16] It is a bad poem. The future lover of the poetess would have done better. If Nietzsche discovered some greatness in those verses, persuaded no doubt by the theme of praise, the great persuasion of the *Sonnets to Orpheus* would have overwhelmed him.

For instance, the sonnet 'Singe die Gärten, mein Herz, die du nicht kennst'. It almost sounds like Lou's 'Hymn to Life' set to music by Rilke (though perhaps in this sonnet the music is actually not very much better than Nietzsche's):

Meide den Irrtum, dass es Entbehrungen gebe
für den geschehnen Entschluss, diesen: zu sein!
Seidener Faden, kamst du hinein ins Gewebe.

Welchem der Bilder du auch im Innern geeint bist
(sei es selbst ein Moment aus dem Leben der Pein),
fühl, dass der ganze, der rühmliche Teppich gemeint ist.

Do not believe you will be deprived
of something by your resolution: to *be*.
Silken thread, you have entered the weaving.

With whatever pattern you are inwardly blended
(and be it a scene from the story of Agony),
feel that the whole, the praiseworthy carpet is meant.

And the sonnet which begins with the beautiful lines:

*Nur im Raum der Rühmung darf die Klage
gehn, die Nymphe des geweinten Quells*

[Only in the realm of Praise may Lamentation move,
naiad of the wept fountain]

is indeed Rilke's 'Trunkenes Lied', the lyrical echo of
Zarathustra's Dionysian song. For in this song too sorrow
transcends itself in the *knowing* certainty of jubilation,
raising to the skies a constellation of immaculate joy:

*Jubel weiss, und Sehnsucht ist geständig,—
nur die Klage lernt noch; mädchenhändig
zählt sie nächtelang das alte Schlimme.*

*Aber plötzlich, schräg und ungeübt,
hält sie doch ein Sternbild unsrer Stimme
in den Himmel, den ihr Hauch nicht trübt.*

(I, VIII)

Triumph knows, and Longing makes confession,—
Lamentation learns: in nightly session
counts, with maiden-hands, old tribulation.

Then, however inexpertly limned,
lifts our voices in a constellation
to the sky her breathing has not dimmed.

Delighted as Nietzsche would have been by these
sonnets, would he necessarily have recognized Orpheus
as their divine inspiration? He himself was preoccupied
with gods of fuller status: with Dionysus and Apollo.
His early *Birth of Tragedy* interpreted the Attic drama
as the outcome of an age-old struggle which these two
gods waged within the Greek soul. In tragedy, at last,
the two hostile gods came together and concluded peace:
Dionysus, the god of chaotic ecstasy, rapturously aban-

doning all claims to form and shape, all individuality, to the amorphous oneness of life; and Apollo, the god with the lyre at whose call all things were arrested within their own contours and their own articulate order. Would Europe, after the end of the 'tragic' period of Greece, ever again know such reconciliation, and achieve so profound a harmony between the deepest and most conflicting impulses of the human soul? Shall we ever create an order which is not, as all our orders are, at the expense of the fullness of life, but its richest unfolding; a pattern which is not imposed upon chaos, but overreaching and surpassing it, its beauty still tremulous with the ancient terror? Or is the ancient god of ecstasy doomed to an ignominious existence in the murky corners of sin and depravity, and the god of order to be imprisoned in the petrified structure of classicism and morality? Or *shall* Dionysus and Apollo be united again, as they were in Attic tragedy?

Such were the youthfully enthusiastic questions which Nietzsche asked in his *Birth of Tragedy*. At the time his equally enthusiastic answer was: the old gods have risen again; they live in the work of Richard Wagner. It was to prove an agonizingly provisional answer. Perhaps Rilke's Orpheus would have made good the promise that Wagner's Parsifal broke.

The attempt of scholars to unravel the complex of historical reminiscences, images, insights, feelings that make up the story of Dionysus, Apollo and Orpheus in modern German literature and thought, and then to relate it to what may be the Greek reality of these divine creatures, is as heroic as it is doomed to failure. For a scholar's guarded steps cannot possibly keep pace with the rush and dance of the passions of the mind swirling around those names and arrested only for brief moments in innumerable figurations. Nietzsche, from *The Birth of Tragedy* onwards, is seeking spiritual employment in the service of a god who is a synthesis of Dionysus and

Apollo. In this composite Nietzschean deity, Apollo, it is true, more and more loses his name to the other god, but by no means the power of his artistic creativeness, for ever articulating the Dionysian chaos in distinct shapes, sounds and images, which are Dionysian only because they are still aglow with the heat of the primeval fire. At the end of his *Will to Power*, that is, at the end of the life of his mind, Nietzsche once more returned to the antagonism within the Greek soul between the Dionysian and Apolline, and once more celebrated the triumph of a god who wrests the utmost of glorifying beauty from the monstrous terror of chaotic passions. This triumphant god, far from suffering the chill of classicism, has, as it were, Apollo's eyes and the heart of Dionysus. In Nietzsche's mature years the real opposition is not Dionysus versus Apollo, but the Apolline Dionysus versus Christ.[17]

And Rilke? In a letter from Rome, written probably in the spring of 1904, eighteen years before the *Sonnets to Orpheus* (it is the last-known letter using undisguised Nietzschean terms), Rilke indulges in a kind of eschatological vision of Apollo's ultimate triumph over the chaotic dominion of Dionysus. The phrases of this letter have not the only ring, but almost the precise wording of Nietzsche's evocations of Apollo-Dionysus. It is chaos itself, says Rilke, which, at the end of days, will stand transformed into 'a million ripe, fine and golden forms', an 'Apolline product, fermented into maturity and still radiant with its inner glow'. And nothing could be more Nietzschean than 'the wakeful, lucid enthusiasm' of Rilke's Apolline world.[18] *

This is the eschatology of an artist; of an artist, at that, whose business is not merely to heighten by his own creations the beauty of a world, beautiful and significant in itself, but to *create* himself the only beautiful and

* The authentic wording of this letter was established with considerable effort and great scholarly care by Eudo C. Mason. (Cf. his *Der Zopf des Münchhausen*, Einsiedeln, 1949, 77.)

significant world that there is or can be. It is astonishing and instructive to see how long an idea, present right at the beginning of a poet's career, takes to mature into great poetry. We may also observe how this same idea, originally part of a quasi-historical or Darwinian theory about the development of man, becomes in the end the timeless assertion, not of a future state, but of existence itself. In 1898 Rilke notes in the *Tuscan Diary*: 'Not for all time will the artist live side by side with ordinary men. As soon as the artist—the more flexible and deeper type among them—becomes rich and virile, as soon as he *lives* what now he merely *dreams*, man will degenerate and gradually die out. The artist is eternity protruding into time.' [19] In the *Sonnets to Orpheus* this eternity not merely protrudes, it has arrived. It *is* the world itself; a world which exists in and through song alone. Song is existence—'Gesang ist Dasein'. A god could easily achieve it: 'Für den Gott ein Leichtes'. But if there are no gods? Then we must become gods ourselves. We? We who hardly *are*? 'Wann aber *sind* wir?' Indeed, man must transform and transfigure himself; and in transfiguring himself he will be the redeemer and transfigurer of all existence: '*der Verklärer des Daseins*'. [20]

This dialogue, made up of verbatim quotations from Rilke and Nietzsche, is about the Orpheus of the sonnets. The other name of this 'Verklärer des Daseins'—the formula is Nietzsche's—is Dionysus Apollo:

Du aber, Göttlicher, du, bis zuletzt noch Ertöner,
da ihn der Schwarm der verschmähten Mänaden befiel,
hast ihr Geschrei übertönt mit Ordnung, du Schöner,
aus den Zerstörenden stieg dein erbauendes Spiel.

. . . .

O du verlorener Gott! Du unendliche Spur!
Nur weil dich reissend zuletzt die Feindschaft verteilte,
sind wir die Hörenden jetzt und ein Mund der Natur.

(1, XXVI)

You that could sound till the end, though, immortal
   accorder
seized by the scorn-maddened Maenads' intemperate
   throng,
wholly outsounded their cries when in musical order
soared from the swarm of deformers your formative
   song.

     .   .   .   .   .

O you god that has vanished! You infinite track!
Only because dismembering hatred dispersed you
are we hearers to-day and a mouth which else Nature
   would lack.

This composite deity is still more obviously present in
the following sonnet, in which allusions to Rilke's imag-
ined family history, repeated in the Third Elegy, are
merged in a kind of Dionyso-Apolline anthropology of
universal significance:

Zu unterst der Alte, verworrn,
all der Erbauten
Wurzel, verborgener Born,
den sie nie schauten.

Sturmhelm und Jägerhorn,
Spruch von Ergrauten,
Männer im Bruderzorn,
Frauen wie Lauten. . . .

Drängender Zweig an Zweig,
nirgends ein frier. . . .
Einer! o steig . . . o steig. . . .

Aber sie brechen noch.
Dieser erst oben doch
biegt sich zur Leier.
           (I, XVII)

L

Undermost he, the earth-bound
root of uprearing
multitudes, source underground,
never appearing.

Helmet and hunting-horn,
words of the ageing,
rage between brothers-born,
women assuaging.

Branch on branch, time on time,
vainly they spire. . . .
One free! Oh, climb . . . oh, climb. . . .

One, though the others drop,
curves, as it scales the top,
into a lyre.

There are also sonnets in which the image of Orpheus could, without imposing the slightest strain on either the poem or our imagination, fade out altogether, making room for Zarathustra himself; for instance, the sonnet which begins

Rühmen, das ist's! Ein zum Rühmen Bestellter,
ging er hervor wie das Erz aus des Steins
Schweigen. Sein Herz, o vergängliche Kelter
eines den Menschen unendlichen Weins.

(I, VII)

Praising, that's it! As a praiser and blesser
he came like the ore from the taciturn mine.
Came with his heart, oh, transient presser,
for men, of a never-exhaustible wine.

and, still more so, the sonnet

Wolle die Wandlung. O sei für die Flamme begeistert

(2, XII)

Choose to be changed. With the flame be enraptured.

in which almost every word—'Wandlung', 'Flamme', 'jener entwerfende Geist, welcher das Irdische meistert', 'Was sich ins Bleiben verschliesst, schon ists das Erstarrte', 'Hammer' and 'Härtestes'—belongs as its most unmistakable property to Zarathustra's prophetic household, although there can be no doubt that they have come into Rilke's possession through perfectly legitimate channels. The seal on the deed is authentic. It shows a lonely priest in a ruined cathedral. The roof is off. Through the vast opening comes down what looks a little like the traditional image of the Holy Ghost. But as it is blurred and indistinct, this may be too hasty an interpretation, merely suggested by the cathedral. It may also be rain. As it descends through the open roof of a ruin, we might perhaps just call it 'openness', 'das Offene'. This seems to be confirmed by the words which are printed around the circumference of the seal. They say: 'Denn offen ist es bei dir und hell', 'Where you are at home, everything is open and light', and 'Mit allen Augen sieht die Kreatur das Offene', 'With all its eyes the creature-world beholds the open'.

The last sentence is the beginning of Rilke's Eighth Elegy; but the first was spoken by Zarathustra on coming home to his lonely cave.* Once more he has left the noisy town—one is irresistibly tempted to say, the 'Leid-Stadt' of Rilke's Tenth Elegy:

> *wo in der falschen, aus Übertönung gemachten*
> *Stille, stark, aus der Gussform des Leeren der Ausguss,*
> *prahlt, der vergoldete Lärm, das platzende Denkmal.*
> *O wie spurlos zerträte ein Engel ihnen den Trostmarkt,*
> *den die Kirche begrenzt, ihre fertig gekaufte:*
> *reinlich und zu und enttäuscht wie ein Postamt am*
> *Sonntag*

* Cf. also Zarathustra's words: 'Only when a clear sky looks down through broken ceilings . . . will my heart turn again towards the places of God'. (M.A., XIII, 116.)

where, in the seeming stillness of uproar outroared,
stoutly, a thing cast out from the mould of vacuity,
swaggers that gilded fuss, the bursting memorial.
How an Angel would tread beyond trace their market
  of comfort,
with the church alongside, bought ready for use: as
  tidy
and disappointed and shut as the Post on a Sunday

for Rilke's is as exact a description as Nietzsche gives of
the town that Zarathustra has left behind in order to
converse with his own solitude:

'Here you are at home with yourself,' he says. . . .
'Here all things come to your speech, caressing and
flattering, for they wish to ride on your back. And you
yourself are riding on many a symbol towards many
a truth. . . .

'Here the words and word-shrines of everything that
is open up before you; everything that is desires to
become word; everything that will become desires to
learn from you how to speak.' [21]

Rilke too was to travel on many a symbol, yielded by
the word-shrines of things, towards many of Zarathustra's
truths. Rilke's youthful *Tuscan-Diary* version of Zarathustra's secret sessions with 'die Dinge' is as follows:
'. . . I feel that more and more I am becoming the
disciple of things (not merely their listener), a disciple
who adds, through comprehending questions, intensity
to their answers and confessions, and who, enticing
them to spend their advice and wisdom, learns how
to reward their generous love with the disciple's humility'.[22]

The aspect of things changes in the new 'openness' of

Nietzsche's, of Rilke's solitude. Within the perspective of this expanded, and yet, as we shall see, more radically confined space, it appears that neither things nor names have ever been really known. With a new consciousness and perception gained, they must be christened anew, baptized, as it were, into a new Church. For another dimension of speech has been thrown open, and all things desire to hear their names once more, uttered in a voice resonant enough to fill the new spaces. Said as they used to be said, words fall flat in these changed acoustical conditions.

What happened to the *form* and *shape* of things at the beginning of the Renaissance seems now to happen to their *names*. With the third dimension *consciously* perceived as an essential aspect of vision, all objects demanded to be seen and painted afresh, and indeed quite new ones called out for recognition. Zarathustra's words of the things that 'come to your speech, caressing and flattering, for they wish to ride on your back', would, with a change from speech to canvas, have made good sense to the first of the great Renaissance painters. If the medieval madonnas and angels seemed to complain that they cut poor figures in their two-dimensional flatness, at the same time an abundance of other images pressed upon the painters' imagination, claiming their right to significance in the new field of vision. Pillars, towers, gates, trees, jugs and windows demanded to be *seen* with an intensity as never before—'wie selber die Dinge niemals innig meinten zu sein'.

Rilke's new dimension is inwardness. As they came to Zarathustra with their novel claims, so the things approach Rilke, asking to be taught how to become words and how to make themselves truly felt in the widened space; and in return they show him that this is precisely his real task in the world: to assimilate them into the new inward dimension:

— Sind wir vielleicht hier, *um zu sagen: Haus,*
Brücke, Brunnen, Tor, Krug, Obstbaum, Fenster,—
höchstens: Säule, Turm . . . aber zu sagen, verstehs,
oh zu sagen so, wie selber die Dinge niemals
innig meinten zu sein. . . .

(Ninth Elegy)

—Are we, perhaps, here in order to say: House,
Bridge, Fountain, Gate, Jug, Peartree, Window,—
at most: Pillar, Tower? . . . but to *say*, remember,
oh, to say this so as never the things themselves
meant so intensely to be. . . .

It has often been said of both Nietzsche and Rilke that
they were masters of new nuances, the one of thought,
and the other of feeling. True, they both felt that their
souls and minds were at the mercy of sensations and
revelations so subtle as had never been received before;
that they were instruments on which the wind of unsuspected spaces played its first tentative tunes. In this
unexplored space, which is, as it were, made up of the
'empty distances' *between* and *around* our normal concepts of thought and feeling, lies our 'wirklicher Bezug',
our *real* 'relatedness' to what really *is*. Like a hymn of
spiritual friendship, addressed to Nietzsche, sounds
Rilke's sonnet:

Heil dem Geist, der uns verbinden mag;
denn wir leben wahrhaft in Figuren.
Und mit kleinen Schritten gehn die Uhren
neben unserm eigentlichen Tag.

Ohne unsern wahren Platz zu kennen,
handeln wir aus wirklichem Bezug.
Die Antennen fühlen die Antennen,
und die leere Ferne trug. . . .

(I, XII)

Hail, the spirit able to unite us!
For we truly live our lives in symbols,
and with tiny steps move our clocks,
beside our real, actual day.

Without knowing our true place
we yet act from real relatedness.
Antennae feel antennae,
and the empty distance carries. . . .

And Nietzsche's response:

Jenseits des Nordens, des Eises, des Heute,
jenseits des Todes,
abseits:
unser *Leben,* unser *Glück!*
Weder zu Lande
noch zu Wasser
kannst du den Weg
zu den Hyperboreern finden:
von uns *wahrsagte so ein weiser Mund.*[23]

Beyond the North, the ice, the present day,
beyond death,
away from it:
our life, *our* bliss!
Neither by land nor by sea
can you find the way
to the Hyperboreans:
it was of *us* that the mouth of wisdom thus prophe-
    sied.

And the solitary figure of Rilke in the Piccola Marina
of Capri, feeling and hardly surviving the

uraltes Wehn vom Meer,
welches weht
nur wie für Urgestein,
lauter Raum
reissend von weit herein. . . .[24]

primeval waft from the sea,
that wafts
only as if for primeval stone,
pure space rushing
in from afar. . . .

easily merges with that of Nietzsche, leaning over a
bridge in the brown Venetian evening:

Meine Seele, ein Saitenspiel,
. . . unsichtbar berührt[25]

My soul, a play of strings
. . . touched by an invisible hand

words which might be followed by Rilke's

Und welcher Geiger hat uns in der Hand?
O süsses Lied.[26]

And who is the minstrel that holds us in his hand?
O sweet song.

Yet these are only lyrical prolegomena or accompani-
ments to the real theme: the radical revision of all frontiers within human experience. The full realization of
this theme comes to both of them in ecstatic states of inspiration. Both Nietzsche and Rilke knew they were inspired, irresistibly commanded to write, the one *Zarathustra* and the other *Duino Elegies*. Theirs are the only
personal accounts we possess in modern literature of

states of inspiration. The reports are almost interchangeable, except that Nietzsche's, written at some distance from the experience itself, is more sober than are Rilke's breathless announcements of victory. 'Has anyone, at the end of the nineteenth century, any clear idea of what poets of more vigorous ages called *inspiration*?' asks Nietzsche in the *Zarathustra* chapter of his *Ecce Homo*, and continues: 'If one were in the least superstitious, one would not know how to reject the suggestion that one is merely an incarnation, merely a mouthpiece, merely a medium of superior powers'.[27] Of 'days of enormous obedience', speaks Rilke, of 'a storm of the spirit' which threatened to annihilate the body. 'O that I was allowed to survive to this day, through everything. Wonder. Grace.' [28] Both Nietzsche and Rilke felt that the very physical surroundings which were the chosen scenes of these Pentecosts were hallowed places. The tenderness with which Nietzsche describes his walks on the hillsides of Genoa and through the Mediterranean pinewoods along the Bay of Santa Margherita, where Zarathustra accompanied him, is equalled by Rilke's stepping out into the cold moonlight, when he had survived the onrush of the Elegies, and stroking the walls of the 'little castle Muzot' 'like an old animal'.

This is not the way mere nuances are discovered. The word nuance presupposes an order of firmly established ideas and objects between which an indefinite number of subtly-coloured shades may playfully mediate, whereas Nietzsche's and Rilke's sensibilities tend towards a radical denial of that very principle of separation—philosophically speaking, the *principium individuationis*, within a world perceived under the dual aspects of immanence and transcendence—on which our intellectual perception has been based throughout the centuries. Nietzsche denounces its results with regard to our thought as that 'barbarism of concepts' which we are still far from fully realizing, and Rilke its effects on our feel-

ing as that pauperism of the heart which makes us out-
casts among angels, men and beasts alike, distressed
vagabonds of the crudely interpreted world—

*dass wir nicht sehr verlässlich zu Haus sind
in der gedeuteten Welt.*

For all men make the mistake of *distinguishing* too
sharply—

*. . . Aber Lebendige machen
alle den Fehler, dass sie zu stark unterscheiden.*

(First Elegy)

But this is an elegiac understatement of the real denun-
ciation implicit in Rilke's mature work, which is that our
traditional way of distinguishing is false throughout the
whole range of our fundamental distinctions between
transcendence and immanence, God and man, man and
things, external reality and inwardness, joy and suffering,
communion of love and separation, life and death—a list
to which Nietzsche's main contribution is: good and
evil. 'To presuppose the *oneness* of life and death,' Rilke
writes, one year after *Duino Elegies* and *Sonnets to
Orpheus*, and again, 'to know the *identity* of terror and
bliss . . . is the essential meaning and idea of my two
books'.[29]

3

We seem to have travelled a fair distance without
being perturbed by our initial scruples which ought to
have cast a shadow over the whole enterprise of relating
the *poet* Rilke to the *thinker* Nietzsche. It appears that
we had neither the courage nor the wisdom to act on
Goethe's advice and 'give ourselves up to impressions', to
allow ourselves freely 'to be amused, moved, and edified'

by Rilke's poetry; nor did we share, or work on, Mr. Eliot's belief that 'the poet who "thinks" is merely the poet who can express the emotional equivalent of thought. But he is not necessarily interested in the thought itself'.[30] For the conviction informing this essay is that Rilke *as a poet* is interested 'in the thought itself', and Nietzsche *as a thinker* also expresses 'the emotional equivalent of thought'; and yet Nietzsche remains a thinker throughout, and is not, as some believe, 'merely a poet', nor does Rilke ever cease to be a poet, even if some complain that he is 'too speculative' in his mature phase. On the contrary, I believe that Nietzsche's and Rilke's distrust of, and opposition to, valid distinctions have some of their roots in their *legitimate* antagonism to one profoundly *invalid* distinction to which their age clung with almost religious passion: the distinction between thought and feeling. It is the distinction on which both rationalism and romanticism throve, spending their forces in an ultimately futile struggle to assert the superiority of the one or the other. Yet it is no good trying to choose between two misfits. Both Goethe and Mr. Eliot, in the quoted instances, attempt to clear up a confusion by using tools of thought manufactured in the very workshop that is responsible for the muddle.

This becomes quite obvious if we look at the concepts to which both Goethe and Mr. Eliot oppose poetry. Goethe says that it has nothing to do with 'ideas'. 'Ideas' always were the *bête noire* as well as the weak point of Goethe. Once, as we have seen, he was on the verge of being very angry with Schiller, who accused his *Ur-pflanze* of belonging to that oppressive and oppressed class. But of course Schiller was right and Goethe was offended only because the word 'idea' suggested to him something 'abstract', something 'thought out' by what he was in the habit of calling 'Verstand': discursive and analytical reason. And throughout the conversation with Eckermann, quoted at the beginning, it is this analytical reason that is set against poetry, this 'Verstand' which Goethe disliked so much as the prosaic enemy of poetry —and, indeed, of science too. It assumes mythological shape in the figure of Newton.°

Mr. Eliot, on the other hand, knows that the meaning of 'thought' does not permit so lighthearted and restrictive a definition. He deplores the difficulty of 'having to use the same words for different things'.[31] But when it actually comes to using 'thought' in *his* sense, this is what happens: 'Champions of Shakespeare as a great philosopher have a great deal to say about Shakespeare's power of thought, but they fail to show that he *thought to any purpose,* that he *had any coherent view of life,* or that he *recommended any procedure to follow'.*[32] In other words, 'thought' in this sense appears to be the preoccupation of a group of men among whom the professional bores are in the majority. The three criteria amount to a definition of a certain type of rationalism. It is a definition that excludes, first, the thinker for whom thinking is not a means to an end, but a passion; secondly, the thinker who knows that no system of thought can ever be completely coherent without the knowledge of the indispensable measure of incoherence worked into the

° A dictionary of Goethe's vacillating use of the word 'idea' would reveal the full measure of ambiguity that besets the problem of 'thought and poetry' in the age of rationalism and romanticism, and the difficulties of a man who is opposed to both. The first essay in this book, 'Goethe and the Idea of Scientific Truth', contains a number of quotations from Goethe that show a much more positive attitude towards 'ideas' than his conversation about *Tasso* would suggest. About *Faust* he said to Luden on August 19th, 1806, that its 'higher interest' lies in 'the idea which has inspired the poet and which is capable of knitting all the details of the poem into a whole, providing norm and significance for its individual elements'. (Cf. also L. A. Willoughby's essay 'Faust als Lebensorganisation' in *Goethe und die Wissenschaft,* Frankfurt a.M., 1951, 37.)

whole structure of the system; and thirdly, the thinker whose thought does not issue in recipes for action, but in invitations to think. In short, it excludes the thinker.

To make poetry is to think. Of course, it is not *merely* thinking. But there is no such activity as 'merely thinking', unless we confine the term to purely logical or mathematical operations. Language is not quite so stupid as some of our analytical philosophers seem to assume. It knows what it does when it allows us to say that we 'think of someone', and when it calls actions deficient in kindness or imagination 'thoughtless'. 'Thinking' and 'thought' in these phrases are no mere manner of speaking. The words mean what they say: thought and thinking. And if we have it on authority still higher than Goethe's or Mr. Eliot's that in the beginning was *logos*, the word, the thought, the meaning, we should think twice before we answer the question whether or not a poet thinks. It is a happy coincidence in German that 'Dichter und Denker', poet and thinker, form an alliterative pair.

Mr. Eliot suggests that Shakespeare, in making Hamlet think in the manner of Montaigne, did not think himself, but merely 'used' thought for dramatic ends. This sounds true enough, and would be even truer if it were possible to 'use' thought without thinking in the process of using it. For thought is not an object, but an activity, and it is impossible to 'use' an activity without becoming active. One can use a table without contributing to its manufacture; but one cannot use thinking or feeling without thinking or feeling. Of course, one can use the results of thought in a thoughtless fashion. In this case, however, one does not use thought, but merely words which will, more likely than not, fail to make sense.

In so far as Hamlet's thought makes sense, Shakespeare must have been thinking it, although not necessarily as the first to do so and certainly in a manner of thinking which is more imaginative and intuitive than rationally deliberate. To define 'thinking' in such a way that the activity which Shakespeare pursued in composing the speeches of Hamlet, or Ulysses, or Lear has to be dismissed as 'non-thought' is to let thinking fall into the rationalist trap from which it is likely to emerge as a cripple, full of animosity against that other deformed creature, mutilated in the same operation: the Romantic emotion. If thought, stripped of imaginative feeling, and emotion, stripped of imaginative thought, become the dominant modes both of thinking and feeling, the outcome is the 'Leid-Stadt', that insufferable city of sorrows, or the Waste Land, in which the spirits of Nietzsche and of Rilke and of Mr. Eliot feel ill at ease. Paradoxically enough, it is precisely this neat separation between thought and feeling which has forced, on the one hand, upon modern philosophy 'the Absurd' as one of its principal themes, and, on the other hand, upon modern poetry an excessive degree of *intellectual* complexity.

Poetry is not, as Goethe would suggest in that conversation with Eckermann, in opposition to 'ideas', nor does it, as Mr. Eliot says, merely give the 'emotional equivalent' of thought. Dante, Shakespeare, Goethe, Rilke and Mr. Eliot, in making poetry, have ideas; and they think. Only in the 'pure' lyric and the 'pure' epic may ideas and thought be so negligible as to be irrelevant to aesthetic or critical appreciation. If Dante's thought is Thomas Aquinas', it is yet Dante's: not only by virtue of imaginative sympathy and assimilation, and certainly not as a reward for the supply of an 'emotional equivalent'. It is Dante's property by birthright. He has recreated it within himself—poetically. For poetry is not a garment around thought, nor is it its shadowy aesthetic reflection. It is a certain kind of thought, hopelessly uncertain of itself at a time when thought is 'merely' thought and poetry 'merely' poetry and therefore, to quote Mr. Eliot's *East Coker*, 'does not matter':

Because one has only learnt to get the better of words
For the thing one no longer has to say, or the way in
   which
One is no longer disposed to say it.

If this happens, the problem of thought and poetry takes on an altogether new complexion. For happy is the poet whose only job is to learn how to get the better of words for things which he *has* to say. He is the poet who thinks with the thought of his age, as Dante thought with the thought of St. Thomas. Whether or not the poet thinks in the thought-mould of his time does not necessarily depend on the goodness or profundity of its thought, and certainly not on its systematic coherence. The question is, rather, whether this thought springs from the same level of spiritual experience on which poetry is formed; and whether it is linked to that reservoir of fundamental intellectual certainties (and be it the certainty of doubt, scepticism or stoicism) from which the poetic impulse must be sustained if it is not to be in danger of breaking under a burden too heavy for its delicate constitution. This danger will arise when the poet, compelled by the peculiar spiritual barrenness of his age, has to struggle for the poetic expression of un-heard-of and unthought-of experiences. It is then that he will have to do *all* the thinking himself, because the experiences for which, as a poet, he has to find the adequate *poetic* thought have not yet become articulate even in terms of *intellectual* thought.

What has become articulate in terms of intellectual thought is experience so prosaic that its mere contemplation paralyzes the poetic imagination. It is the situation that Hegel had in mind when in his *Aesthetics* he wrote: 'If the mode of prose has absorbed all the concepts of the mind and impressed them with its prosaic stamp, then poetry has to take on the business of so thorough a recasting and remodelling that, faced with the unyielding mass of the prosaic, it finds itself involved everywhere in manifold difficulties'; and which led him to the pessimistic dictum that therefore 'art . . . is and will remain for us a thing of the past'.[33] In such conditions a kind of poetry will be produced for which, anomalously enough, the *intellectual* thinking has to be done after the event. Whole gangs of interpreters will rush in, intellectually to prepare the ground for what has already grown—ploughboys of the sparse harvest.

Yet Mr. Eliot is not, I suspect, concerned as much with the question of thought in poetry as with the problem of belief. For the assumption underlying his essay is that the thinker is interested in the *truth* of thought, but the poet merely in its fitting expression. In other words, the thinker invites us to *believe* what he says, whereas the poet aims only at our being *moved* or *pleased* by the way he puts it. This is indeed a very relevant problem at a time when more and more people try to believe in poetry as in a religion. Around Rilke, for instance, a vast body of literature has grown up that appears to aim not at gaining comprehending readers for the poet, but at making proselytes.

The question, then, is: is the poet a trustworthy counsellor? Does he himself believe what he says? Is he committed to his truths, as the thinker appears to be committed to his? Without going into the endless intricacies of this problem, I would say that it has nothing to do with the nature of either poetry or thought as such, but with the character of any particular poet or thinker, or with the character of any particular poetry or thought. There *are* poetic creations which bear the unmistakable stamp of convictions deeply held by the poet; and the *aesthetic* success of this kind of poetry is inextricably bound up with the sincerity of the personal beliefs expressed in them. This applies, for instance, to the poetry of St. John of the Cross. But it applies, also, on varying levels and in different degrees, to less extreme examples: to George Herbert, John Donne, Milton, Andreas Gryphius, Claudius, Hölderlin—and Mr. T. S. Eliot. It does not matter in the slightest whether such a poet is, while writing, *preoccupied* with his beliefs. Of course, in the act of writing he is preoccupied with the business of writing as well as possible. But what does matter is the fact that such poets could not produce good poetry if they were prepared to betray their beliefs for the sake of occasional heresies offering a more felicitous phrase. On a profounder level it would even be true to say that such a poet, in writing his poetry, *discovers* the precise nature of the beliefs to which he is, or ought to be, really committed. Whether he remains committed to such beliefs, whether he is a believer all the time, realizing what he believes through his actions, is another matter, again wholly irrelevant to the specific problem of poetry. Few men are like Pascal, and even he had to remind himself continually, by a sheet of paper sewn into his jacket, of what he had on one sacred occasion recognized as wholly true.

Naturally, the beliefs of such a poet, as proclaimed in his poetry, may be of so subtle, esoteric and even eccentric a sort that it would be unwise to try to live by them. But he is not necessarily less 'trustworthy' as a prophet of truths than any other type of prophet. The difficulty does not lie in the fact that he is a poet, but is of a universal nature. It is the difficulty of translating spiritual convictions into living convictions. If this were an easy matter, the Christian Church would have no 'history'. Her practices would be as unchanging and unchangeable as the core of her spiritual beliefs. The reasons why one should, or should not, accept the beliefs inherent in Rilke's later poetry are not different in kind from the reasons why one should, or should not, accept the beliefs of Marxism, or of the Oxford Group, or of anthroposophy. To say, 'but he is merely a poet' (and not, I suppose, a sectarian hawker, an ideologist or a political propagan-

M

dist) is to suggest that, by his profession, he is less capable of perceiving truth than others; to say, 'but his poetry is too beautiful to be true' is to insinuate that the closer the poetry is to truth, the less successful it will be as art, because all truth is necessarily ungainly. This is a point to which we shall return at the end of this essay.

I am not concerned with advocating Rilke's beliefs. But I am concerned with a dangerous type of aesthetic fallacy: that Rilke's ideas do not matter because they are a poet's ideas. If I could see a choice where, in fact, I believe there is none, between the ideas and the poetry, I think I should rather be inclined to say with Mr. Eliot that it is the poetry which 'does not matter'. But there is no such choice. In *Duino Elegies* the poetry is the ideas, and the ideas are the poetry. If the ideas were all humbug, or if, as Herr Holthusen suggests in his book on Rilke, they were all 'wrong', in the sense of contradicting that 'intuitive logic' which tells us what is a true and what is a false picture of man,[34] then the poetry would have little chance of being what he believes it to be: *great* poetry.

The appreciation of poetry is not like looking at a beautiful apple; it is rather like looking and eating. If the core is rotten, the outside beauty will soon be felt to be a mockery. Herr Holthusen's way out of the dilemma between his Christian beliefs, which make him condemn Rilke's ideas, and the pagan enchantment that impels him to acknowledge the greatness of Rilke's poetry, is, I think, the way of spiritual timidity. Its coarser symbols are the fig-leaves of the Vatican museum. Let us enjoy the pagan beauty, but not go too far. How far? Not as far as the *whole* poetry. For the poetry of the *Duino Elegies* is indivisible. There is no poetry left if we *feel* that the 'ideas' are false to the point of being a distortion of the true image of man. If, on the other hand, we merely *know* this, not by that 'intuitive logic' of which Herr Holthusen speaks, but by theological deliberations, we are by no means immune from sharing the beliefs of the *Duino Elegies*. Why not accept a situation which for most Christians in Europe is at least as old as the Renaissance? The characteristic spiritual quality of that long period of history of which we are the bewildered heirs was not only a dissociation of faith from knowledge; this was a comparatively harmless episode, lasting from the seventeenth century to the age of Victoria, a mere surface repercussion of that mightier earthquake which severed faith from sensibility. It is this rift which has made it impossible for most Christians not to *feel*, or at least not to feel *also*, as true many 'truths' which are incompatible with the truth of their faith. If this is agony, it must be borne by those who are incapable of Keats's '*Negative Capability*, that is, when a man is capable of being in uncertainties, mysteries, doubts, without any irritable reaching after fact and reason'. Such an 'irritable reaching' is the all too facile distinction between the 'truth' of a poem and its 'aesthetic appeal', between the 'idea' and the 'poetry', a separation which can only do damage to the resources, meagre as they are, with which we have to carry on in our modest efforts to get a little nearer the spiritual integrity within which, in Nietzsche's words, 'the religious, aesthetic and moral perceptions are at one'. For the time being, which does not seem to be God's good time:

Jede dumpfe Umkehr der Welt hat solche Enterbte,
denen das Frühere nicht und noch nicht das Nächste
  gehört.

(Seventh Elegy)

Each torpid turn of the world has such disinherited
  children,
to whom no longer what's been, and not yet what's
  coming, belongs.

This again is spoken, not only from the heart of Nietzsche, but almost with his tongue, suggesting that we should resume the discussion of the particular poet and the particular philosopher.*

* In his essay on Dante, written in 1929, two years after 'Shakespeare and the Stoicism of Seneca', Mr. Eliot discusses once more the question of belief and poetry. 'There is a difference,' he says, 'between philosophical *belief* and poetic *assent*' (*Collected Essays*, p. 257). This is undoubtedly true in an age in which 'the religious, aesthetic and moral perceptions' are *not* at one. We may, however, disregard the word 'philosophical' in Mr. Eliot's phrase, for his context is more strictly a religious or theological one. An agnostic can give his poetic assent to Dante and a Christian withhold it from every single hymn sung on a Sunday in his church. Yet there will be a certain strain in such a situation. The more *serious* becomes a reader's love for Dante's poetry, the more will he be tempted to accept his beliefs, or else be exasperated by the poet's wrongheadedness in holding them or his own inability to share them; and exasperation detracts from enjoyment. Differences of opinion are more worrying between lovers than between superficial acquaintances; in fact, they tend to become or reveal something else: flaws in mutual understanding. And because this is so, Mr. Eliot's discussion of this particular problem comes to nothing. His statement on page 258: 'You are not called upon to believe what Dante believed, for your belief will not give you a groat's worth more of understanding and appreciation' is, after its more forceful reiteration in a postscript (p. 269), crossed out again by 'So I cannot, in practice, wholly separate my poetic appreciation from my personal beliefs' (p. 271). The question is extremely difficult, so difficult that both assertions, blatantly contradictory, are in some measure true. It seems to me that two points could be added to make them a few degrees truer and less incompatible. 1. Where beliefs embodied in poetry are as important as they are in what one may call confessional poetry, we cannot fully appreciate the poetry without being at least *tempted* to accept the beliefs as well. The measure of our appreciation will be the degree

4

We observed them, each in his own way, working, thinking and feeling towards a radical revision of the frontiers between traditionally articulated concepts of thought and, as it were, units of feeling. There remains the question of how and why they came to undertake such a stupendous labour of thought and feeling—'Herzwerk', 'work of heart', as Rilke called it. The answer was given for both of them by Nietzsche: because God is dead. And God was so powerful, efficient and secretive a landlord that to look after His Estate all by ourselves involves us in great difficulties. What under His management used to be clearly defined spheres are now objects of confused and conflicting claims. Much that we were powerfully persuaded to accept as true dissolves into sheer illusion. For all the land appears to have been heavily mortgaged. We have lived in splendour, but the splendour was merely loaned. Payment was due on the death of God, and the unknown transcendental creditor lost little time in claiming it. A tremendous effort has to be exacted to restore the glory.

Both Nietzsche and Rilke have made themselves administrators of the impoverished estate. The enormous complexity of their works must not deceive us; the struc-

---

to which we experience the poem's strength in persuasion and our weakness in the face of the challenge. With such poetry before us, complete immunity from infection would prove either the bluntness of our perception or the worthlessness of the poetry. 2. There are ideas and beliefs so prosaic, outlandish or perverse in their innermost structure that no great or good poetry can come from them: for instance, Hitler's racialism. It is this *negative* consideration that to me finally proves the intimate *positive* relation between belief, thought and poetry. If there were no relation, there would be no reason either why the most perverse or idiotic beliefs should not be convertible into *great* poetry. They are not.

ture behind it is consistently simple; it has the simplicity of that immense single-mindedness with which they, consciously or intuitively, dedicated their lives to the one task: to re-assess and re-define all experience in thought and feeling; to show that the traditional modes of thought and feeling, in so far as they were determined, or decisively modified, by Christian transcendental beliefs—and to which of them does this not apply?—had been rendered invalid by the end of religion; to replace them; to overcome the great spiritual depression, caused by the death of God, through new and ever greater powers of glory and praise; to adjust, indeed to revolutionize, thought and feeling in accordance with the reality of a world of absolute immanence; and to achieve this without any loss of spiritual grandeur. 'Indeed,' writes Nietzsche (to Overbeck, May 21st, 1884), 'who can feel with me what it means to feel with every shred of one's being that the weight of all things must be defined anew,' and Rilke (to Ilse Jahr, February 22nd, 1923): 'God, the no longer sayable, is being stripped of his attributes; they return to his creation'; [35] and in 'The Letter from the Young Workman' (reversing the debtor-creditor relationship and presenting the bill to Heaven): 'It is high time for the impoverished earth to claim back all those loans which have been raised at the expense of her own bliss for the equipment of some super-future'. [36] Nietzsche spoke for himself as well as for Rilke when at the time of writing *Zarathustra* he made the following entry in his notebook: 'He who no longer finds what is great in God will find it nowhere—he must either deny or create it'. [37] It is the most precise formula for the religiously disinherited religious mind.

Nietzsche and Rilke experienced and explored this situation with the utmost consistency, courageously facing the paradox to which it leads: the paradox of affirming from negation, and creating from denial. For the denial of God involves for both Nietzsche and Rilke the denial of man *as he is*. Even before Zarathustra proclaimed the rule of the Superman, Nietzsche, knowing that man has become 'impossible' after doing away with God, 'the holiest and mightiest that the world possessed', asked: 'Is not the greatness of this deed too great· for us? To prove worthy of it, must not we ourselves become gods?' [38] And Rilke said of his *Malte Laurids Brigge* that it almost 'proved that this life, suspended in a bottomless pit, is impossible'.[39]

How is this impossible life to become possible again? How is the vanished glory issuing from a transcendental god to be recreated by a world gloomily imprisoned in its own immanence? At this point both Nietzsche and Rilke indulge in the same alchemy that we have seen employed in their transmutation of pain and suffering. The idea of even heightening the agony of existence in order to increase the resources from which ultimate bliss will be sustained is familiar to both of them. Nietzsche once quoted Cardanus as having said that one ought to seek out as much suffering as possible in order to intensify the joy springing from its conquest; [40] and Rilke wrote of the 'holy cunning of the martyrs', taking 'the most concentrated dose of pain' to acquire the immunity of continual bliss.[41] Now again they seek in the greatest possible intensification of immanence salvation from the inglorious prison. They almost invent more and more deprivations of transcendence to heighten the pressure within the hermetic vessel. In that, Nietzsche's Eternal Recurrence and Rilke's 'Einmal und nichtmehr', 'Once and no more', are contrasts merely in verbal expression, but identical in meaning. This identity lies in the emphasis both these symbols place on the *eternity* of the moment here and now, the *irrevocability* of the one and unique opportunity and test of living.

The idea of Eternal Recurrence seeks to bestow the paradox of an eternity of finite time on the transient moment, which Rilke, in his turn, eternalizes in the hermetical flame of inner experience, consuming all that is merely corruptible ma.ter and concreteness in our world and leaving us with an essence as imperishable as it is invisible. Rilke states this theme of his mature work with explicit precision as early as his *Tuscan Diary*: 'We need *eternity*; for only eternity can provide space for our gestures. Yet we know that we live in narrow finiteness. Thus it is our task to create infinity within these boundaries, for we no longer believe in the unbounded.'[42] And the imaginations of both Nietzsche and Rilke have given birth to symbolic creatures moving with perfect grace and ease in a sphere to which man can attain only in the utmost realization of his spiritual powers. These creatures of immanence, transcending immanence in the achievement of a yet profounder immanence, are Nietzsche's Superman and Rilke's Angel. Both are terrible to man, threatening with annihilation the image that, fondly and lazily, he has built up of himself, an image resting on the illusion of transcendence and now shattered in the great undeceiving: 'To create the Superman after we have thought, indeed rendered thinkable, the whole of nature in terms of man himself' and then 'to *break all your images of man* with the image of the Superman— this is Zarathustra's will . . .'[43] says one of Nietzsche's notebooks from the time of *Zarathustra*; and Rilke's *Duino Elegies* begin with the invocation of the angelic terror:

Wer, wenn ich schriee, hörte mich denn aus der Engel Ordnungen? und gesetzt selbst, es nähme einer mich p ɔtzlich ans Herz: ich verginge von seinem stärkeren Dasein . . .

(First Elegy)

Who, if I cried, would hear me among the angelic orders? And even if one of them suddenly

pressed me against his heart, I should fade in the
    strength of his
stronger existence . . .

and

Jeder Engel ist schrecklich. Und dennoch, weh mir,
ansing ich euch, fast tödliche Vögel der Seele,
wissend um euch. . . .

(Second Elegy)

Every angel is terrible. Still, though, alas!
I invoke you, almost deadly birds of the soul,
knowing of you. . . .

The supreme realization of immanence and its metamorphosis into everlasting inwardness is man's task in a
world dominated by Rilke's Angel, in the same way in
which Nietzsche conceives Eternal Recurrence as the
terrifying discipline which must break man and make the
Superman. Only he, in the glory of his own strength, joy
and power of praise, can *will* again and again a life
which, even if lived only once, must be all but unendur-
able to man, as soon as he is exposed to the full impact
of its absolute godlessness and senselessness, and no
longer sheltered from it by the ruins of Christianity
among which he exists. 'I perform the great experiment:
who can bear the idea of Eternal Recurrence? He who
cannot endure the sentence, "There is no redemption",
ought to die out.' [44] The Superman is for Nietzsche what
Orpheus is for Rilke: the transfigurer of unredeemable
existence, with the 'mystery of its unending repetition
issuing from superhuman delight'.[45]

Und so drängen wir uns und wollen es leisten,
wollens enthalten in unseren einfachen Händen,
im überfüllteren Blick und im sprachlosen Herzen.
Wollen es werden. . . .

(Ninth Elegy)

And so we press on and try to achieve it,
try to contain it within our simple hands,
in the gaze ever more overcrowded and in the speech-
     less heart.
Try to become it. . . .

But what we try to achieve here and what overcrowds
our gaze and heart—with 'überzähliges Dasein', 'Super-
numerary existence'—is not the vision of Eternal Recurrence, but, on the contrary, of

          Einmal
jedes, nur einmal. Einmal und nichtmehr. Und wir
     auch
einmal. Nie wieder. Aber dieses
einmal gewesen zu sein, wenn auch nur einmal:
irdisch gewesen zu sein, scheint nicht widerrufbar.
                      (Ninth Elegy)

              Just once,
everything only for once. Once and no more. And
     we, too,
once. And never again. But this
having been once, though only once,
having been once on earth—can it ever be cancelled?

Nietzsche's Eternal Recurrence and Rilke's eternally
reiterated 'Once' are both the extreme symbols of the determination to wrest the utmost of spiritual significance
from a life that, in traditional terms, has ceased to be
spiritually significant. How to cast eternity from the new
mould of absolute transience, and how to achieve the
mode of transcendence within the consciousness of pure
immanence, is one of the main concerns of Nietzsche as
well as of Rilke. This problem links Rilke (and, of course,
Nietzsche) with the philosophers of Existence; Heidegger, for instance, is said to have remarked that his philosophy is merely the unfolding in thought of what Rilke
has expressed poetically; [46] but even without this con-

fession the affinity would be obvious. What, above all, Rilke and the existentialists have in common is the experience of the utter exposure and defencelessness of the frontiers of human existence against the neighbouring void, that area which was once established as the divine home of souls and is now the unassailable fortress of the *nihil*, defeating for ever every new and heroic attempt of man to assert himself in that region: hence Jasper's *Scheitern*, Heidegger's *Geworfensein* and, long before them, Kierkegaard's—and even Pascal s—*Angst*. The focal point of all existentialist philosophies is this 'marginal situation' of man in the border-districts of immanence and the realization of the existence of a sphere which seems to invite and yet relentlessly beat back every attempt at transcendence.

It is this impenetrable void against which Zarathustra hurls his armies of men, knowing that they will not be victorious, but utterly routed; yet a few will return in triumph, having gained the strength of supermen in the purifying defeat. For life is a 'Wagnis', a perpetual staking of existence, man a mere 'essay in existence' and lovable only because he is 'ein Übergang und ein Untergang',[47] at once transition and perdition. The same frontier is the defeat of Malte Laurids Brigge, until the mature Rilke succeeds in concluding an everlasting truce with the anonymous powers on the other side—by appropriating their territory 'inwardly'. Where man knew merely the terror of the monstrous emptiness beyond, there is now the peace of 'reiner Bezug', 'pure relatedness', which is so pure because no real 'otherness' enters into it. In this 'reiner Bezug' life and death are one. As soon as it is achieved,

> *entsteht*
> *aus unsern Jahreszeiten erst der Umkreis*
> *des ganzen Wandelns. Über uns hinüber*
> *spielt dann der Engel. . . .*
>
> (Fourth Elegy)

arises
from our seasons the cycle
of the entire motion. Over and above us,
then, there is the Angel's play. . . .

Or, one is tempted to add, the Superman's dance, the joy
of the creatures who have gained eternity in the resigned
and yet victorious return to themselves. Rilke, in the
Super-Narcissus image of his Angels, at the same time
expresses the essence of Nietzsche's race of Supermen
who assert their power and beauty in the cycle of Eternal
Recurrence:

> . . . *die die entströmte eigene Schönheit*
> *weiderschöpfen zurück in das eigene Antlitz.*
>
> (Second Elegy)

> . . . drawing up their own
> outstreamed beauty into their faces again.

It is not correct to say that after the *Duino Elegies*
Rilke returned, as some critics suggest, to a 'simpler' and
'purely lyrical' mode of expression. The apparent simplicity and pure lyricism of the final phase are not different in kind from the simplicity and lyricism of *Sonnets to Orpheus*. There is, indeed, repose; but it is the
repose of a poetry that appears to have settled peacefully
on the very pastures which had for so long been the goal
of the struggle. If the *Duino Elegies* were the invocation
of the Angel, some of the poems that come afterwards
sound like the Angel's own poetry; and it is hardly surprising that it could also be said: like the poetry of the
Superman. This, indeed, does not make them easier to
understand. It is the poetry of achievement, and not the
poetry of return. There is little gain in it for those who
find the 'ideas' of the preceding period disturbing. The
ideas are not abandoned, but realized; for instance, in
the poem written in 1924:

Da dich das geflügelte Entzücken
über manchen frühen Abgrund trug,
baue jetzt der unerhörten Brücken
kühn berechenbaren Bug.

Wunder ist nicht nur im unerklärten
Überstehen der Gefahr;
erst in einer klaren reingewährten
Leistung wird das Wunder wunderbar.

Mitzuwirken ist nicht Überhebung
an dem unbeschreiblichen Bezug,
immer inniger wird die Verwebung,
nur Getragensein ist nicht genug.

Deine ausgeübten Kräfte spanne,
bis sie reichen, zwischen zwein
Widersprüchen. . . . Denn im Manne
Will der Gott beraten sein.[48]

As the winged ecstasy
has borne you over many an early abyss,
now, with mathematical audacity
build the arches of unheard-of bridges.

Wonder is not merely in the inexplicable
surviving of danger;
only in the clear and purely granted
achievement is the miracle miraculous.

To participate in the indescribable
relating, is not presumption,
ever more intense becomes the pattern,
only being borne along will not suffice.

Stretch your practised powers till they span
the distance between two contradictions,
for the god must find
counsel in the man.

Or in Rilke's last known poem in German, which, if it is simple, has the inexhaustibly complex simplicity of a sphere so esoteric that it renders it completely untranslatable, defeating even the attempt to give a prose version of it in English. Yet all that has been said here about Rilke and Nietzsche could easily be based on this one poem alone and would need no further support. It is dated August 24th, 1926, four months before Rilke's death, and is dedicated to Erika Mitterer 'for the feast of praise':

Taube, die draussen blieb, ausser dem Taubenschlag,
wieder in Kreis und Haus, einig der Nacht, dem Tag,
weiss sie die Heimlichkeit, wenn sich der Einbezug
fremdester Schrecken schmiegt in den gefühlten Flug.

Unter den Tauben, die allergeschonteste,
niemals gefährdetste, kennt nicht die Zärtlichkeit;
wiedererholtes Herz ist das bewohnteste:
freier durch Widerruf freut sich die Fähigkeit.

Über dem Nirgendssein spannt sich das Uberall!
Ach der geworfene, ach der gewagte Ball,
füllt er die Hände nicht anders mit Wiederkehr:
rein um sein Heimgewicht ist er mehr.[49]

5

Both Nietzsche and Rilke, experiencing life as wholly immanent, irrevocable in its transience and unredeemable in its imperfection, stake it on the supreme 'Wagnis', the daring experiment: man himself must become the redeemer of existence. This is the ultimate consequence of the Will to Power, or of humanism thought out and felt to its radical conclusion by the *anima naturaliter religiosa*. Nietzsche replaces the mystery of the Incarnation by the Superman, the Will to Power incarnate; and Rilke by the

angelic vision of a world disembodied in human inwardness. 'We must transform our prayers into blessings,' [50]
says Nietzsche; and Rilke:

> *Erde, ist es nicht dies, was du willst: unsichtbar*
> *in uns erstehen?—Ist es dein Traum nicht,*
> *einmal unsichtbar zu sein?—Erde! unsichtbar!*
> *Was, wenn Verwandlung nicht, ist dein drängender*
> *   Auftrag?*

(Ninth Elegy)

> Earth, isn't this what you want: an *invisible*
> re-arising in us? Is it not your dream
> to be one day invisible? Earth! invisible!
> What is your urgent command, if not transformation?

Only on the discovery of this redeeming mission follows
Rilke's final affirmation: 'Erde, du liebe, ich will'.

Interpreting the Elegies to his Polish translator, Rilke
wrote: *'There is neither a Here and Now nor Beyond, but
only the great Oneness,* in which the creatures surpassing
us, the Angels, are at home. . . . *We are the bees of the
Invisible. Nous butinons éperdument le miel du visible,
pour l'accumuler dans la grande ruche d'or de l'Invisible.'*
And after denouncing the ceaselessly progressing depreciation of the spiritual value of all 'things', he continues:
'The earth has no other refuge except to become invisible: *in us* . . . only *in us* can this intimate and enduring
transformation of the Visible into the Invisible . . . be
accomplished. . . . The Angel of the *Elegies* has nothing to do with the angel of the Christian Heaven. . . .
He is the creature in whom the transformation of the
Visible into the Invisible, which is our task, appears already accomplished. . . .' [51] But for all this, the most
illuminating part of Rilke's much-quoted letter is the
statement that the ultimate affirmation of life, achieved
in the *Elegies*, is sustained by precisely the same aware-

ness that persuaded Malte Laurids Brigge of life's 'impossibility'. Malte's disgust and the Ninth Elegy's praise spring from an identical source. In other words, the Angel did for Rilke what the Superman did for Nietzsche: he supplied the philosophers' stone with which to make gold from base matter. Yet it appears that of the two Rilke was the more successful alchemist. The letters he wrote after the *Duino Elegies* lavished the precious stuff from the poet's workshop on as many needy as cared to apply for it. Nietzsche, on the other hand, while writing *Zarathustra* and expounding the doctrines of Eternal Recurrence, praise and affirmation, made the following entry in his notebook: 'I do not wish to live *again*. How have I borne life? By creating. What has made me endure? The vision of the Superman who *affirms* life. I have tried to affirm it *myself*—but ah!' [52]

These two confessions of Rilke and Nietzsche clinch the whole excruciating problem that besets the spiritually disinherited mind of Europe, and raise anew the question of poetry and truth in an age dispossessed of all spiritual certainties. Without that all-pervasive sense of truth which bestows upon happier cultures their intuition of order and reality, poetry—in company with all the other arts—will be faced with ever increasing demands for ever greater 'creativeness'. For the 'real order' has to be 'created' where there is no intuitive conviction that it exists. The story of the rise of the poet from the humble position of a teller of tales and a singer of songs to the heights of creation, from a lover of fancies to a slave of the imagination, from the mouthpiece of divine wisdom to the begetter of new gods, is a story as glorious as it is agonizing. For with every new gain in poetic creativity the world as it is, the world as created without the poet's intervention, becomes poorer; and every new impoverishment of the world is a new incentive to poetic creativeness. In the end the world as it is is nothing but a slum to the

spirit, and an offence to the artist. Leaving its vapours behind in audacious flight, his genius settles in a
world wholly created by the creator-poet: *Gesang ist
Dasein.*

'Only after the death of religion will the imagination
be able to luxuriate again in divine spheres,'[53] said
Nietzsche, perhaps not knowing that in saying it he was
merely echoing one of the favourite ideas of the Romantics whom he so much disliked. For it was Friedrich
Schlegel who wrote: 'Only he can be an artist who has a
religion of his own, an original view of infinity',[54] and it
was Novalis who added to this dictum the marginal note
'The artist is thoroughly irreligious. Hence he can work
in the medium of religion as though it were bronze.' [55]
But the original views of infinity cannot for ever remain
unaffected by the spiritual destitution of the finite. There
must come a time when owing to excessive mining bronze
is devalued and the soil becomes too dry for anything to
grow luxuriantly, except in artificial conditions.

Neither Rilke nor Nietzsche praises the praiseworthy.
They praise. They do not believe the believable. They
believe. And it is their praising and believing itself that
becomes praiseworthy and believable in the act of worship. Theirs is a *religio intransitiva.* Future anthropol-
ogists may see in it the distinctive religious achievement
of modern Europe, the theological equivalent of *l'art pour
l'art.* For the time being, it may help us to assess the rank
of Rilke as a poet, and to clear up some of the confusion
into which we are plunged by dissociating his 'great poetry' from his 'false ideas'.

In a sense Rilke's poetry is as 'false' as are his ideas.
This sense, however, is not simply derogatory. There is
a kind of falseness which, quite legitimately, affords the
most refined aesthetic pleasure: at the point, that is, at
which consistently sustained artificiality assumes the semblance of spontaneity, and the most elaborate magical

N

procedure the appearance of the naïvely miraculous. In this sense both Rilke's poetry and his ideas show the intrinsic falseness of a self-created reality and a self-induced love for it. In defending a sense and vision of reality different from Rilke's, the critic implicitly upholds, often against his explicit intentions, standards of poetry by which the poetic work of Rilke's mature years stands judged as too eccentric to be really great. Rilke poetically exploits a marginal position, precariously maintained on the brink of catastrophe. The catastrophe, perpetually threatening and only just warded off by the most dazzling acrobatics of soul and mind, is the loss of significant external reality. In the great poetry of the European tradition the emotions do not interpret; they respond to the interpreted world. In Rilke's mature poetry the emotions do the interpreting and then respond to their own interpretation.

All great art (and, for that matter, every human order stabilized by tradition) rests on a fundamentally fixed correspondence between the impact of external experience on man and man's articulate answers. These answers may be given on varying levels of profundity and with varying degrees of precision, but they are all recognizable by, as it were, their basic colour as the more or less right answers. Indeed, the imagination, this kingfisher after new experiences and new articulations, may discover new waters in lands which have long remained inaccessible and unexplored. But there will be a place for them, hitherto left blank, on the maps of the familiar world.

Rilke, however, is the poet of a world of which the philosopher is Nietzsche. Its formations evade all traditional systems of cartography. Doubt has dislodged all certainties. The unnameable is christened and the unsayable uttered. It is a world in which the order of correspondences is violently disturbed. We can no longer be sure that we love the lovable and abhor the detestable.

Good does no good and evil no harm. Terror and bliss are one. Life and death are the same. Lovers seek separation, not union. All the sweetness of the visible world is stored in invisible hives.

Unembarrassed greatness is not to be expected from the poetry of such a world.* Yet Rilke is uniquely successful in evoking the traditional responses of the emotions to fundamentally new impacts. At his bidding the soul travels as though through familiar land; but on arrival it finds itself in a place where it never meant to be. It is not for nothing that the central position in the

* Mr. Eliot, in discussing the question of whether a poet 'thinks', says: 'We talk as if thought was precise and emotion was vague. In reality there is precise emotion and there is vague emotion. To express precise emotion requires as great intellectual power as to express precise thought.' This is an important point admirably put, although it would be difficult to find a word other than 'thought' for the *intellectual* power required to express precise emotion. Yet the passage continues; 'But by "thinking" I mean something different from anything that I find in Shakespeare'—namely, as we saw, 'thinking to a purpose', etc. (*Selected Essays*, p. 135).

Asked for a definition of the 'unembarrassed greatness of poetry' I should accept Mr. Eliot's sentence and say that, among other things, it is 'the precise expression of precise emotion'. But I should add that precise emotion is a mode of response or even of comprehension, closely linked to thought. Their common medium is language. Indeed, precise emotion is the result of that sustained and refining interaction between thought and emotion to which we give the name of culture. The only measure for the precision of emotion is in its articulation. Inarticulate emotion is vague and thoughtless. And precise emotional articulation in language is possible only within a definite 'system of correspondences' between thought, feeling and external impacts. This, however, is hardly provided by the situation in which modern poetry finds itself involved. This situation is inimical to such precision partly because by 'thought' we have come to 'mean something different from anything' we may find in Shakespeare or Dante.

Duino Elegies—the fifth among the ten—is occupied by *Les Saltimbanques*. There is an acrobatic element in Rilke's poetry itself which tinges its greatness with the hue of the abstruse. For his most superb accomplishment is the *salto mortale* of despair which lands the soul in a 'Raum der Rühmung', a sphere of praise, where all the praise is sung in honour of the singer while the voiceless world, deranged and dizzy, is left behind to face the music.

'What was it that Zarathustra once told you? That poets lie too much?—But Zarathustra too is a poet. . . . *We* lie too much.' [56] These words of Nietzsche's sound like an anticipated motto to Rilke's letters. For the utter precariousness of Rilke's vision is exposed most painfully in endless prose variations which form a large part of his correspondence. Only a generation of recipients and readers benumbed and befogged by every conceivable spiritual deprivation, and insensitive to the intimate relation between language and authenticity, could accept as genuine spiritual guidance pronouncements which more often than not show the unmistakable stylistic imprint of untruth; of that most dangerous kind of untruth which does not spring from fraudulent intent, but from a self-deception so profound that nothing less powerful than a false inflection, a hollow adjective or a synthetic noun can undeceive us of its hypnotic persuasion. Rilke takes the unending curtain-calls which acknowledge his poetic achievement, in the costume of his inspiration. Then, and only then, the prophecy turns to performance, and the visionary glance seems produced by make-up. But it was Nietzsche, the thinker, not Rilke, the poet, who was obsessed with the problem of the actor-artist, as it was Nietzsche who wrote the lines:

Dass ich verbannt sei
von aller Wahrheit!
Nur Narr! *Nur* Dichter! . . . [57]

Oh, that I am banished
from all Truth!
Mere *fool*! Mere *poet*! . . .

This fact brings to its paradoxical conclusion an argument that took its bearings from a theory expounding that, while the poet merely makes poetry, it is the thinker who is unequivocally committed to his thought.

'My earliest serious concern was with the relationship between Art and Truth,' wrote Nietzsche in 1888, right at the end of his conscious life, in a renewed attempt to understand the mind that in 1870 conceived *The Birth of Tragedy*. 'And even now,' the meditation continues, 'I am seized with holy terror in the face of that dilemma. The belief that informs *The Birth of Tragedy* is a belief in Art, against the background of yet another belief: that it is *impossible to live with Truth*. . . . The will to *illusion* . . . is profounder, more "metaphysical", than the will to Truth, Reality and Being'.[58] And in *The Will to Power* we read: 'For a philosopher it is an abomination to say, "the Good and the Beautiful are one"; and if he dares to add, "also the True", then one ought to beat him. Truth is ugly. . . . We have *Art* in order *not to perish of Truth*.'[59] Thus the essential function of art is, according to Nietzsche, to think and feel existence to that conclusion which convinces us of its perfection, 'to create perfection and the fullness of life', to '*affirm, bless* and *deify* existence'.[60]

This is the perfect definition of Rilke's poetic project. It also marks the summit reached by art and poetry in its steep ascent to the heights of absolute creativeness. At this point the separation between art and reality appears to be complete. Reality is the death of the spirit and art its salvation. Where does truth reside? Is it in the deadly real world or in the saving vision of the artist? The question lingers on the all but imperceptible borderline between delusion and lunacy, between Nietzsche's madness and Rilke's prophetic pose, tenaciously maintained even beyond the confines of poetic inspiration. Nietzsche, believing that truth was insufferable and that poetry was an illusion, continually suspected that at least some of his thought was 'merely poetry.' Rilke, on the other hand, succeeded most of the time in convincing himself that the thought behind his poetry was the mind of truth. Illusion or truth, Superman or Angel, Will to Power or the Will to Inwardness—in both Nietzsche and Rilke the human mind and imagination are engaged in the ultimate task of creating a world to take the place of the spiritually useless productions of God.

'Indeed, the whole book acknowledges only an artist's meaning behind everything that happens—a "god" if you like, but certainly only an artist-god . . .' desirous of achieving his delight and sovereignty through making things and unmaking them . . . and who, in creating worlds, frees himself from the agony . . . of his inner conflicts. The world . . . seen as the successful salvation of god, as a vision . . . of one who suffers most, one who is the richest in conflicts and contradictions and can only save himself by creating illusion. . . .' [61] The book in question is *The Birth of Tragedy*, thus described by Nietzsche himself in 1886, sixteen years after it was written. A critic could hardly do better in the case of *Duino Elegies* and *Sonnets to Orpheus*.

In January, 1889, Nietzsche, then in Turin, became clinically insane. On the fourth of that month the uncanniest of all calls to Orpheus was posted at the Turin railway station. The note was addressed to Nietzsche's friend, the composer Peter Gast. It ran: 'To my maestro Pietro. Sing a new song for me: the world is transfigured and all the heavens rejoice.' It was signed 'The Crucified'.

Sharing with each other the fruits of defeat, inflicted upon all besiegers of the Absolute in a world without Truth, thought ceases to be merely thought and poetry is no longer merely poetry. Song, trying to prove the glory, and thought, determined to dispel the illusion, are adventurers in the same heroic saga. It tells the story of one Tantalus who has deprived the gods of their seats at the banquet. Sitting all by himself at the divinely laid table, he yet cannot eat without letting them into his own secret: that he does not think well enough of himself to believe in the reality of his triumph. This is their curse, which he cannot escape. Intoxicated with their wine, he glories in their absence; but with the sobriety of his thought returning, he sees the water of life receding before the hollow of his outstretched hand.

It is the redeeming achievement of Nietzsche and Rilke that they have raised, the one in the intensely felt plight of his thought, the other in his intensely meditated poetry, the abysmal contradictions of their age to a plane where doubt and confusion once more dissolve into the certainty of mystery.

OSWALD SPENGLER AND THE

PREDICAMENT OF THE

HISTORICAL IMAGINATION

Oswald Spengler, who died in 1936, performed one of the most curious feats in the history of modern thought: in a remarkably short time he has achieved a kind of highly topical oblivion. The first volume of his great work *The Decline of the West* appeared in 1918, and the second followed in 1922.[1] It was passionately debated at the time. A special issue of the philosophical journal *Logos* was published in which the headmasters of all the schools of German philosophy launched critical campaigns for or against this surprisingly learned and alarmingly catastrophe-minded *Oberlehrer*. Furthermore, a book called *Der Streit um Spengler* assembled the numerous expert voices of critics into a confused chorus which left behind the effect of agitated historical embarrassment. And now, when the author of *The Decline of the West* would be only just over seventy, his work is by general consent utterly out of date.

Yet the 'utterly' carries a suspicious emphasis. It sounds a little like the comforting agreement of a party of grown-up empiricists who all saw the ghost of a very unpleasant uncle during the preceding night: 'But he has been utterly dead for the last fifteen years!' And so he has; yet his ill-tempered prophecies have unfortunately come true; the family was called together to discuss the impending auction of the family estate.

The uneasiness is not surprising. For the history of the West since 1917 looks like the work of children clumsily filling in with lurid colours a design drawn in outlines by Oswald Spengler. The spiritual exhaustion of the age has been the dominant theme of our most-discussed writers, of D. H. Lawrence, Franz Kafka, T. S. Eliot, not to mention the gloomily vigorous Americans; and when they indulge in prophetic visions of the future, in the manner of Aldous Huxley, George Orwell or even the dying Fabian H. G. Wells, the emerging picture is invariably an elaboration of themes from *The Decline of the West*. Spengler even predicted the disappointing behaviour of that god who has since so sadly failed many of our intellectuals. Some time before the Russian revolution he wrote: 'Socialism, only half-developed to-day, is indeed fighting against Imperialism; yet one day it will become arch-expansionist itself with all the vehemence of Destiny'.[2]

Destiny—this brings us to the very centre of Spengler's vision of history. History is Destiny, unfolded through the life and death of cultured human societies. All these societies share a common rhythm of development, which Spengler sees in analogy with the life-and-death rhythm of living organisms. Cultures—this and not 'civilization' is the proper term to use with Spengler—come into being, are young and full of vigorous metaphysical sap, flower like splendid vegetables on the herbaceous borders of an indifferent cosmos, and decay—or rather, are frozen into rigid forms by the metaphysical winter of their old age. It is this petrified stage of a culture which Spengler calls 'civilization'. With our Western culture the great chill finally descended in the course of the nineteenth century.

It is amazing how far Spengler is carried along by his precarious analogy. For according to him, when the freezing-point of a culture is reached, it expands and breaks whatever may try to contain it. Then, with its spiritual substance exhausted, outward expansion is the only gesture of life that is left. The age of Caesarism is upon us. A strict and rigid order of the molecules within is the condition of successful raids on the outward world; or in terms of government and foreign policy: the totalitarian State becomes the instrument of inevitable imperialist wars. Their outcome is, however, of little importance to the spiritual existence of the members of such a society. In victory or defeat their spirits will remain sterile—as barren, Spengler says, as the society of the Romans under their conquering Caesars. After some time, however, this powerful structure, spiritually dead as it is, is bound to fall to pieces, probably under the elusive but irresistible impact of new forces, alien and hostile to the existing order, and possessed of the stuff of which cultures are made: creative spontaneity and religious devotion.

In this struggle between the civilized engineers and barbaric, but God-inspired men, the barbarians will win. But before the time of a new culture comes, for Destiny's sake, Spengler proclaims, be an engineer! Don't waste your life in the futile agony of trying to realize what you may have left of a soul. This is no time for souls. If you become a painter, a poet, a composer, he says, you will find yourself in no time whatever frustrated, or else corrupted by those aesthetic cliques which offer, in terms of power, influence, licentiousness, easy sales of bogus wares, some compensation for the pains of a spiritual vocation gone astray. For the *Zeitgeist* is inexorable:

as inexorable now as it was in Roman times. Then, too, it would have been absurd for a young intelligent citizen to hatch out some irrelevant variation of post-Platonic philosophy, if he was clever enough to organize armies and provinces, and to plan new cities and roads.[3] Then as much as now, all spiritual, aesthetic, philosophical resources had been spent. Culture was, as it were, put into inverted commas and reduced to a museum, or a pleasure-garden, exhibiting the past together with its contemporary parodies. To-day, Spengler says, there is more intelligence, taste, character and ability in the technical staff of any first-rate engineering works than in the whole of contemporary music and painting.[4] His conclusion is: 'I can only hope that men of the new generation may be moved by my book to take up engineering instead of poetry, join the Navy rather than an art school, become politicians rather than philosophers'.[5]

Yet *The Decline of the West* is by no means a pamphlet written for boys. It contains the results of an enormous amount of learning and intellectual labour. Its scope— all the major societies in traceable human history—is as fantastic as its claim: to give the philosophy of the West to end all Western philosophies. Thus its subject is not history in any conventional sense of the term, but what the author calls 'the world-as-history'.[6]

It is impossible to refute such a mighty enterprise by listing, as so many of its opponents did, factual inaccuracies. There will always be sufficient indisputable facts left to support the structure, if one allows such a structure to be supportable at all. The proper tools of empiricism can only deal with Spengler's brushwood, and inflict a few scratches on his landscape of peaks and valleys. The assertion, for instance, that Spengler's culture-organisms have no real historical existence goes right outside the range of empiricism. It is impossible to destroy an analogy 'empirically', however much 'evidence' is assembled for the campaign. All historical generalizations are the defeat of the empiricist; and there is no history without them. Apply the strict empiricist test to the concept of 'nation', 'class', 'economic trend' or 'tradition', and the concept dissolves into a host of unmanageable *minutiae*. In every single case the question is merely how profound and subtle a generalization it is, or how much of the generalizing manoeuvre passes unnoticed; and it has every chance of not being recognized for what it is, if it is in keeping with the silent agreements and prejudices, the prevalent generalizing mood of society.

Professor Toynbee (whom Mr. E. H. Carr accuses of wanting to have Spengler metaphysically and eat him empirically) finds it disappointing that the author of *The Decline of the West* has nothing to say about the genesis of his cultures. It seems to him, so he says, a defect 'unworthy of Spengler's brilliant genius'.[7] But if one grants Spengler the power of genius, then it is as meaningless to blame him for his shortcoming as it would be to reproach Picasso for sometimes ignoring the rules of perspective. For what Toynbee finds disappointing is the very core of Spengler's method.

This method can best be illustrated by taking the following facts from Greek antiquity, a necessarily restricted and random collection. The figure of Alexander the Great merged even for his contemporaries with the myth of Dionysus. The Doric column was a prominent feature of a certain period of Greek architecture. Greek thinkers knew the strict chronology and calendar of the Babylonians and Egyptians, and yet that highly sophisticated way of measuring time never became integrated into Greek life. Neither Plato nor Aristotle had observatories. In the last years of Pericles the Athenians passed a decree by which all who propagated astronomical theories were made liable to impeachment. Thucydides states right at the beginning of his history that before his time (about 400 B.C.) no events of importance had occurred in the world.[8]

Let us assume that these facts are all soundly established. Let us further take it for granted that very many more such facts, useful for the purposes of a certain interpretation, can be added to the list. With these data before us, and with our historical imagination bent upon discovering some characteristics of the world of the mind which the ancient Greeks inhabited, a certain picture, however blurred at the beginning, is bound to emerge from the contemplation of the facts themselves. In other words, *the facts are the interpretation*, and facts from Greek antiquity, as chosen by Spengler, are Spengler's interpretation of Greek antiquity.

This, however, ought not to be used rashly as an argument against Spengler, for it applies to all written history that is more than an arbitrary list of data. Differences in quality between historians cannot solely be established by measuring the relative degrees of their selectivity or comprehensiveness, but mainly by appreciating the relative subtlety, accuracy, intelligence and sensitivity of the mind, reflected in the meaningful, and therefore selective, ordering of the facts. And Spengler's assembly of facts from Greek antiquity adds up to, briefly, the following picture. Greek consciousness differed from ours by the absence of any distinct historical or astronomical sense. It revolved around a centre of Pure Present. It interested itself not in the political or psychological biography of Alexander the Great, but in his kinship with a god, his mythological significance. The Greeks rejected instinctively the time-obsession of the Egyptians, and found it appropriate to burn their dead rather than mummify them for all time to come. They even went so far as to defend actively their particular vision of the world against astronomical encroachments, very much in the manner in which the Church once defended the central position of the earth against the Copernican attack. Compare the Doric architecture with, say, the Gothic and you will behold two fundamentally different visions of

space; static and earth-bound the one, the other struggling with outstretched arms to grasp some glory above.

Professor Toynbee, when he first read Spengler, was
afraid that his own inquiry 'had been disposed of . . .
before even the questions, not to speak of the answers,
had fully taken shape in my mind'; and it was only
when he looked in Spengler's book for an answer to the
question of *how* civilizations come into being that he saw
that there was still work for him to do.[9] One is tempted
to imagine Darwin on the point of throwing in his hand
at the sight of Michelangelo's Creation of Man, and only
regaining his self-assurance on discovering that the
painter does not show us exactly how the job was done.
For the question which Toynbee asks is indeed the question of empiricism, and the inability or unwillingness to
answer it is not a flaw in Spengler's 'brilliant genius', but
the secret of his ingenious brilliance. The empiricist
would account for the prevalent use of, for instance, the
Doric column at a certain time in terms, say, of building
techniques, of available building materials, of economic
conditions, perhaps even in terms of the psychology of
the subconscious. Spengler, however, exposes himself to
the ridicule of the empiricist by insisting that the Doric
column, in whatever way one may describe the processes
and causal connections involved in its manufacture, is
the expression of the soul of a cultured community and
a symbol of Pure Present. Now, it is no good believing
that this can be *shown* to be wrong by saying: 'Nonsense; the Doric column came into use because such and
such a tribe at such and such a time, prompted by certain
economic and technical changes, succeeded in convert-
ing into stone their original primitive buildings made of
tree-trunks, airy structures which had proved quite agree-
able and adequate for certain functions in this particular
climate'.

This way of reasoning may be very illuminating and
even completely satisfying to certain intellectual tem-

o

peraments; yet it would be quite useless as a tool for undermining Spengler's position. For *what* a thing is raises a question categorically different from the question of *how* it came about; and the contention that the Doric column is a symbolic creation of the Greek soul is entirely untouched by the explanation that it is a petrified tree-trunk. The two lines of interpretation never meet. Yet modern consciousness is inclined to take for granted that they do meet and clash, and that the symbol lies smashed under the weight of the tree-trunk. The superstition is due to a squint: the same kind of squint which looks expectantly to the newest cosmologists for some information about God, and to the psychologists for the forgiveness of sins. This state of intellectual affairs may have been brought about by the enormous birth-rate of modern science, which has overpopulated our minds with most successful answers to questions of *How*, and left little breathing-space for questions of *What* even to be asked without a sense of embarrassment. But not to distinguish between the two is a vulgar mental habit which has been unduly encouraged throughout a whole period of intellectual education, a period which has been too exclusively fascinated by the virtues—indisputable in their proper fields—of the empiricist and scientific discipline.

This, in turn, also accounts for the uncouthness of Spengler's attempt to break the empiricist spell. But the very violence of his attack exposes a genuine predicament of the historical imagination. He wished to provide radical solutions for two cardinal problems of historiography. The first of these problems concerns a hidden conflict between facts and meaning, objectivity and pattern. For the facts of history, as distinct from the facts of natural science, are men, or groups of men, and the circumstances and events in which they find themselves involved, or which they bring about. Even if we limit our interest to the shortest period, the question of selection arises. Clearly, the historian is not concerned with *all* men, circumstances and events; he has to pick and choose. And what is his criterion of choice? However warily the answer is formulated, it will trap the mind in a vicious circle. For it is the historian's view of what is historical that determines his selection. The 'historical' facts are singled out from the inarticulate mass of facts that constitute 'the past'. These selected facts must then be recorded in a coherent manner: in words, and with a view to plausible causal connections. Having been unavoidably biased in his selection of facts, either by the socially predominant or by his personal view of what is 'historical', now, at least, the good historian may hope to be 'objective' or 'purely technical'. But by describing in words men, human actions and human motives, he *implicitly* conveys and evokes emotions and passes moral judgments. If he is wise and subtle, the emotions evoked will be complex, the moral judgments fine and just. Yet they will be there, for they are in the words themselves and in our responses to human behaviour.

The goal of objectivity proves still more unattainable as soon as we are faced with the problem of establishing causal connections. For history is, of course, not concerned with physical pulls and pushes, or chemical reactions, which can be reproduced in the laboratory for experimental purposes. The stuff of history is made of unique situations, singular and complex because they are brought about not by scientifically ascertainable causes but by human motives. And however many 'facts' the searching scholar may unearth to support his conclusions, these must finally be reached through the full exercise of his imaginative sympathy. Thus, in every single case, the historical picture is established by the historical imagination, not by scientific reason, and proved not by objective experiment, but by the persuasiveness of the historian's vision. This vision, to be persuasive, must have force; and its force lies in the quality of its order or pattern. In this last respect history is like a work of art, and what has happened in recent historiography has happened time and again in the history of art: a nervous quest for a constant, or a centre, capable of imposing order and pattern on the confusing wealth of sensations and impressions. The crises in art as well as in thought—and therefore also in historiography—occur in periods when the centre of gravity ceases to be 'attractive', is rendered ineffectual by a new vision of reality and the ensuing perception by the human mind of new relevancies among the profusion of facts that surround him at all times. If, moreover, the demand for realistic accuracy in the minutest detail is met by increasingly prolific techniques to supply it, the old centre of gravity will fail completely, overwhelmed by the impossible task of holding together so many unexpected things. Such a time was the seventeenth century, and at its beginning stands John Donne's lamentation:

And new Philosophy calls all in doubt,
The Element of fire is quite put out;
The Sun is lost, and th' earth, and no man's wit
Can well direct him where to look for it.

'Tis all in peeces, all cohaerence gone;
All just supply, and all Relation.

To-day, our historical consciousness teems with Relation and Function. Everything seems to depend on everything else, and we are unable to say precisely for what. Coherence can only be established within tiny fragments, and the general effect is one of over-subtlety, irrelevance and confusion. It is a situation similar to that in painting at the end of the Middle Ages when significance began to be attached to realistic detail and spatial perspective. If one compares the first fumbling attempts to make pictures from the unwieldy mass of accurately reproduced detail in accurately rendered space with the assured and unrealistic order of medieval altar-paintings, one can scarcely help feeling that the new realism is but a triumph of mediocre pedantry. The whole mastery of the later Renaissance masters was needed in order to merge all the pieces into a new coherence, a new vision of pattern and order.

Oswald Spengler believed that he had found the new centre of gravity for history. Clearly, it cannot be supplied by a purely 'naturalistic' historiography, intent on disentangling the endless and chaotically complicated world of 'Relation', the events as they hang together by virtue of cause and effect. Spengler once said that the only difference between the opposed schools of historians, all labouring under the empiricist spell, lies in the conclusions which they reach after having observed for long enough the movements of a pair of scales. Some, seeing one side go up, find a perfectly satisfactory cause for the event in attributing it to the going-down of the other side. Some again would rather say that one side sinks because the other rises.[10] And had he had a chance of contemplating the opening sentence of the second chapter of Mr. E. H. Carr's *The New Society*, he might have added: 'And some even say it sinks because it sinks'. For Mr. Carr states: 'Experience shows that the structure of society at any given time and place, as well as the prevailing theories and beliefs about it, are largely governed by the way in which the material needs of the society are met'.[11] Experience seems to show very little indeed; for the ways in which the material needs of a society are met do not 'largely govern', but largely *are* the structure of society. And, naturally, the theories and beliefs about the structure of a society largely depend on a large part of this structure, in the same way in which a theory about a house must be largely governed by what is a large part of the house. On the other hand, the 'structure of society' is, of course, a more elusive object of investigation than the structure of a building; for what *actually is* of structural significance is intimately bound up with the *consciousness and feeling* of this society regarding the question of what is important for the ordering of its collective existence. If, for instance, a society feels that it is its foremost concern to make a success of its arrangements in the eyes of God, then its organized religion will form that prominent structural feature which economic affairs claim in our society. This is what Spengler means by his overstatement: 'It is possible to understand the Greeks without mentioning their economic relations; the Romans, on the other hand, can *only* be understood through these'.[12]

An ordered and at the same time objective vision of history, Spengler maintains, can only be achieved by cutting right through the cause-and-effect tangle. For no meaning or order can ever emerge unless we discover how *all* things in history are related, not merely one to the other, but to something else: to a constant, a crystallizing principle. And Spengler's constant is the Soul, or the Destiny, of a cultured society. Now at last all historical facts add up to a definite shape—*morphe*, in Greek —and Spengler's 'morphological' history saves the perplexed historical mind from being led back and back along the dull thread of cause and effect. There is no clash between objectivity and pattern; on the contrary, only within their appropriate pattern can the facts be seen for what they really are: symbols of Destiny. Coin-currency, the nude statue, the city-state are all symbolic expressions of the Greek Soul; and a more modern Destiny and unified Culture-Personality will be seen at work in the discovery of perspective in painting, the invention of the printing-press, long-range weapons, the credit system and contrapuntal music.[13]

It is, I think, a perfectly legitimate problem which Spengler attacks with so much force, learning and imagination, and which he solves in so catastrophic a fashion.

The problem was present right at the beginning of modern historical thought. Vico knew it, and, of course, Herder. Hegel tried to solve it in one way, Karl Marx in another. If, as a Marxist scholar said, Spengler has corrupted the 'concept of history', then Hegel and Karl Marx are his fellow-corrupters. For the purely empiricist concept of history is hopelessly spoilt as soon as the question of meaning or pattern is raised. It matters little whether the 'corrupting' is done in the name of the *Weltgeist*, or supplied by the goal of a classless society, dialectically driving history on towards its final scoring, or by Destiny presenting a cycle of dramas about a common theme, or by a court of divine justice passing judgment on a lot of original sinners. But, of course, the concept cannot really be corrupted. It is itself a corruption, the distorted shadow of the idea of a 'pure' natural science.

Spengler must be rejected on different grounds: not because his history is incorrect, but because it is untrue. And between the two reasons lies a world of difference. Spengler's history is untrue because the mind which has conceived it is, despite its learning and seeming subtlety, a crude and wicked mind. The image of man which lurks behind Spengler s vast historical canvas is perverted, and could only be accepted by a hopelessly perverted age. For Spengler has no idea of the true stature of the problem of human freedom. Therefore his historical vision is lacking in depth as well as in love, pity and pathos. It is a worthless and deeply untruthful sort of history which lacks these qualities, for they are the proper tools of human understanding.

If Spengler's men were real men, his Culture-Souls real souls, and his Destiny really destiny; if, in other words, Spengler had realized the full pathos of human freedom under the shadow of necessity, his historical plot would move us with the force of tragedy. As it is, there is no terror and no pity in his acceptance of Destiny, but merely a conscious decision for the false values; and this is the classical definition of sin and wickedness. Destiny, he says, has decreed that our spiritual values should be frustrated in this period of history; therefore let us join the enemies of the spirit. Thus Spengler is not a historian, but a false prophet. For whether a prophet is true or false does not depend on the correctness of his predictions. It depends on the purity and sincerity of his concern for the things threatened by human sin and divine anger. Indeed, his predictions are the more likely to be correct, the less he is a true prophet and the more affinities he has within himself to the destructive tendencies of his age, that is, to the very stuff that will determine the evil future. And Spengler appears merely concerned with lending Destiny a hand in the business of destruction.

Yet this deliberate choice of the wrong is again intimately linked with another very real perplexity of the historical imagination: the relativity of all values. History shows that men of different societies lived by different values; and all these different values, embodied in various religious beliefs, moral and legal codes, works of art, were effective in their own way and satisfactory within the limits of the general unsatisfactoriness of human affairs. From history itself no absolute values will ever emerge. For our historical consciousness differs profoundly from that of the Old Testament, or that of Thucydides. Our history is a variety-show of gods of every description, and as historians we could not care less if at least one of them is outraged by all the others; and Thucydides' opening statement that before his time nothing really important ever happened is the denial of our sense of historical proportion.

If there is any valid philosophy of history, it is scepticism; and an age which is as historically minded as ours is necessarily a sceptical age. But nothing is more difficult than to be a consistent sceptic, and nothing easier than to slip on the sceptical road and, in a crisis of balance, embrace the nearest absolute lamp-post. With the possible exception of Montaigne, there is no sceptical thinker who could not be caught out in some such embarrassing embrace. During the nineteenth century the broadest emergency exit from the embarrassment of historical relativity led into history itself as the progressive unfolding of the Absolute. Hegel flung it wide open, and Karl Marx guided a whole mass movement through the gate.

Spengler, however, radically renounced the idea of progress. He assumed the part of the long-awaited hero who freed the historical imagination from the last shackles of the Absolute, and boasted of his courage to face the Medusa of limitless historical relativism, calling himself the Copernicus of historiography. History, he says, does not revolve around our system of values or virtues. The real meaning of all religions, all thoughts, all works of art can only be experienced within the particular culture that has produced them. Nothing is universal. History does not write anything with capital letters. We must cease to speak of the forms of Thought, the principles of Tragedy, the truth of Religion, the function of the State.[14] Whenever we are tempted to believe in the universal validity of anything, we are merely lending our ears to the whispers of ghosts which may still haunt for a while this age of absolute historical scepticism.

What, then, according to Spengler, are the values left to us? Even if we feel they are there, must not this tempestuous insight rob them of their power to guide our actions? Luckily, says Spengler, we do not need them any longer. The new insight takes their place: the insight into our historical Destiny written with the only surviving capital letter. Questions about ultimate values must not be asked in the presence of the *Zeitgeist*. Ours is the business of 'civilization'. Let us build aeroplanes, no matter what they carry; roads, no matter where they lead; weapons, no matter what 'values' they defend or attack. For absolute scepticism is our intellectual fate, and absolute engineering our historical Destiny.

Again, as with Hegel and Marx, history itself arises as an Absolute from the vast bankruptcy of traditional values. This fact was still hidden behind clouds of idealism —of a metaphysical brand in the case of Hegel, of a messianic-social kind in the case of Marx. With Spengler, however, the mists have lifted: the spiritual bankruptcy itself is our history, our Absolute, our guiding principle. If Spengler is, after all, not quite out of date, this is because he has reduced to a wicked kind of absurdity a tendency of the mind which is certainly not unfashionable yet: the habit of applying to historical necessity for the marching orders of the spirit.

The late Munich comedian, Karl Vallentin—one of the greatest of the rare race of metaphysical clowns—once enacted the following scene: the curtain goes up and reveals darkness; and in this darkness is a solitary circle of light thrown by a street-lamp. Vallentin, with his long-drawn and deeply worried face, walks round and round this circle of light, desperately looking for something. 'What have you lost?' a policeman asks who has entered the scene. 'The key to my house.' Upon which the policeman joins him in his search; they find nothing; and after a while he inquires: 'Are you sure you lost it here?' 'No,' says Vallentin, and pointing to a dark corner of the stage: 'Over there'. 'Then why on earth are you looking for it here?' 'There is no light over there,' says Vallentin.

History, maybe, is the circle of light. But the key we are looking for is likely to be in a place unillumined by the street-lamps.

THE WORLD OF FRANZ KAFKA

Sometimes I feel I understand the Fall of Man better than anyone.—Franz Kafka.

1

The relationship of Kafka's heroes to that truth for which they so desperately search can best be seen in the image through which Plato, in a famous passage of his *Republic*, expresses man's pitiable ignorance about the true nature of the Ideas. Chained to the ground of his cave, with his back towards the light, all he perceives of the fundamental reality of the world is a play of shadows thrown on to the wall of his prison. But for Kafka there is a further complication: perfectly aware of his wretched imprisonment and obsessed with a monomaniac desire to know, the prisoner has, by his unruly behaviour and his incessant entreaties, provoked the government of his prison to an act of malicious generosity. In order to satisfy his passion for knowledge they have covered the

walls with mirrors which, owing to the curved surface of
the cave, distort what they reflect. Now the prisoner sees
lucid pictures, definite shapes, clearly recognizable faces,
an inexhaustible wealth of detail. His gaze is fixed no
longer on empty shades, but on a full reflection of ideal
reality. Face to face with the images of Truth, he is yet
doubly agonized by their hopeless distortion. With an
unparalleled fury of pedantry he observes the curve of
every line, the ever-changing countenance of every figure, drawing schemes of every possible aberration from
reality which his mirror may cause, making now this angle and now that the basis of his endless calculations
which, he passionately hopes, will finally yield the ge-
ometry of truth.

In a letter (December 16th, 1911) Kafka says: 'I am
separated from all things by a hollow space, and I do
not even reach to its boundaries'. In another (November
19th, 1913): 'Everything appears to me constructed . . .
I am chasing after constructions. I enter a room, and I
find them in a corner, a white tangle.' And as late as 1921:
'Everything is illusion: family, office, friends, the street,
woman, all illusion, drawing nearer and further away;
but the nearest truth is merely that I push my head
against the wall of a cell without doors or windows.' [1]
And in one of his aphorisms he says: 'Our art is dazzled
blindness before the truth: the light on the grotesquely
distorted face is true, but nothing else is.' [2]

Kafka's novels take place in infinity. Yet their atmosphere is as oppressive as that of those unaired rooms in
which so many of their scenes are enacted. For infinity
is incompletely defined as the ideal point where two
parallels meet. There is yet another place where they
come together: the distorting mirror. Thus they carry into
the prison-house of their violently distorted union the
agony of infinite separation.

It is a Tantalus situation, and in Kafka's work the ancient curse has come to life once more. Kafka says of

himself: 'He is thirsty, and is cut off from a spring by a mere clump of bushes. But he is divided against himself: one part can see the whole, sees that he is standing here and that the spring is just beside him, but another part notices nothing, has at most a divination that the first part sees all. But as he notices nothing he cannot drink.' [3] Indeed, it was a curse, and not a word of light, which called the universe of Kafka's novels into existence. The very clay from which it was made bore the imprint of a malediction before the creator had touched it. He builds to a splendid design, but the curse runs like a vein through every stone. In one of his most revealing parables Kafka shows himself completely aware of this: 'Everything seemed to fit the design of his edifice magnificently. Foreign workmen brought the marble, quarried for the purpose, each block fashioned for its proper place. The stones lifted themselves up and moved along in obedience to his measuring fingers. No edifice ever grew so smoothly as this temple, or rather this temple grew truly in the way in which temples ought to grow. Only there were cut into every stone, obviously with wonderfully sharpened instruments, clumsy scribblings from the hands of senseless children, or perhaps inscriptions of barbaric mountain-dwellers: mischievous texts, blasphemous, or totally destructive, fixed there for an eternity which was to survive the temple.' [4]

It is the reality of the curse that constitutes the ruthlessly compelling logic of Kafka's writings. They defy all attempts at rational interpretation, for Kafka is the least problematic of modern writers. He never thinks in disputable or refutable generalities. His thinking is a reflex movement of his being and shares the irrefutability of all that is. He thinks at an infinite number of removes from the Cartesian *Cogito ergo sum*. Indeed, it sometimes seems that an unknown 'It' does all the thinking that matters, the radius of its thought touching the circumference of his existence here and there, causing him infinite pain, bringing his life into question and promising salvation on one condition only: that he should expand his being to bring it within the orbit of that strange Intelligence. The formula has become: 'It thinks, and therefore I am not', with only the agony of despair providing overpowering proof that he is alive. He says of himself that he *is* the problem, and 'no scholar to be found far and wide'.[5]

There is, outside this agony, no reality about which he could entertain or communicate thoughts, nothing apart from the curse of his own separation from that Intelligence. Yet it is a complete world that is to be found within that pain, the exact pattern of creation once more, but this time made of the stuff of which curses are made. Like sorrow in the tenth of Rilke's *Duino Elegies*, despair is given a home of its own in Kafka's works, faithfully made in the image of customary life, but animated by the blast of the curse. This gives to Kafka's writings their unique quality. Never before has absolute darkness been represented with so much clarity, and the very madness of desperation with so much composure and sobriety. In his work an intolerable spiritual pride is expressed with the legitimate and convincing gesture of humility, disintegration finds its own level of integrity, and impenetrable complexity an all but *sancta simplicitas*. Kafka establishes the moral law of a boundlessly deceitful world, and performs in a totally incalculable domain, ruled by evil demons, the most precise mathematical measurements.

Small wonder at the pathetic plight of critics in the face of Kafka's novels. It was with incredulous amazement that I noticed extracts from reviews which appear as advertisements of the English translation of Kafka's *The Castle*: 'One reads it as if one were reading a fairy tale . . .', 'What a lovely, moving, memorable book!', 'A book of curious and original beauty'. All this, attributed by the publishers to critics of some repute, is, of course, perverse. A nightmare is not a lovely fairy-tale, and a torture-chamber of the spirit not full of original beauty. More serious, however, are the misinterpretations of Kafka by those who have undoubtedly made an honest effort to understand him. In the introduction to his own and Willa Muir's translation of *The Castle* Edwin Muir describes the subject-matter of this novel (very much in keeping with Max Brod's interpretation) as 'human life wherever it is touched by the powers which all religions have acknowledged, by divine law and divine grace', and suggests that it should, with some reservations, be regarded 'as a sort of modern *Pilgrim's Progress*', the reservation being that 'the "progress" of the pilgrim here will remain in question all the time'. According to him '*The Castle* is, like the *Pilgrim's Progress*, a religious allegory'.[6]

From a great number of similar attempts to elucidate the darkness of Kafka's world I am choosing these sentences as a starting-point for a discussion of the work of this writer, and of *The Castle* in particular, because they express most succinctly what seems to me a disquieting misconception of its nature, the more disquieting because it is harboured by men of letters who are seriously concerned with literature and have, like Max Brod, Kafka's lifelong friend and editor of his writings, and Edwin Muir, his English translator, grasped the religious relevance of their author. Thus their misapprehension would seem to reflect a very profound religious confusion, so profound indeed that one can scarcely hold the individual critic responsible for it. It is the very spiritual uprootedness of the age which has deprived us of all sureness of religious discrimination. To men suffering from spiritual starvation even a rotten fruit of the spirit may taste like bread from Heaven, and the liquid from a poisoned well like the water of life. If the critic is, moreover, steeped in psychology and comparative religion (as we all unwittingly are) the difference may ap-

P

pear negligible to him between Prometheus clamped to
the rock, and the martyrdom of a Christian saint; between an ancient curse and the grace that makes a new
man.

The Castle is as much a religious allegory as a photo-
graphic likeness of the Devil could be said to be an allegory of Evil. Every allegory has an opening into the
rarefied air of abstractions, and is furnished with sign-
posts pointing to an ideal construction beyond. *The
Castle*, however, is a terminus of soul and mind, a *non
plus ultra* of existence. In an allegory the author plays
a kind of guessing game with his reader, if he does not
actually provide the dictionary himself; but there is no
key to *The Castle*. It is true that its reality does not precisely correspond to what is commonly understood in our
positivist age as real, namely, neutral sense-perception
of objects and, neatly separated from them, feelings;
hence our most authentic and 'realistic' intellectual pursuits: natural sciences and psychology; and our besetting
sins: the ruthlessness of acquisitive techniques and sentimentality. In Kafka's novels there is no such division
between the external sphere and the domain of inwardness, and therefore no such reality.

Kafka's creations are at the opposite pole to the writings of that type of Romantic poet, the true poetical representative of the utilitarian age, who distils from a
spiritually more and more sterile external reality those
elements which are still of some use to the emotions, or
else withdraws from its barren fields into the greenhouse
vegetation of inwardness. The author of *The Castle* does
not select for evocative purposes, nor does he project his
inner experience into a carefully chosen timeless setting.
He does not, after the manner of Joyce, give away, in the
melodious flow of intermittent articulation, the secret bedroom conversations which self conducts with self. There
are no private symbols in his work, such as would be

found in symbolist writing, no crystallized fragments of inner sensations charged with mysterious significance; nor is there, after the fashion of the Expressionists, any rehearsing of new gestures of the soul, meant to be more in harmony with the 'new rhythm' of modern society. Instead of all this, the reader is faced with the shocking spectacle of a miraculously sensitive soul incapable of being either reasonable, or cynical, or resigned, or rebellious, about the prospect of eternal damnation. The world which this soul perceives is unmistakably like the reader's own; a castle that is a castle and 'symbolizes' merely what all castles symbolize: power and authority; a telephone exchange that produces more muddles than connections; a bureaucracy drowning in a deluge of forms and files; an obscure hierarchy of officialdom making it impossible ever to find the man authorized to deal with a particular case; officials who work overtime and yet get nowhere; numberless interviews which never are to the point; inns where the peasants meet, and barmaids who serve the officials. In fact, it is an excruciatingly familiar world, but reproduced by a creative intelligence which is endowed with the knowledge that it is a world damned for ever. Shakespeare once made one of his characters say: 'They say miracles are past, and we have our philosophical persons, to make modern and familiar things supernatural and causeless. Hence it is that we make trifles of terrors, ensconcing ourselves in seeming knowledge when we should submit ourselves to an unknown fear.' In Kafka we have the abdication of the philosophical persons.

In his work the terror recaptures the trifles, and the unknown fear invades all seeming knowledge—particularly that of psychology. Any criticism of the current religious interpretation of Kafka (which, at least, meets the religious aspect of his work on its own plane) is, I think, well advised to avoid the impression that it sides

surreptitiously with other equally well-established dog-
mas about this writer. One of them, the psychological,
is laid down by critics fascinated by Kafka's indubitably
strained relationship with his father. But to interpret
Kafka's novels in the perspective of the Oedipus complex is about as helpful to our understanding of his work
as the statement that Kafka would have been a different
person (and perhaps not a writer at all) if he had had
another father: a penetrating thought, of which even psy-
chologically less initiated ages might have been capable
if they had deemed it worth thinking. This kind of psychology can contribute as much to the explanation of a
work of art as ornithological anatomy to the fathoming
of a nightingale's song. But so deeply engrained is positivism in the critics of this age that even when they are
genuinely moved by the symbolic reality which the
author has created, they will soon regain the balance of
mind required for the translation of the symbol into what
it 'really' means; and by that they mean precisely that
meaningless experience which the artist has succeeded in
transcending through his poetic creation. If, for instance,
to the author the *meaning* of his senselessly tormenting
feud with his father has been revealed through the discovery (which, in creating his work, he has made) that
what he is *really* called upon to find is his place within
a true spiritual order of divine authority, the interpreter
will insist that what the author 'really' means by talking
about God is that the quarrels with his father should
stop.

In Kafka we have before us the modern mind, seemingly self-sufficient, intelligent, sceptical, ironical, splendidly trained for the great game of pretending that the
world it comprehends in sterilized sobriety is the only
and ultimate reality there is—yet a mind living in sin with
the soul of Abraham. Thus he knows two things at once,
and both with equal assurance: that there *is* no God, and
that there *must* be God. It is the perspective of the curse:

the intellect dreaming its dream of absolute freedom, and the soul knowing of its terrible bondage. The conviction of damnation is all that is left of faith, standing out like a rock in a landscape the softer soil of which has been eroded by the critical intellect. Kafka once said: 'I ought to welcome eternity, but to find it makes me sad'.[7]

This is merely an exhausted echo of the fanfares of despair with which Nietzsche (in many respects a legitimate spiritual ancestor of Kafka) welcomed his vision of eternity. In one of the posthumously published notes on *Zarathustra* he says about his idea of the Eternal Recurrence: 'We have produced the hardest possible thought—now let us create the creature who will accept it lightheartedly and blissfully!' [8] He conceived the Eternal Recurrence as a kind of spiritualized Darwinian test to select for survival the spiritually fittest. This he formulated with the utmost precision: 'I perform the great experiment: who can bear the idea of Eternal Recurrence?' [9] And an ever deeper insight into the anatomy of despair we gain from his posthumous aphorisms and epigrams, which were assembled by his editors in the two volumes of *The Will to Power*, many of which refer to the idea of Eternal Recurrence: 'Let us consider this idea in its most terrifying form: existence, as it is, without meaning or goal, but inescapably recurrent, without a finale into nothingness . . .' [10] Nietzsche's Superman is the creature strong enough to live for ever a cursed existence, even to derive from it the Dionysian raptures of tragic acceptance. Nietzsche feels certain that only the Superman could be equal to the horror of a senseless eternity, and perform the great metamorphosis of turning 'this most terrifying knowledge' into the terror of superhuman delight. And Kafka? On most of the few occasions when, in his diary, he speaks of happiness he registers it as the result of a successful transformation of torture into bliss. This is one of his most horrible entries

(November 21st, 1911): 'This morning, after a long time, I again took pleasure in imagining that a knife is turned in my heart'. And in 1921, in the account of a dream: 'There was bliss in my welcoming, with so deep a sense of freedom, conviction and joy, the punishment when it came'.[11] If Nietzsche's Superman is the aesthetic counterbalance to the weight of the curse, then Kafka is its chosen victim. What some of his critics interpret as signs of religious achievement in his later writings is merely the all-engulfing weariness of a Nietzschean Prometheus, which Kafka expressed in the fourth of his Prometheus legends: 'Everyone grew weary of the meaningless affair. The gods grew weary, the eagles grew weary, the wound closed wearily.'[12]

Thus Kafka's work, as much as Nietzsche's, must remain a stumbling-block to the analysing interpreter to whom, in the enlightened atmosphere of modern Europe, the word 'curse' comes only as a faint memory of Greek tragedy, or as a figurative term for a combination of ill-luck and psychological maladjustments. Yet the grey world of Kafka's novels is luminous with its fire. Perhaps one cannot expect from modern man that, when he sees light, he should be able to distinguish between burning sulphur and the radiance of Heaven. And although Mr. Muir is right in saying that Kafka's novels are about life in the grip of a power 'which all religions have acknowledged', this power is certainly not 'divine law and divine grace', but rather one which, having rebelled against the first and fallen from the second, has, in its own domain, successfully contrived the suspension of both. Undoubtedly, the land-surveyor K., hero of *The Castle*, is religiously fascinated by its inscrutably horrid bureaucracy; but again it is a word from Nietzsche, and not from the Gospels, that sums up the situation: 'Wretched man, your god lies in the dust, broken to fragments, and serpents dwell around him. And now you love even the serpents for his sake.'[13]

2

The Castle is not an allegorical, but a symbolic novel.
A discussion of the difference could easily deteriorate
into pedantry, the more so as, in common and literary
usage, the terms are applied rather arbitrarily and have
established themselves as meaning more or less the same
thing. It will, however, help our understanding of Kafka's
work if we distinguish, in using these two terms, two
different modes of experience and expression. I shall
therefore define my own—probably not less arbitrary—
use of the terms.

The symbol *is* what it represents; the allegory represents what, in itself, it is *not*. The terms of reference of
an allegory are abstractions; a symbol refers to something specific and concrete. The statue of a blindfolded
woman, holding a pair of scales, is an *allegory* of Justice; bread and wine are, for the Christian communicant,
symbols of the Body and Blood of Christ.* Thus an allegory must always be rationally translatable; whether a
symbol is translatable or not depends on the fundamental
agreement of society on the question of what kind of
experience (out of the endless range of possible human
experience) it regards as significant. The possibility of
allegorizing will only vanish with the last man capable
of *thinking in abstractions*, and of forming *images* of
them; yet the validity of symbols depends not on rational
operations, but on complex experiences in which thought
and feeling merge in the act of spiritual comprehension.
The sacramental symbols, for instance, would become
incommunicable among a race of men who no longer regarded the life, death, and resurrection of Christ as spir-

* At this point I should like to beg the indulgence of the
reader for disregarding the established theological termi-
nology. The following discussion will, I hope, to some extent
justify my apparent arbitrariness, which I do not wish to
maintain outside the scope of this particular argument.

itually relevant *facts*. An allegory, being the imaginary representation of something abstract, is, as it were, doubly unreal; whereas the symbol, in being what it represents, possesses a double reality.

Goethe, summing up in one line at the end of *Faust II* the mature experience of his life, attributes whatever permanent reality there may be in a transient world, to its symbolic significance. What is is only *real* in so far as it is symbolic. Earlier in his life he defined the 'true symbol' as that 'particular' which represents the 'universal', not, however, 'as a dream or shadow, but as the revelation of the unfathomable in a moment filled with life.' [14]

The predicament of the symbol in our age is caused by a split between 'reality' and what it signifies. There is no more any commonly accepted symbolic or transcendent order of things. What the modern mind perceives as order is established through the tidy relationship between things themselves. In one word: the only conceivable order is positivist-scientific. If there still is a—no doubt, diminishing—demand for the fuller reality of the symbol, then it must be provided for by the unsolicited gifts of art. But in the sphere of art the symbolic substance, dismissed from its disciplined commitments to 'reality', dissolves into incoherence, ready to attach itself to any fragment of experience, invading it with irresistible power, so that a pair of boots, or a chair in the painter's attic, or a single tree on a slope which the poet passes, or an obscure inscription in a Venetian church, may suddenly become the precariously unstable centre of an otherwise unfocused universe. Since 'the great words, from the time when what *really* happened was still visible, are no longer for us' (as Rilke once put it in a Requiem for a young poet), the 'little words' have to carry an excessive freight of symbolic significance. No wonder that they are slow in delivering it. They are all but incommunicable private symbols, established beyond any doubt as symbols by the quality and intensity of artistic experience behind them, but lacking in any representative properties. Such is the economy of human consciousness that the positivist impoverishment of the one region produces anarchy in the other. In the end, atomic lawlessness is bound to prevail in both.

The intellectual foundation of every human society is a generally accepted model of reality. One of the major intellectual difficulties of human existence is, I think, due to the fact that this model of reality is in every single case a mere *interpretation* of the world, and yet exerts, as long as it seems the valid interpretation, the subtly compelling claim to being accepted as the only true picture of the universe, indeed as truth itself. This difficulty, manifesting itself in the deeper strata of doubt, by which, at all times, certain intellectually sensitive men have been affected, develops easily into a mental epidemic in epochs in which a certain model of reality crumbles and collapses. It seems that we have lived in such an epoch for a long time. One of its main characteristics was the uncertainty, steadily increasing in the minds and feelings of men, about the relation between mundane and transcendental reality, or, in other words, about the meaning of life and death, the destiny of the soul, the nature and sanction of moral laws, the relative domains of knowledge and faith. As far as Christianity was the representative religion of the Middle Ages, their model of reality was essentially sacramental. A definite correspondence prevailed between the mundane and transcendental spheres. Faith was not established in any distinct 'religious experience', nor, as a particular 'mode of comprehension', kept apart from 'knowledge'. It was an element in *all* experience, indeed its crystallizing principle. Only within a mould and pattern determined by faith did experiences make sense and impressions turn to knowledge.

This correspondence between the two spheres was so close that at every important stage of a man's life they met and became one in the sacraments.

The sacramental model of reality, intermittently disputed and questioned throughout the whole development of Christian theological thought, was upset in an historically decisive fashion at the time of the Reformation. During that period an intellectual tension, inherent in Christian dogma, developed into a conflagration of vast historical consequences. It produced an articulate climax —which was, however, a mere symptom of a more inarticulate, yet more comprehensive process—at a particularly exposed point of dogmatic faction: the sacramental dispute between Luther and Zwingli. Luther, despite his divergent interpretation of the traditional dogma, represents in it the essentially medieval view, whereas Zwingli, disciple of the humanist Pico della Mirandola, is the spokesman of modernity. To Luther the sacrament of the Last Supper *is* Christ (the bread and the wine *are* what they represent), while Zwingli reduces it to the status of an allegory (as merely representing what, in itself, it is not). From then onwards the word 'merely' has been attaching itself ever more firmly to the word 'symbol', soon gaining sufficient strength to bring about a complete alienation between the two spheres. Finally a new order of things emerged. Within it the transcendental realm is allotted the highest honours of the spirit, but, at the same time, skilfully deprived of a considerable measure of reality; the mundane, on the other hand, is recompensed for its lowering in spiritual stature by the chance of absorbing all available reality and becoming more 'really' real than before.

The sudden efflorescence of physical science in the seventeenth century is the positive result of this severance. Its successes have further contributed to the 'lower realm' setting itself up as the only 'really' real one, and as the sole provider of relevant truth, order and lawfulness. Scientific and other positivist pursuits owe the unchallenged dominion which they have wielded ever since over the intellectual life of Europe to the ever more exclusive fascination which the new model of reality has had for the European mind.

As an unavoidable corollary of this state of affairs, religion and art lost their unquestioned birthright in the homeland of human reality, and turned into strange messengers from the higher unreality, admitted now and then as edifying or entertaining songsters at the positivist banquet. What had once been a matter-of-fact expression of life became a 'problem', worthy of a great deal of intellectual fuss and a negligible assignment of reality. As far as the arts are concerned, it is most revealing that the only *distinctive* artistic achievement of Europe since the end of the seventeenth century was accomplished by the art with the least claim to 'reality': music, while the most 'real' of all arts, architecture, degenerated more and more until it gained new vitality as the unashamed functional servant of technology.

In Germany, a country which, for historical reasons too complex ever to be unravelled, suddenly rose in the eighteenth century to the heights of European consciousness and to the fulfilment of the most extravagant intellectual aspirations (without any gradual transition from the Middle Ages), the plight of the poet within the new model of reality is most conspicuous. The artist as an exile from reality—this is one of the most authentic themes of German literature, from Goethe's *Tasso* and Grillparzer's *Sappho* to Thomas Mann's *Tonio Kröger*. Kleist, Hölderlin, Nietzsche are the greatest among the victims of a hopeless collision between the minority demand for a realization of the spirit and a spiritualization of reality on the one hand, and, on the other, the inexorable resistance of a safely established spirit-proof view of life. Hölderlin is the greatest poet among those involuntary desperadoes of the spirit. His work is one continuous attempt to recapture the lost reality of the symbol and the sacramental experience of life. And for Goethe, to preserve his life, exposed at every point to the revengeful blows of the banished spirit, was, from beginning to end, a terrible struggle, entailing the most precarious manoeuvres of compromise, irony and resignation. It was only—ironically enough—in his scientific activities that he gave vent to his unrestrained fury against the analytical-positivist view of the world and its scientific exposition through mathematics and Newtonian physics. How gloriously he blundered into physical science, determined to meet the enemy on his own ground, and how stubbornly convinced he was of being right! He once said to Eckermann (February 19th, 1829): 'Whatever I have achieved as a poet is nothing to be particularly proud of. Excellent poets are my contemporaries, still better poets lived before me, and others will come after me. But in my own century I am the only man who knows what is right in the difficult science of colours; and this is something that gives me real satisfaction and a feeling of superiority over many.' His own idea of science was, as we have seen, based on the *Urphänomen*, a striking assertion of the symbol as the final and irreducible truth of reality.

Goethe lost the battle for the symbol. In the century that stretches between his death and Kafka's writing, reality has been all but completely sealed off against any transcendental intrusion. But in Kafka's work the symbolic substance, forced back in every attempt to attack from above, invades reality from down below, carrying with it the stuff from Hell. Or it need not even invade: Kafka writes at the point where the world, having become too heavy with spiritual emptiness, begins to sink into the unsuspected demon-ridden depths of unbelief. In this cataclysm, the more disastrous because it overtakes a world which has not even believed in its own unbelief, Kafka's heroes struggle in vain for spiritual sur-

vival. Thus his creations are symbolic, for they are in-
fused with (and not merely allegorical of) negative transcendence.

Kafka knew the symbolic relevance of his work; he
knew, too, of the complete alienation of modern man
from the reality of the symbol. One of his profoundest
meditations runs as follows:

Many complain that the words of the wise are always merely symbols and of no use in daily life, which
is the only life we have. When the wise man says:
'Go over', he does not mean that we should cross
to some actual place, which we could do anyhow if
it were worth the effort; he means some miraculous
beyond, something unknown to us, something that he
too cannot define more precisely, and which therefore cannot help us here in the least. All these symbols
merely express the fact that the incomprehensible is
incomprehensible, and we knew that already. But the
cares we have to struggle with every day: that is a
different matter.

Concerning this a man once said: Why such reluctance? If you only followed the symbols you would
become symbols yourselves, and thus be rid of all your
daily cares.

Another said: I bet this is also a symbol.

The first said: You have won.

The second said: But unfortunately only symbolically.

The first said: No, in reality; symbolically you have
lost.[15]

3

There are, however, allegorical elements to be found
in *The Castle*: for instance, the names of many of the
characters. The hero himself, who is introduced to us

with the bare initial K. (undoubtedly an autobiographical hint,* and at the same time, through its very incompleteness, suggesting an unrealized, almost anonymous personality) is a land-surveyor. Kafka's choice of this profession for his hero has clearly a meaning. The German for it is *Landvermesser*, and its verbal associations are significant. The first is, of course, the land-surveyor's professional activity, consisting precisely in what K. desperately desires and never achieves: to produce a workable order within clearly defined boundaries and limits of earthly life, and to find an acceptable compromise between conflicting claims of possession. But *Vermesser* also alludes to *Vermessenheit*, hubris; to the adjective *vermessen*, audacious; to the verb *sich vermessen*, commit an act of spiritual pride, *and* also, apply the wrong measure, make a mistake in measurement. The most powerful official of the castle, (for K., the highest representative of authority) is called *Klamm*, a sound producing a sense of anxiety amounting almost to claustrophobia, suggesting straits, pincers, chains, clamps, but also a person's oppressive silence. The messenger of the castle (as it turns out later, self-appointed and officially never recognized) has the name of *Barnabas*, the same as that man of Cyprus who, though not one of the Twelve, came to rank as an apostle; 'Son of Consolation', or 'Son of Exhortation', is the biblical meaning of his name, and it is said of him that his exhortation was of the inspiring kind, and so built up faith. And the Barnabas of the novel is indeed a son of consolation, if only in the desperately ironical sense that his family, whom the curse of the castle has cast into the lowest depths of misery and wretchedness, in vain expects deliverance through his voluntary service for the authority. To K., however, his messages, in all their obscurity and pointlessness, seem the only real link with

* The first draft of the novel was written in the first person.

the castle, an elusive glimmer of hope, a will-o'-the-wisp of faith. Barnabas's counterpart is *Momus*, the village secretary of Klamm, and namesake of that depressing creature, the son of Night, whom the Greek gods authorized to find fault with all things. In the novel it is he whose very existence seems the denial of any hope which Barnabas may have roused in K. *Frieda* (peace) is the girl through whose love K. seeks to reach the goal of his striving; *Bürgel* (diminutive of *Bürge*, guarantor), the name of the little official who offers the solution, without K.'s even noticing the chance; and the secretary through whom K. does expect to achieve something, and achieves nothing, is called *Erlanger* (citizen of the town of Erlangen, but also suggestive of *erlangen*, attain, achieve).

This discussion of names provides an almost complete synopsis of the slender plot of *The Castle*. Someone, a man whose name begins with K., and of whom we know no more, neither whence he comes nor what his past life has been, arrives in a village which is ruled by a castle. He believes that he has been appointed land-surveyor by the authorities. The few indirect contacts that K. succeeds in establishing with the castle—a letter he receives, a telephone conversation he overhears, yet another letter, and above all the fact that he is joined by two assistants whom the rulers have assigned to him—*seem* to confirm his appointment. Yet he himself is never fully convinced, and never relaxes in his efforts to make quite sure of it. He feels he must penetrate to the very centre of authority and wring from it a kind of ultra-final evidence for his claim. Until then he yields, in paralyzed despair, broken by only momentary outbursts of rebellious pride, to the inarticulate, yet absolutely self-assured refusal of the village to acknowledge him as their land-surveyor: 'You've been taken on as land-surveyor, as you say, but, unfortunately, we have no need of a land-surveyor. There wouldn't be the least use for one here.

The frontiers of our little estates are marked out and all neatly registered. . . . So what would be the good of a land-surveyor?' [16] says the village representative to him.

K.'s belief appears, from the very outset, to be based both on truth and illusion. It is Kafka's all but unbelievable achievement to force, indeed to frighten, the reader into unquestioning acceptance of this paradox, presented with ruthless realism and irresistible logic. Truth and illusion are mingled in K.'s central belief in such a way that he is deprived of all order of reality. Truth is permanently on the point of taking off its mask and revealing itself as illusion, illusion in constant danger of being verified as truth. It is the predicament of a man who, endowed with an insatiable appetite for transcendental certainty, finds himself in a world robbed of all spiritual possessions. Thus he is caught in a vicious circle. He cannot accept the world—the village—without first attaining to absolute certainty, and he cannot be certain without first accepting the world. Yet every contact with the world makes a mockery of his search, and the continuance of his search turns the world into a mere encumbrance. After studying the first letter from the castle, K. contemplates his dilemma, 'whether he preferred to become a village worker with a distinctive but merely apparent connection with the castle, or an ostensible village worker whose real occupation was determined through the medium of Barnabas'.[17] From the angle of the village all K.'s contacts with the castle are figments of his imagination: 'You haven't once up till now come into real contact with our authorities. All those contacts are merely illusory, but owing to your ignorance of the circumstances you take them to be real.' [18] The castle, on the other hand, seems to take no notice whatever of the reality of K.'s miserable village existence. In the midst of his suffering the indignity of being employed as a kind of footman to the schoolmaster, he receives the following letter from Klamm:

'The surveying work which you have carried out thus far has my recognition. . . . Do not slacken in your efforts! Bring your work to a successful conclusion. Any interruption would displease me. . . . I shall not forget you.' [19] From all this it would appear that it is, in fact, the village that disobeys the will of the castle, while defeating K. with the powerful suggestion that he misunderstands the intentions of authority. And yet the authority seems to give its blessing to the defiance of the village, and to punish K. for his determination to act in accordance with the letter of its orders. In his fanatical obedience it is really he who rebels against the castle, whereas the village, in its matter-of-fact refusal, lives the life of the law.

Kafka represents the absolute reversal of German idealism. If it is Hegel's final belief that in the Absolute truth and existence are one, for Kafka it is precisely through the Absolute that they are for ever divided. Truth and existence are mutually exclusive. From his early days onwards it was the keenest wish of Kafka the artist to convey this in works of art; to write in such a way that life, in all its deceptively convincing reality, would be seen as a dream and a nothing before the Absolute: 'Somewhat as if one were to hammer together a table with painful and methodical technical efficiency, and simultaneously do nothing at all, and not in such a way that people could say: "Hammering a table together is really nothing to him", but rather "Hammering a table together is really hammering a table together to him, but at the same time it is nothing", whereby certainly the hammering would have become still bolder, still surer, still more real and, if you will, still more senseless'.[20] This is how Kafka describes the vision of artistic accomplishment which hovered before his mind's eye when, as a young man, he sat one day on the slopes of the Laurenziberg in Prague. Has he, in his later works, achieved this artistic justification of nonentity? Not

Q

quite; what was meant to become the lifting of a curse through art, became the artistically perfect realization of it, and what he dreamed of making into something as light as a dream, fell from his hands with the heaviness of a nightmare. Instead of a vindication of nothingness, he achieved the portrayal of the most cunningly vindictive unreality. He had good reason for decreeing that his writings should be burned.

It is hard to see how *The Castle* can possibly be called a religious allegory with a pilgrim of the type of Bunyan's as its hero. Pilgrimage? On the contrary, the most oppressive quality of Kafka's work is the unshakable stability of its central situation. It takes place in a world that knows of no motion, no change, no metamorphosis. Its caterpillars never turn into butterflies, and when the leaves of a tree tremble it is not due to the wind: it is the stirring of a serpent coiled round its branches. There is, in fact, no pilgrimage to be watched in *The Castle*, and the progress not merely 'remains in question all the time', but is not even possible, unless we agree to call progress what Kafka once described in his fable of the mouse: ' "Alas," said the mouse, "the world is growing smaller every day. At the beginning it was so big that I was afraid, I kept running and running, and I was glad when at last I saw walls far away to the right and left, but these long walls have narrowed so quickly that I am in the last chamber already, and there in the corner stands the trap that I must run into." "You only need to change your direction," said the cat, and ate it up.' [21] Of the two points on which Kafka and Bunyan, according to Edwin Muir's introduction, are agreed: 'that the goal and the road indubitably exist, and that the necessity to find them is urgent', only the second is correct, and, indeed, to find them is so urgent for Kafka that life is impossible unless they are found. But do they exist? 'There is a goal, but no way; what we call way is only wavering,' [22] is what Kafka says about it. And *is* there really a goal for him? This is Kafka's self-reply: 'He feels imprisoned on this earth, he feels constricted; the melancholy, the impotence, the sickness, the feverish fancies of the captive afflict him; no comfort can comfort him, since it is merely comfort, gentle, head-splitting comfort glozing the brutal fact of imprisonment. But if he is asked what he actually wants he cannot reply, for— that is one of his strongest proofs—he has no conception of freedom.' [23]

Kafka's hero is the man who *believes* in absolute freedom, but cannot have any conception of it because he *exists* in a world of slavery. Therefore it is not grace and salvation that he seeks, but either his right, or—a bargain with the powers. 'I don't want any act of favour from the castle, but my rights,' [24] says K. in his interview with the village representative. But convinced of the futility of this expectation, his real hope is based on Frieda, his fiancée and Klamm's former mistress, whom he is obviously prepared to hand back to him 'for a price'.

In K.'s relationship to Frieda the European story of romantic love has found its epilogue. It is the solid residue left behind by the evaporated perfume of romance, revealing its darkest secret. In romantic love, as it has dominated a vast section of European literature ever since the later Middle Ages, individualism, emerging from the ruins of a communal order of the spirit, has found its most powerful means of transcendence. The spiritually more and more autonomous, and therefore more and more lonely, individual worships Eros (and his twin deity within the romantic imagination: Death) as the only god capable of breaking down the barriers of his individualist isolation. Therefore love becomes tragedy: overcharged with unmanageable spiritual demands it must needs surge ahead of any human relationship. In its purest manifestations, romantic love is a glorious disaster of the soul, carrying frustration in its wake. For what the romantic lover seeks is not really the beloved. Intermixed with his erotic craving, inarticulate, diffuse, and yet dominating it, is the desire for spiritual salvation. Even a 'happy ending' spells profound disillusionment for the romantic expectation. Perhaps it is Strindberg who wrote the last chapter of its history. It is certainly Kafka who wrote its postscript.

For K. loves Frieda—if he loves her at all—entirely for Klamm's sake. This is not only implied in the whole story of K. and Frieda, but explicitly stated by Kafka in several—afterwards deleted—passages of the book. It is contained in the protocol about K.'s life in the village which Momus has drawn up, and in which K. is accused of having made up to Frieda merely because he believed that in her he would win a mistress of Klamm's 'and so possess a hostage which could only be redeemed at the highest price'.[25] On the margin of the protocol there was also 'a childishly scrawled drawing of a man holding a girl in his arms; the girl's face was hidden in the man's breast, but he, being much taller, was looking over her shoulders at a paper in his hand on which he was gleefully entering some figures'.[26] But perhaps still more conclusive than Momus's clearly hostile interpretation is another deleted passage giving K.'s own reflections on his love for Frieda: '. . . And soon afterwards—and there was not even time to think—Frieda had entered his life, and with her the belief (a belief which he was quite unable to abandon completely even now) that through her there was established an almost physical connection with Klamm, intimate to the point of whispered communications; perhaps, for the time being, it was only K. who knew of it, but it needed a mere touch, a word, a raising of eyes, to reveal itself first to Klamm, but then to everybody, as something unbelievable but yet self-evident by virtue of the irrefutability of life itself, the irrefutability of the embrace of love. . . . What was he without Frieda? A nonentity, staggering after glittering will-o'-the-wisps. . . .' * 27

The desperate desire for spiritual certainty is all that is left of romantic love. K. *wills* his love for Frieda because he *wills* his salvation. He is a kind of Pelagius believing that he 'can if he ought', yet living in a relentlessly predestined world. This situation produces a theology very much after the model of Gnostic and Manichaean beliefs. The incarnation is implicitly denied in an unmitigated loathing of 'determined' matter, and the powers which rule are perpetually suspected of an alliance with the Devil because they have consented to the creation of such a loathsome world. Heaven is at least at seven removes from the earth, and only begins where no more neighbourly relations are possible. There are no real points of contact between divinity and the earth, which is not even touched by divine emanation. Reality is the sovereign domain of strangely unangelic angels, made up of evil and hostility. The tedious task of the soul is, with much wisdom of initiation and often with cunning diplomacy, gradually to by-pass the armies of angels and the strongpoints of evil, and finally to slip into the remote kingdom of light.

The castle of Kafka's novel is, as it were, the heavily fortified garrison of a company of Gnostic demons, successfully holding an advanced position against the manoeuvres of an impatient soul. I do not know of any conceivable idea of divinity which could justify those interpreters who see in the castle the residence of 'divine law and divine grace'. Its officers are totally indifferent

* These, and the passages from the Pepi and Bürgel episodes which will be quoted later, have not yet appeared in English. Max Brod published them from Kafka's manuscripts only with the second and third editions of *Das Schloss*, volume IV of *Gesammelte Schriften*. All references to volume IV are to the third edition, New York, 1946.

to good if they are not positively wicked. Neither in their decrees nor in their activities is there discernible any trace of love, mercy, charity or majesty. In their icy detachment they inspire certainly no awe, but fear and revulsion. Their servants are a plague to the village, 'a wild, unmanageable lot, ruled by their insatiable instincts . . . their shamelessness knows no limits',[28] an anticipation rather of the blackguards who were to become the footmen of European dictators than the office-boys of a divine ministry. Compared to the petty and apparently calculated torture of this tyranny, the gods of Shakespeare's indignation who 'kill us for their sport' are at least majestic in their wantonness.

From the very beginning there is an air of indecency, indeed of obscenity, about the inscrutable rule of the castle. A newcomer in the village, K. meets the teacher in the company of children. He asks him whether he knows the Count and is surprised at the negative answer: ' "What, you don't know the Count?" "Why should I?" replied the teacher in a low tone, and added aloud in French: "Please remember that there are innocent children present".' [29] And, indeed, what an abhorrent rule it is! The souls of women seem to be allowed to enter the next realm if they surrender, as a sort of pass, their bodies to the officials. They are then married off to some nincompoop in the village, with their drab existence rewarded only by occasional flashes of voluptuously blissful memories of their sacrificial sins. Damnation is their lot if they refuse, as happened in the case of Amalia, Barnabas's sister, who brought degradation upon herself and her family by declining the invitation of the official Sortini.

The unfathomable depths of nonsense into which an interpretation can be lured by its own mistaken assumptions is revealed in Max Brod's critical dealings with that crucial point in the story of Barnabas's family. In his epilogue to *The Castle* Max Brod writes: 'The connection between the castle—that is divine guidance—and the women . . . may appear mysterious and even inexplicable in the Sortini episode, where the official (Heaven) requires the girl to do something obviously immoral and sordid; here a reference to Kierkegaard's *Fear and Trembling* may be of value. . . . The Sortini episode is literally a parallel to Kierkegaard's book, which starts from the fact that God required of Abraham what was really a crime, the sacrifice of his child; and which uses this paradox to establish triumphantly the conclusion that the categories of morality and religion are by no means identical.' [30] This is, for the believer, downright blasphemy, and a critical insult to the intelligence of a reader able to read for himself the Bible, Kierkegaard and Kafka. The comparison between Kierkegaard and Kafka would indeed be relevant. It might bring home, even to a modern reader, the difference between Purgatory and Hell. For this is the precise relationship between Kierkegaard's *Fear and Trembling* and Kafka's *Castle*. The sacrifice of Isaac a parallel to Sortini's designs on Amalia? But this means, without any polemical exaggeration, to ascribe to the God of Abraham a personal interest in the boy Isaac worthy rather of a Greek demi-god. Moreover, He, having tested Abraham's absolute obedience, did not accept the sacrifice. Yet Sortini (who conveys to Max Brod the idea of divine guidance and Heaven itself) can, to judge by the example of his colleagues, be relied upon not to have summoned Amalia to his bedroom merely to tell her that one does not do such a thing.

To return from the comic escapades of literary criticism to Franz Kafka's novel: the castle represents neither divine guidance nor Heaven. It is for K. something that is to be conquered, something that bars his way into a purer realm. K.'s antagonism to the castle becomes clear from the very first pages of the book. This is how he responds to the first telephone conversation about his appointment which, in his presence, is conducted between the village and the authorities: 'K. pricked up his ears. So the castle had recognized him as the land-surveyor. That was unpropitious for him, on the one hand, for it meant that the castle was well informed about him, had estimated all the probable chances and was taking up the challenge with a smile. On the other hand, however, it was quite propitious, for if his interpretation were right they had underestimated his strength, and he would have more freedom of action than he had dared to hope.' [31]

The correspondence between the spiritual structure of *The Castle* and the view of the world systematized into Gnostic and Manichaean dogma is indeed striking. There is, however, no reason to assume that Kafka had any special knowledge of those ancient heresies. In their radical dualism they are merely the model systems of a deep-rooted spiritual disposition, asserting itself over and over again in individuals and whole movements. Gnostic and Manichaean is, above all, 'the face that is filled with loathing and hate' at the sight of physical reality. Kafka refrains from any dealings with nature. There is, apart from the mention of a starry sky, wind and snow, not one description of nature in *The Castle*. Within the human sphere everything that is of the flesh is treated with a sense of nausea and disgust. All the habitations of men are lightless, airless and dirty. The nuptial embrace between K. and Frieda takes place amidst puddles of beer on the floor of a public bar, the room still filled with the stale smells of an evening's business, while mass prostitution is carried on in the stable of the inn.

But Kafka has also found subtler means of conveying his revolt against the 'real'. One evening K. is waiting in the dark courtyard of the inn for Klamm to emerge from his village room and enter his sledge. The coachman, noticing K., encourages him to wait inside the sledge and have a drink from one of the bottles kept in the side-pockets. K. opens the bottle and smells: 'Involuntarily he smiled, the perfume was so sweet, so caressing, like praise and good words from someone whom one loves very dearly, yet one does not quite know what they are about and has no desire to know, and is simply happy in the knowledge that it is he who is saying them. Can this be brandy? K. asked himself doubtfully and tasted out of curiosity. Yes, surprisingly enough, it was brandy, and it burned and warmed. How strangely it transformed itself, as he drank, from something which was hardly more than a medium of sweet perfume, into a vulgar drink, fit for a coachman!' [32] Whether intentional or not, this profanation of the aroma of a spirit in the process of being 'realized' is a wonderfully subtle symbol of a Manichaean perspective of the world. And the most telling formula of this Manichaean disposition Kafka once found after finishing one of his stories: 'I can still derive some temporary satisfaction from a work of this kind . . . but happiness only if I ever succeed in lifting the world into a sphere pure, true, unchangeable' (diary note of September 25th, 1917).[33]

Is his castle of that sphere? It is, no doubt, the highest realm K. is capable of perceiving. This is what misled the critics, but not Kafka himself, into equating it with God. But it is certainly not quite irrelevant that in his personal confessions Kafka never, not once, utters the belief that the incessant striving of his spirit was directed towards God, or prompted by *amor Dei*. All the time his soul is preoccupied with the power of Evil; a power so great that God had to retreat before it into purest transcendence, for ever out of reach of life. Life itself is the incarnation of Evil: 'Knowledge of the diabolical there can be, but not belief in it, for there is nothing more diabolical than what exists'.[34] And then again the reality of life, still identified with Evil, is denied completely: 'There is only a spiritual world; what we call the physical world is the evil in the spiritual one . . .'.[35] Thus the idea of final authority, merely by assuming the shape of physical reality in *The Castle*, falls, without the author's either willing it or being able to help it, under the spell of Evil. It is the paradox of spiritual absolutism that the slightest touch of concreteness will poison the purest substance of the spirit, and one ray of darkness blot out a world of light.

Yet Kafka is neither a dogmatic follower of the Gnosis nor a Manichee; he is an artist, and although the cursed rule of the castle is the furthest point of the world to which his wakeful mind can reach, there dawns, at its extreme boundaries, a light, half suspectingly perceived, half stubbornly ignored, that comes from things outside the scope of Klamm's authority. K. knows only one thing: that he must come to grips with Klamm; yet at the same time he knows that his very obsession with this thought precludes him from reaching what he mistakenly believes only Klamm can give. He senses dimly that humility and humour would bring him the possession of which he deprives himself by his very striving for it. In Pepi who, for a short time, was promoted to the rank of barmaid in the local inn (and thus to the opportunity of serving beer to Klamm), now trembling at the prospect of losing her position again, K. meets the caricatured embodiment of his own ambition. In giving advice to her he shows a remarkable knowledge of his own disease: 'It is a job like any other, but for you it is the kingdom of Heaven. Therefore you set about your business with exaggerated zeal . . . you tremble for your position, feel constantly persecuted, try, by overdoing your friendliness, to win over those who you believe could help you; but you merely annoy and repel them; for what they look for in a bar is peace, and not the barmaid's worries on top of their own.' [36] And later: 'In comparing myself with you, I suspect that both of us have tried, in too noisy, too childish, too inexperienced a fashion, to get something which is to be had easily and simply through Frieda's matter-of-factness. We cry and scratch and toss about, like little children tugging at the tablecloth and getting nothing for it, but only making all the nice things tumble down so that they are unobtainable for ever.' [37]

But it is in K.'s adventure with the castle official Bürgel that this insight finds its most striking parable. K., summoned in the middle of the night to an interview with the official Erlanger, has, in his weariness and exhaustion, forgotten the number of the right door, and enters (more in the hope of finding an empty bed there than an official of the castle) another room. There he encounters, lying in bed, the official Bürgel. The ensuing dialogue, or monologue rather, is one of Kafka's greatest feats in the art of melting the solid flesh of a grotesque reality and revealing behind it the anatomic structure of the miraculous. Bürgel promises K. to settle once and for all his affairs in the castle. K. is not in the least impressed by this offer. He waves it aside as the boast of a dilettante: 'Without knowing anything of the circumstances in which K.'s appointment had been made, of anything of the difficulties which it met in the village and in the castle, and of the complications which had either already arisen or were in the air; without knowing anything of all this, indeed without even showing—and might one not take that for granted with a secretary?—that he had at least a faint notion of it, he offered, by sleight of hand, and with the help of a little pad of notepaper, to settle the matter up there.' [38] It is the unbelief of a labyrinthine mind in the very existence of simplicity. And while K. grows ever more weary, Bürgel delivers, in a rapturous crescendo, the message of the miracle: if a man takes a secretary of the castle by surprise; if, in the middle of the night, the applicant, almost unconscious of what he does, slips, like a tiny grain through a perfect sieve, through the network of difficulties that is spread over all approaches to the centre of authority, then the castle, in the person of this one secretary, must yield to the intruder, indeed must almost force the granting of the request upon the unsuspecting subject: 'You believe it cannot happen? You are right, it cannot happen at all. But one night—who can vouch for everything?—it does happen after all.' It is an event so rare that it seems to occur merely by virtue of rumour, and even if it does occur, one can, 'as it were, render it innocuous by proving to it—and this proof is easy enough—that there is no room for it in this world'.³⁹ And Bürgel goes on with his rhapsody, describing the shattering delight with which a secretary responds to this situation. But when he ends, K. is sound asleep, and, with the conditions of the miracle fulfilled before his eyes, as unaware of its possibility as he had been in his tortured wakeful pursuit of it.

Indeed, no comfort can be found *within* this world. Yet the power not only to experience but poetically to create this world must have its source *outside*. Only a mind keeping alive in at least one of its recesses the memory of a place where the soul is truly at home is able to contemplate with such creative vigour the struggles of a soul lost in a hostile land; and only an immensity of goodness can be so helplessly overcome by the vision of the worst of all possible worlds. This is the reason why we are not merely terrified by the despair of this book, but also moved by its sadness, the melancholy of spiritual failure carrying with it a subtle promise.

In one of his most Manichaean sayings Kafka speaks of the power of a single crow to destroy the heavens; but, he adds, this 'proves nothing against the heavens, for the heavens signify simply: the impossibility of crows'.⁴⁰ And although these birds swarm ceaselessly around *The Castle*, its builder built it from the impulse to render them impossible. Is it, one wonders, yet an-. other phantom hope in a deluded world that prompts, in the book, a child, a simple girl and a wretched family to turn with a mysteriously messianic expectation to the land-surveyor K.? And makes, on a deleted page of the unfinished manuscript, a mother invite the homeless stranger to her house with the words: 'This man should not be allowed to perish'? [41] Or is it perhaps the reflection of a faith, maintained even in the grip of damnation, which Nietzsche once expressed: 'Whosoever has built a new Heaven has found the strength for it only in his own Hell'[42].*

* Long after this essay was written, I found the following passage in a (then still) unpublished letter of Kafka's: 'No people sing with such pure voices as those who live in deepest Hell; what we take for the song of angels is their song'. (Now published in Franz Kafka, *Letters to Milena*, London, 1953, p. 186).

KARL KRAUS:

SATIRIST IN THE MODERN WORLD

1

Confucius was once asked what he would do first if it were left to him to administer a country. The Master said: 'It would certainly be to correct language.' 'Surely,' they said, 'this has nothing to do with the matter. Why should language be corrected?' The Master's answer was: 'If language is not correct, then what is said is not what is meant; if what is said is not what is meant, then what ought to be done remains undone; if this remains undone, morals and art will deteriorate; if morals and art deteriorate, justice will go astray; if justice goes astray, the people will stand about in helpless confusion. Hence there must be no arbitrariness in what is said. This matters above everything.'

It mattered above everything to the Austrian satirist

Karl Kraus. He examined the language spoken and written by his contemporaries, and found that they lived by wrong ideas. Listening to what they said, he discovered the impure springs of their actions; reading what they wrote, he knew that they were heading for disaster. To him the style of the diplomatic correspondent's report revealed more of the political situation than the conference thus reported. The diplomats may have had reasons to be optimistic, but portents occurred in their reported speeches – wrong subjunctives and false inflections. The hopes of the world, proclaimed in manifestoes of good-will, came to grief at the barrier of a misplaced comma, and the highest expectations of mankind were frustrated by their verbal alliance with a cliché. Phrases, for Karl Kraus, were more germane to the matter of war or peace than the number of cannons carried by each side, and while he defied the auguries of politicians, he saw a special providence in the fall of a relative clause.

Karl Kraus's satire is more deeply rooted in its own medium than the work of any other recent writer of German prose. 'The German language,' he said, 'is the profoundest of all languages, but German speech is the shallowest.' The genius of Karl Kraus could not have arisen from the ground of another language; for the inspiration of his satirical work is the contrast between his faith in words and the speech of the faithless: and it is German that offers the biggest scope for this faith as well as its blasphemers.

His thinking was a voyage of exploration in a landscape of words. No other western language allows adventures on such a scale, for every other language has been more thoroughly explored, surveyed and ordered. What in modern English may be a wrestle with words, is a vast conflagration in German, with victories more glorious and defeats more devastating; and what, in the workaday life of words, is a relaxed walk through an English park, is in German a venture into exposed territory. While the English writer or speaker, over long stretches of his verbal enterprise, is protected by the tact and wisdom of the linguistic convention itself, his German counterpart risks revealing himself as an idiot or a scoundrel through the ring and rhythm of his first sentence. Had Hitler's speeches been accessible to the West in their unspeakable original, we might have been spared a war. For this war was partly caused by Hitler's innocent translators, unavoidably missing in smooth and diplomatic French or English the resonance of the infernal sphere. Only German, in all its notorious long-windedness, offers such shortcuts to the termini of mankind. It was Karl Kraus who knew them all.

With only a few exceptions, his work must remain untranslated; and it is untranslatable because he did not write 'in a language,' but through him the German language seemed to assume personal shape in order to become the crucial witness in the case this great prosecutor brought against his time. Thus his work does not convey through the written word something which, if needs be, could be conveyed in another medium; he merely confronts with the uncorrupted spirit of language the representative idiom of his society; and at the approach of his words the language-scene of the age is uncannily illuminated, showing souls and minds corrupted by untruth and self-deception.

In 922 numbers of his journal *Die Fackel* there is not one polemical essay which does not begin and end with an opposition of this kind. His campaigns are not aimed at hostile opinions or ideologies. In every single case his field of action is the ever-widening no-man's-land between appearance and reality, expression and substance, word-gesture and personality. The tirades of rhetoricians, the pamphlets of politicians, the *feuilletons* of renowned authors are passed through the filter of language, leaving behind mere dregs of folly and residues of false pretence. The dead word is resurrected and comes back as a spirit of destruction. Men, having tried to live on empty

phrases, die of their own clichés. The triumphs of medical
science are undone by the products of the printing-press,
and the effect of the ink used by journalists is seen to be
as deadly as the Black Death.

For Karl Kraus the word has personal life. Language,
passion and thought are one and the same for him. Language is the name of the activity of his passionate
thinking; his passion and his thought are identical with
their articulation. This is as much as to say that the
objects of his thinking and writing are not concepts, but
ideas; and not ideas which he 'holds,' but ideas by which
he is held. 'Poetry and passionate speech,' said Goethe,
'are the sources of the life of every language.' In this sense
every word which Karl Kraus wrote is alive with the life
of language, every sentence the result not of construction,
but of creation and growth. This was difficult to grasp
for an age which betrayed on every level of intellectual
activity a preference for constructed abstractions. A noble
conspiracy of hard precision seemed at work to save us
from the embarrassments of highfalutin' vagueness and
sentimental inexactitude. But intermingled with this
brave renunciation of imprecise feeling was the terror
of an age that had lost its soul and made an artistic and
intellectual virtue of a terrible emergency. Karl Kraus
did not simply accept the loss. He discovered sin where
others submitted to fate. He attempted atonement where
others resigned themselves to the curse. It is this that
makes him a prophet. Others may tell their dreams,
their nightmares, as Joyce, Kafka and Picasso do. He was
wide awake and was seized by the word. It is a biblical
happening in a modern setting: 'The prophet that hath
a dream, let him tell a dream; and he that hath my word,
let him speak my word faithfully . . . For ye have perverted the words of the living God . . .' The word for
Karl Kraus was as concrete as the word that 'the Lord
sent . . . unto Jacob, and it has lighted upon Israel.'

The work of Karl Kraus is rich in words; and every single word is of the greatest possible precision. It is precise through its infinite ambiguity. He intended it to be like that, in protest against the rationalist superstition that a word could ever create or convey a clear-cut concept, and fix a definite object in the void of the universe. For Karl Kraus all thoughts are in the world even before they are thought. They are dispersed among the elements of language. The artist gathers them together and welds them into his thought. He once said: 'Language is the divining-rod which discovers wells of thought.' Thus language, for him, is a means not so much of communicating what he knows, but of finding what he does not yet know. Words are living organisms, not labels stuck to things. They are at home in a cosmos of the spirit, not in a chance assembly of 'atoms of perception'. Each of them holds secrets of its own and, once struck, opens up mines of thought. The greater the number of associations into which a word enters, the greater is its value in a piece of writing. This again must come as a surprise to intellectuals whose sharpest weapon in dispute is the question: 'What do you mean by that?' It is a double-edged weapon: useful in combating confused minds, it yet may defeat language itself if it will not rest until the linguistic emptiness of mathematical precision is reached. Applied excessively, it must destroy all the indefinable and imponderable agreements upon which any cultured community is based; and, indeed, much of modern philosophizing is merely the intellectual symptom of the loss of spiritual community.

Karl Kraus's answer to the stock question would be: 'I mean what I say; yet what I say has, with all its apparent ambiguities, a precision which may well be beyond your sense of exactitude. For the world of the word is round, and language is Delphi.'

Textbooks would call Karl Kraus a master of language; but he is its master by being its slave. He has no 'command of words'; he is at their command, avenging their honour upon all who violate them. Thus this implacable enemy of all phrase-ridden traditionalism and nationalism is most deeply steeped in a national tradition.

2

Karl Kraus was born in 1874 as the son of wealthy Jewish parents in a little town in Bohemia. Most of his life he spent in Vienna, where he died in 1936. In 1899 he founded the periodical *Die Fackel*. In it the young Franz Werfel published his poems; other contributors were Else Lasker-Schüler, Frank Wedekind, Peter Altenberg, Wilhelm Liebknecht. But soon all the contributions were written by the editor himself – satirical essays, aphorisms and poems. From time to time he collected his writings according to certain themes and published them as books. The result was seven volumes of essays, three volumes of aphorisms and nine volumes of poems. Yet the central place in any list of Karl Kraus's works must be allotted to his immense drama of the first world war, *Die letzten Tage der Menschheit* (The Last Days of Mankind.) It was followed, in the genre of drama, by five minor satirical plays, by revised translations of a number of Shakespeare's tragedies and comedies, by new versions of the libretti of Offenbach's operettas, and by adaptations of some of Nestroy's comedies.*

*When the first and shorter version of this essay appeared, the works of Karl Kraus were hardly accessible. They seemed to be buried under the ruins left behind by Hitler and the Second World War. Now, however, they are in print again, a fact that both reflects and commendably perpetuates a Karl Kraus renaissance in German literature. Their publisher is Kösel-Verlag, Munich. In 1952 they published for the first time *Die dritte Walpurgisnacht* (The Third Walpurgisnight), the diatribe Karl Kraus wrote in Vienna, not yet occupied at the time, against Hitler's Germany, but deliberately withheld because it did not and could not, as he thought, succeed in its satirical purpose and, indeed, might have only increased the fury of the regime. The editor of the whole remarkable publishing venture (which before long will include a

What was the inspiration of this enormous productivity? The answer is Hamlet's: 'Words, words, words.' And the commas between them; and the deeds they beget; and the deeds they leave undone; and the word that was at the beginning and above all those that were at the end. These were printed in newspapers. Hence newspapers were Karl Kraus's main theme; and the men who wrote them, and the things about which they wrote: society, law-courts, sex and morality, literature, theater, war, commerce and merchandise, in brief, the whole world that is called into being by a headline, organized by a leading article and sold by an advertisement. But his contrast-theme was the words that make up a drama by Shakespeare or a poem by Goethe. Thus his theme behind the themes was the culture of Europe, its glory, its berayal and its doom. Exploring the labyrinths of contemporary verbiage, Karl Kraus never lost the thread. His purpose was 'to show the very age and body of the time his form and pressure.'

When in 1899 he founded *Die Fackel*, his subjects seemed of little more than local interest; but as the locality was Vienna, it was the heart of a European empire that was examined, and its beat was found defective. His Vienna was easily recognized as the cherished city of the world's tourists, but under his gaze the waltz was performed under the threat of the Day of Judgment. *Heurigenstimmung* faded into a hangover of eternity, and at the end of the Kärtnerstrasse passengers came to the parting of the way where a king of Babylon stood. Even if to a superficial observer it may have seemed that a brilliant polemical talent had launched out against what was merely a typical Austrian form of corruption, more perceptive minds already recognized that behind every dwarf that Karl Kraus attacked there loomed the shadow of a giant. Indeed, it was an Austrian *débâcle* of the spirit

---

facsimile edition of all the volumes of *Die Fackel*) is Heinrich Fischer, Karl Kraus's friend and devoted literary editor.

from which his first diatribes took their cue. Yet there was no need for him to change his satirical method when the domestic scene of discontent broadened into a European disaster. Into his language he had gathered the storm at a time when his age was still busy sowing wind.

Three currents from heterogeneous sources came together to form his character: the ethical radicalism of an Old Testament prophet, the conservatism and the anti-plebeian idiosyncracies of an Austrian aristocrat from before 1848, and that mystical relationship to language which characterized some of the German Romantics and enabled them to achieve one of the greatest feats in the history of translation – the rendering in German of Shakespeare's dramas. Of these three ingredients it is the second which is the most puzzling in a man who was regarded as a destructive revolutionary by the majority of his conservative, liberal and social-democratic fellow-citizens. And, indeed, his conservatism was different from what an age that knew only of political allegiances meant by 'conservative'. For him it was not an ideology. He hated all ideologies. He saw them as what they were and are: the intellectual pretence of a spiritually impoverished age, the inflated paper currency of the bankruptcy of culture.

After 1848 ideologies spread in Austria like an infectious disease. They emerged from the stagnant waters of discontent which the unfinished revolution had left behind. Unrealized political desires rationalized themselves into bogus systems of political thought, and emotional frustration developed into mental hysteria. Go-getting journalists stirred Austrian *Urgemütlichkeit* into paroxysms of discomfort, and the lower strata of alpine feeble-mindedness worked their way to the surface and became politically conscious. Hungarian pig-breeders and Viennese stockbrokers struggled for an intellectual articulation of their demands for greater profits. From the ethnical hotch-potch of the Sudeten Germans sprang the doctrine of racial purity, and racially pure but cosmopolitan Jews became ardent propagandists of the Teutonic mythology of Richard Wagner. In a pandemonium of *Gemütlichkeit* and confused political aspirations, where commercial travellers hobnobbed with *Geist,* priests with corrupt journalists, bankers with saviors of the people, and advertising agents with artists, the last remnants of Austrian culture dissolved. And this culture had proved particularly corruptible. Its very generosity and blissful lack of articulate moral convictions, its baroque taste for untidiness, its sense of drama and dramatic upheavals, and its childlike trust in its own everlastingness, made it the more susceptible to the poison of industrialization and commercialization. A people, in whom faith had always had preponderance over the intellect, enthusiastically embraced political ideologies which offered a substitute for the evaporating certainties of religion.

In Karl Kraus's satirical work this dissolute scene is confronted with the integrity of a tradition and culture which in him had preserved itself and retained an amazing vigor. He had an unfailing ear for two kinds of sound: the common talk of the town which he reproduced with flawless precision, and the language of prophecy which he discerned as the whispered accompaniment of the degraded vernacular, suddenly forcing it into a key of ultimate significance. Oppressed by the confusing chorus of apparent triviality, his ear was tuned to the pitch of the Absolute. People gossiped about the war; he heard them lament the loss of their souls. At every streetcorner acts of high treason were committed. The shouts of newspaper-boys announcing in mysterious vowels latest editions, became monstrous threats to man's spiritual safety or shrieks of anguish from the lowest deep.

This metamorphosis of the commonplace will for ever remain one of the greatest achievements in the German language. For the technique of Karl Kraus, if indeed it was technique, was literal quotation. He took the material of experience as it was: the coffee-house conversation of the journalists, the stock exchange rendezvous of the racketeers, the fragments of talk that reached his ear in the streets of Vienna, the judgments of the law courts, the leading articles of the newspapers and the chatter of their readers – in fact, all that looks like the triviality of daily life – and endowed it with a soul: an anti-soul, as it were. This he did not by recasting, shaping, modifying his material. No, he quoted verbatim. 'The most improbable deeds which are here reported,' he says in the Preface to the *Last Days of Mankind*, 'really happened; I have registered only what was done. The most improbable conversations which are here conducted took place; exaggerations and inventions are quotations . . . Documents assume a living shape, reports come to life as persons, persons die as leading articles. The *feuilleton* is given a mouth to deliver itself as a monologue; phrases walk on two legs – men have kept only one. Inflections of voices rush and rustle through our days and grow into the chorus of the unholy plot. People who have lived amidst mankind and have survived it, the executive organs and spokesmen of an age that has no flesh but blood, no blood but ink, are reduced to shadows and marionettes, that is, to the form befitting their busy sham-existences. Cyphers and lemurs, masks of the tragic carnival, have living names because this must be so, and because nothing is accidental in this time conditioned by chance. This gives nobody the right to regard it as a local affair. Even the noises of a Viennese rush-hour are directed from a cosmic point.'

Leaving the material of actuality intact, he yet gave it the deeper significance of satire, drama, and tragedy – by creating another context for it. He took the frivolous seriously, and discovered that the situation was desperate. Thus he did 'invent' after all; but his invention was of the simplest kind. It consisted in assuming the existence of natural states of culture and of self-evidently correct norms of human conduct; for instance, that modesty befits the mediocre – and instantly mediocrity was seen to have risen to demonic heights from which it ruled the world. Or he assumed that the prominent German writers and journalists of his time wrote in the German tongue – and the German tongue answered back, saying that they were illiterates. He dealt with the practice of the law courts as though it were based upon justice; with the theatre as though it were concerned with the art of drama; with journals as though they intended to supply correct information; with politicians as though they desired the promotion of communal prosperity, and with philosophers as though they were seekers after truth. The satirical effect of these inventions was annihilating.

Beginners in the study of physics are shown an experiment with a little balloon, sealed but not inflated, an inconspicuous little object put under a jar-bell which is then emptied of its content of air. The minute quantity of air which had remained in the shrivelled balloon, now, in the new medium, suffices to make it into a full-blown globe. The material of the balloon has not changed, but its appearance and shape are transformed. In the work of Karl Kraus something similar takes place. He transfers his characters, all these leader-writers and leader-readers, shareholders and opinion-makers, war-reporters and truth-distorters, into a medium the laws of which issue from a 'cosmic point.' And there he shows, on a full-blown and transparent object, the diabolic structure of what before looked merely like innocuous mediocrity and banality. Thus his apocalypse has found its appointed executors. In the absence of a valid mythology, it is Tom, Dick and Harry who charge through the world as apocalyptic horsemen.

3

The Last Days of Mankind is not a drama in any accepted sense of the word. Its book edition has eight hundred pages, and its list of characters thirteen. It has no hero, no unity of space, time or action. In time it stretches from 1914 to 1919. It takes place on the battle-fields of Europe, in stock exchanges and hospitals, the offices of journals, the lecture-rooms of universities, the headquarters of armies, and again and again in the streets of Vienna. The author says in the Preface that the drama which, if performed on earth, would last for ten evenings is meant to be enacted in a theater on Mars. 'Audiences here would not be able to bear it. For it is blood of their blood, and its contents are those unreal, unthinkable years, out of reach for the wakefulness of mind, inaccessible to any memory and preserved only in nightmares – those years when characters from an operetta played the tragedy of mankind.' That is the pervasive theme of this incommensurable satirical work: the discrepancy between the stature of the protagonists and the weight and significance of the play which they have succeeded in getting up.

In 1914 it may have seemed an exclusively Austrian theme. Only in Vienna could it first have forced itself upon a satirical mind. With inimitable *vis comica* Karl Kraus's satires bring out the incongruity between the kindheartedness and nonchalance of the inhabitants of that country and the 'iron rule' of war and conquest, between the soft and sentimental ring of their dialects and the heroic accents of *Nibelungentreue*, between their excessive admiration of waltz-enchanted soubrettes and the worship of the god Mars. And with equal power the satirist conveys the terror and the pity of the creature helplessly caught in a tragedy and unable to recognize his own guilt.

This theme has ceased to be a provincial one. There is no other which throws so much light on the particular character of our time. We are imbued with the idea that it is greatness and strength of personalities which account for dramatic events, achievements and catastrophes alike, and that it is in mediocrity that safety lies. In that we are the involuntary heirs of the Renaissance and of Romanticism. We deplore that a man like Hitler ever came to power. But behind our regret may lurk a suspicion that he was a 'great man' after all, an evil genius, but a genius none the less. For we judge by the spectacular consequences of his dominion. We have not yet grasped the demonic possibilities of mediocrity, believing as we do that the only appropriate partner for Mephisto is a Faustian genius. It was Karl Kraus who discovered to what satanic heights inferiority may rise. He anticipated Hitler long before anyone knew his name.

Thus, through him, the theme of literature has undergone a radical change. In by-gone days it was the business of the imagination to create within the world of the senses the image and symbol capable of expressing the wealth of inner experience. It was in art that man, dissatisfied with the meagre scope of his 'real' life, found a reality more adequate to what he felt to be the truth of his existence. To-day it is different: our task – and difficulty – is rather to find within ourselves something big enough to be charged with the responsibility for the monstrous dimensions of our external reality. In a better age the disaster of the world which we have caused, and the still greater destruction which we face, would have been the doing of mythological creatures, enemies of mankind, hostile gods who tear open the mountains and burn the habitations of man in the volcanic fire; of giants, cyclops and sinister magicians who have robbed Olympus of its secrets and with them threaten to extinguish life. In our uncanny and enlightened epoch all this is merely the result of a conspiracy of sobriety, scientific planning, mediocrity and human insignificance. The demonstration of this terrifying incongruity fills the pages of *The Last*

Days of Mankind. Its heroes are troglodytes living in the skyscrapers of history, barbarians having at their disposal all the amenities and high explosives of technical progress, fishmongers acting the role of Nelson, ammunition salesmen crossing Rubicons, and hired scribblers tapping out the heroic phrases of the bards. And there are, on the more passive and pathetic side, their victims on active service: farm laborers with a few weeks of battle training, honest-to-goodness little people with pensionable salaries and paid holidays, decent folk whose imagination is unable to grasp even a fragment of the horror which they are commanded to inflict upon the world by faithfully serving machines, pulling levers and pressing buttons. And the effects are registered by men whose imagination is blunted and whose moral judgment is corrupted by the insidious poison of journalistic language which has emptied the word of all its reality and meaning.

This is Karl Kraus's thesis: If our imagination sufficed to visualize the reality behind the news column of one morning paper, this reality would not and could not exist. And if one man's imagination were inspired by it and gave expression to it, all the tragedies of ancient Greece would dwindle into idyllic sentimentalities before such a drama of human corruption and human agony. But such an imagination does not exist, and therefore there exists such a reality; there exists such a reality, and therefore no such imagination. This is the last wonder of the world, and compared to it all the others are children's playthings. Man has achieved a technical superiority over himself which threatens him with unavoidable disaster. The combined employment of technique and 'man-power' has got the better of the power of his humanity. Between his technical mastery (which would have terrified Prometheus) and his imagination (which not even pigmies could eke out to make from it fairy tales for their children), he has fixed a gulf spacious enough for Armageddon to take place.

Vacuous spirits and enfeebled souls, living in a world replete and luxuriant with the riches of Hell – and (most perverse of miracles!) in a world of their own making; minds as hopelessly muddled and impoverished as the language of their psychology, and as diabolically exact as the formulae of their missile engineering; intelligences defeated by the task of writing a correct sentence but triumphantly equal to the commission to destroy the world: such is the occasion of Karl Kraus's prophecy. Compared with its satirical vigor, the moralizing aestheticism of his contemporary, the prophet-poet Stefan George, was a mere whim and an elegant superficiality of the spirit, displayed with sincere but incongruous earnestness at a prolonged heroic carnival. While Stefan George built ostentatious castles of words and waved elaborately designed flags of beauty, Karl Kraus lived in the old house of language and, listening to the war-like noises outside, knew that this was a time for sober vigilance; and as for flags, handkerchiefs would do where there was weeping.

Through *The Last Days of Mankind* go, as the chorus of the tragedy, two figures called the Optimist and the Grumbler. The Grumbler is the author himself, and by choosing this denigrating name he has made ironical use of a title bestowed upon him by some of his contemporaries. The Optimist is the reasonable man (and it is important that he is not satirically caricatured, but is throughout the Grumbler's intelligent partner), showing a great deal of common sense, psychological understanding and historical appreciation. He is balanced, while the Grumbler is desperate. The Optimist always sees both sides of a problem, whereas the Grumbler refuses to learn how to squint. The Grumbler speaks in eschatological terms, the Optimist in terms of history. 'I don't know what you are talking about,' the Optimist would say, 'our situation is far from being unique. Life has always been precarious; there has always been a crisis.'

'Profound indeed,' the Grumbler would reply, 'if only I did not suspect that you use this insight as an excuse for behaving as though there were no crisis at all.' 'We have lived in illusory and artificial safety up till now,' the Optimist would assert, 'and what we witness is a return to normal.' 'No,' would be the Grumbler's retort, '*you* have lived in illusory safety, and what *I* witness is a deadly complication of abnormality.'

The dialectic of these dialogues consists in the perpetual juxtaposition of psychological understanding and moral experience. In a world abounding with psychologists and analytical literature, the work of Karl Kraus was of the greatest value for a generation lost in relativities. He, who spent hours over the decision where to put a comma, would yet be able to decide instantly on a moral issue. His moral word was 'Yea, yea' or 'Nay, nay,' but his sentences were complex organisms of the subtlest structure. In the moral sphere where most contemporary writers would lose their way in a tangle of problems he would see none; but he would prove to all of them that they had given too little thought to the sound of their words and to the rhythm and syntax of their sentences. And what, above all, he taught those who were able to hear him was the meaning and extent of moral responsibility. His unfailing and instinctive response to what are 'strictly moral' questions was the result of his having pondered over them endlessly in 'strictly amoral' fields: in the sphere of aesthetics and language. *Language* – the collection of his essays on this subject – is probably the profoundest book that exists on style and the use of German. It is the work of an artist and moralist, not of a pedant and grammarian. There it becomes clear that the ruthlessness of his moral judgment sprang from the delicate tact and care which he showed in his dealings with the 'crystallized tradition of the spirit of man.' To his impatience with the wrongdoers corresponded his infinite patience with language, and to his relentless ethical determination his compassion for the maltreated word. He knew what few critics know: that the aesthetic judgment is a moral judgment if it is to be more than the diffuse reaction of a vaguely refined sensitivity. For him *De gustibus non est disputandum* was an alarming advertisement of a *moral* bankruptcy. He saw the connection between maltreated words and the maltreatment of human souls and bodies, and he avenged lives by restoring words to their state of integrity, health and vigor in which, of their own accord, they could 'speak to the yet unknowing world how these things came about.' Through him it is language itself that opens its mouth and speaks to those who use it deceitfully: 'But ye are forgers of lies, ye are all physicians of no value.'

There were in German literature men before, and contemporary with, Karl Kraus who had recognized the immense dangers, indeed the apocalyptic character, of their age and whose works were prompted by this sense of urgency; there were, for instance, Nietzsche and – at a considerable distance from him – Stefan George. But with them the experience of their time inspired the attempt to transcend it in the dimension of time itself, and to redeem it in the vision of a future which would be greatness and purity of spirit. Karl Kraus, on the other hand, insisted upon the timeless significance of the contemporary scene. For him it was not a cacophonous overture, played in the dark, before the curtain rose on a stage of light; it was itself the drama, redeemable not through the expectation of future goodness, but only through the faithful realization of present evil. It was Kierkegaard who said (and Karl Kraus who quoted) that 'the individual cannot help his age; he can only express that it is doomed'. And this is the only way in which he can bring help to it. This paradox links the work of Karl Kraus with the prophecies of the Old Testament.

S

4

In one of his dialogues with the Optimist; the Grumbler asserts that Germany and Austria were more deeply affected by the corruption of the spirit than the West. The corruption of England, for instance, could not suffice to produce and maintain a satirist.

The Grumbler: There is no English satirist.

The Optimist: Bernard Shaw.

The Grumbler: Precisely.

The kind of literary work commonly called 'satire' is rather vaguely defined. If, for instance, Heinrich Heine and Bernard Shaw are satirists, then one must find a different name for Karl Kraus. If, however, he is a satirist – and I believe he is the first European satirist since Swift – then Heine and Shaw are merely earnest jesters. The difference lies in the natures of their negative enthusiasm. Is its *positive* pole love, or sentimentality? Faith, or an expectation? An idea, or an intellectual concept? Is its creation therefore the other side of poetry, or of *belles-lettres* (though they may be rhymed as in the case of Heine, or concerned with social reforms as in the case of Shaw)? Is the writer of satires a wit thriving on the foolishness of society, or a genius whose soul is wounded by the sinfulness of his age?

Schiller, in his essay *Uber naive und sentimentalische Dichtung,* says of the true satirist that he would have been a poet had 'the moral perversity of his age not filled his heart with bitterness'. If there could be any doubt left about the authenticity of Karl Kraus's satire, it would be removed by his lyrical poetry. Although some of his verse is part and parcel of his satirical campaigns, most of his poems are untouched by the spirit of satire, meeting it only at the source of their common inspiration: language. A first and superficial judgment may class this poetry as *'Epigonendichtung'*; and this is what, in a particular sense, he called it himself. Its forms, metres, rhythms and rhymes are traditional. It is determined by the history of German poetry from Goethe to Liliencron, yet by-passes that poet whose genius was to direct, or misdirect, distinctly 'modern' trends: Hölderlin. He had to remain outside the poetic orbit of Karl Kraus; for with Hölderlin's later and greatest poems poetry leaves its articulate German tradition, achieving the miracle of speechlessness bursting into speech.

If Goethe had the gift of his Tasso: to say what he suffered, and say it at a level of experience where others would be silenced by agony, then Hölderlin sought, and often miraculously found, the word with which anguish speaks its own silence without breaking it. The paradox is indeed alarming, as alarming as the spiritual distress of which it is the expression. Short of miracles surpassing the miracle, from Hölderlin's poetry the way leads either to silence itself or to poetic mischief, the verbose stammer of those who have never learned to speak or to be silent, or the professional ecstasies of souls that, only because they are uninhabitable, are constantly beside themselves. Karl Kraus's poetry, on the other hand, is the poetry of speech. He never allows his genius to busy himself in regions beyond the beginning that began with the word. But there he is at home and at his '*Ursprung*'. It is this beginning that is his end. He is identical with one of the '*Zwei Läufer*' who in his poem of this name compete for the prize: one who, coming from nowhere, reaches his goal, while the other, starting at the beginning, the '*Ursprung*,' dies on the way, humbly and yet triumphantly attaining his end:

> *Und dieser, dem es ewig bangt,*
> *ist stets am Ursprung angelangt.*

Yet is would be a mistake to interpret this poem in terms suggested by its obvious thought-resemblance to T. S. Eliot's 'In my beginning is my end.' Karl Kraus did not commune with St. John of the Cross. He had no access to mysticism and, of course, deeply suspected the mystical flirtations practised in the Expressionist nightclubs of the soul, or in the Freud-Jungian mysticological consulting-rooms. And as for psychology, 'I combine in myself a great capacity for psychology with the still greater capacity to disregard a psychological state,' he said, or 'Psychoanalysis is the disease of which it pretends to be the cure.'

It was Nietzsche who defined mysticism as the marriage between skepticism and the craving for the transcendent. Karl Kraus was free from either. His '*Ursprung*' was the force that is expressed in the purest forms of human culture. In apprehending them, his vision was never unsteadied by skepticism. They were self-evidently true if they had the blessing of language, that language of which he naively believed that it could say everything worth saying, and was incapable of deceiving him who spoke it truthfully. He knew not the suspicion that there might be a 'deeper truth' beneath what was thus said with truth – the presistent suspicion of transcendentalism as well as psychology. The suspicion itself was suspect to him, and within his contemporary world he had little difficulty in showing that it rose like a miasma from the corruption of language.

The unity of thing and word, of feeling and its articulation, which is the essence of poetry, has in Karl Kraus's verse a distinctly erotic character. He was in love with language, but not in the manner of those promiscuous affairs with sounds so liberally encouraged in the society of Symbolists. His passion aimed at a more real possession – the body and soul of words. The subject of his poems is often language itself, and like a true lover he believed in the purifying effect of his love. In the most striking epigramm addressed to his mistress, she appears as a harlot transformed into a virgin by his very approach:

> *Mit heissem Herzen und Hirne*
> *naht ich ihr Nacht für Nacht.*
> *Sie war eine dreiste Dirne,*
> *die ich zur Jungfrau gemacht.*

In the poetic dialogue 'Eros and the Poet,' in which the poet boasts of having defeated the distracting god by a final escape into work, Eros yet overtakes and conquers him by rising from the words themselves, even though there is 'no trace of woman':

Hier ist keine Spur vom Weibe
und ich hab' dich doch besiegt!

And in a rhymed *tour de force* about the nature of rhyming, the most memorable lines are those in which rhyme is defined as the landing-place of two thoughts which have found each other in mutual agreement:

Er ist das Ufer, wo sie landen,
sind zwei Gedanken einverstanden.

It is revealing that the agreement is between two thoughts, for much of Karl Kraus's poetry is *Gedankenlyrik*. But it would be misleading to think of Schiller. The lyrical thought of Karl Kraus is as concrete and sensuous as any 'object' that has ever been received into poetic diction. With him both trees and thoughts grow in precise articulation from the soil of language, and both thoughts and fountains rise and fall with the exact rhythm of Nature breathing through the mouth of Art. And it is surely not only against the background of the thinker's thought and the satirist's Herculean labor that those moments when his poetry relaxes in the purest lyrical concentration are so deeply moving. On the contrary, they are in themselves enhanced by the energy set free through the release from the arduous task. There is indeed enough even of such purely lyrical poems to build up for their maker a poetic reputation of high order, poems in which the world is irradiated with the peace that is in the perfect concord of man, things, sounds and rhythms, leaving us with nothing else to be desired:

Staunend stand ich da
und ein Bergbach rinnt
und das ganze Tal
war mir wohlgesinnt.

Or else, leaving us with everything to be desired in the *cadenza* and desolation of a lost love:

Wie mag es sein, aus meinem Feuerkreise
geflohen sein!
Nun zieht nach ungewohnter Weise
die Seele auf die lange Reise
allein.

Another part of Karl Kraus's poetic work was his Theater of Poetry. He 'founded' it in opposition to the industrialized metropolitan theater of the day where resourceful directors, electrical engineers, brilliant designers of décor and costume, mixers of off-stage sounds, and dictatorial controllers of masses had become the real protagonists. They were unable to see Macbeth for the Birnam wood, and while the former was a poor actor, the latter was designed by a first-class landscape-gardener. Where Reinhardt dreamt his Midsummer Night's Dream, the glow-worm was the thing. The poetry could look after itself and did so with the embarrassment of an uninvited guest. The Theater of Poetry attempted to redress the balance. It knew of no productions, no décor, and no ensemble. Karl Kraus was its sole actor. He sat at a table and read *King Lear* or *Timon* or *Measure for Measure*:

. . . My business in this state
Made me a looker-on here in Vienna,
Where I have seen corruption boil and bubble
Till it o'er-run the stew . . .

Of course, he excelled in the delivery of Shakespeare's great invective and indignation; but while the world seemed still to smart with the wounds inflicted by Timon's curses, an inimitable movement of Karl Kraus's hands would set the scene for pure affection and tenderness. His voice, face and hands were perfect instruments conveying all the moods that lie between the soul's most passionate denials and its gentlest affirmations. The range of his dramatic expressiveness was equalled by the precision of his poetic sympathy, rendering with exact

imagination the prayer of Matthias Claudius's *Abendlied*
as well as Thersites's blasphemies, the gentle pathos of
Hauptmann's *Hannele* as well as the grand heroic manner
of Goethe's *Pandora*. It was on such occasions that the
'one-sidedness' of his satirical preoccupation was most
clearly seen to be to one side of an argument beyond
which was the faith in a life secure in its own riches and
vindicated by every flicker of man's goodness, the potential depth and rightness of his responses. Who would
then have denied him the right to say that everything
was surpassingly good if only God willed it so, and that
the satirist's denials were not of God's world but only of
those who denied Him:

Nicht Gott, nur alles leugn' ich, was ihn leugnet,
und wenn er will, ist alles wunderbar.

In the later years of his life he began to 'perform'
Offenbach's operettas. It was then that the satirist's ideal
dramatic unity seemed established. For him Offenbach's
satirical wit and charm effected a home-coming. The
mature satirist, remaining a satirist, recaptured the innocent theatrical enchantment of his childhood summer
days, the magical hours spent by the boy in the *Sommer-
theater,* preserved for us in the poem *Jugend:*

Da ward mir frei und froh
vor bunter Szene.
Liebte Madame Angot,
schöne Helene.
Blaubarts Boulotte und,
nicht zu vergessen,
Gerolstein, Trapezunt,
alle Prinzessen.

When Karl Kraus sang (almost more with his eyes than
with his voice) and danced (with the fingers of his hand)
the roles of 'all princesses', unforgotten by the satirist
from those remote days in the summer resort of Weid-
lingau where 'the sky was blue and red the butterfly';

and when, singing the last lines of the farewell letter of an Offenbach soubrette:

Lebe wohl! – Deine Perichole,
die vor Liebe und Hunger verght

his voice faded with the sadness of poverty and love, and yet merged with a gentle and kind infinity where all parted lovers are reunited, then his satirical relentlessness was revealed as the accidental form into which an ineluctable nostalgia for grace was driven by a corrupted world.

5

Satire ends at the very point where hatred of the world's abuses becomes irrelevant. This point is reached when absurdity gains control of that plane of experience at which men, throughout the ages, have formed their idea of order and normality; when, as in Shakespeare's vision of the ultimate disorder, right and wrong

Between whose endless jar justice resides,
Should lose their names, and so should justice too.
Then everything includes itself in power,
Power into will, will into appetite;
And appetite, an universal wolf,
So doubly seconded with will and power,
Must make perforce an universal prey,
And last eat up himself.

That there was a comma missing in Hitler's nation-wide appeal *'Deutschland erwache!'* was a satirical observation wasted on a humanity that, in its universal sleep, was oblivious even of its main clauses. Commas no longer mattered in the face of such a full stop.

When Hitler came to power, Karl Kraus realized that it was the end of his satirical world. In 1919 he said of

The Last Days of Mankind that its satirical inventions
and exaggerations were mere quotations of what was said
and done. Hitler's Germany reversed the situation: her
words and deeds merely quoted, and by quoting exaggerated beyond belief, the satirist's inventions. Where the
truth of facts took on the shape of inflated lies, truth
became truly unspeakable. If proof was needed for the
authenticity of Karl Kraus's satirical work, it was provided by his knowledge that satire was defeated. '*Mir
fällt zu Hitler nichts ein*' was his shatteringly nonchalant
formula for an agony of the spirit.

All he published in 1933 was one number of *Die
Fackel,* consisting of four pages and containing the farewell he spoke at the funeral of his friend Adolf Loos, the
architect. On the fourth page was printed a short poetic
declaration of silence: '*Ich bleibe stumm,*' ending with
'*Das Wort entschlief, als diese Welt erwachte*' – the word
expired with the awakening of that world. What none
the less he wrote and did not publish – *The Third Walpurgisnight,* a doubly posthumous work – is variations
upon the great theme: the incommensurability of the
material provided by the age with the conditions of
imaginative contemplation. For this material was more
than material; it was in itself perversely realized art, the
ne plus ultra of an infernal spiritualization of the real.
Indeed, the events of that epoch 'took place', but the place
they took was in a world too densely populated with
real demons to leave any room for the liberating work
of the satirist's art. It was a world the daily routine of
which consisted in murder with robbery; among its
victims was the human imagination.

Thus Karl Kraus has taught from beginning to end the
lesson of language and silence. The last words of *The
Last Days of Mankind* were spoken by the Lord into the
silence of a horribly devastated world. They were the
words that were once attributed to the old Austrian
Emperor who died during the First World War: *Ich*

habe es nicht gewollt – It has not been my will. The *satirist* Karl Kraus brought to life a world whose every breath was a denial of God's designs, and was the chaos that decided that His will should not be done. The *poet* Karl Kraus praised the order of a universe in which all is well if only He wills it so. The *silent* Karl Kraus bore witness to an unspoken faith that lies on the other side of speechless despair. It is a faith inaccessible to those who are never at a loss for words – not even when *'das Wort entschlief'*.

THE HAZARD OF MODERN POETRY

1

It is on an Easter Sunday that Goethe's Faust comes
back to his study from one of the most lyrical walks of
German literature. He is accompanied by a strange black
poodle that, out in the fields, insisted on joining him.
Faust opens the Gospel according to St. John, determined to translate it into his 'beloved German'. He is
defeated by the very first line. What is it that was in the
beginning? *Logos*—the Word. No, it seems impossible to
rate the word so high. 'Meaning' might be better. Yet it
sounds too feeble to be placed at the source of everything that is. And Faust tries 'Force'; but having moved
away so far from the original text, why should the translator not go further in his freedom? 'In the beginning
was the Deed'. This satisfies Faust—and excites the poo-

dle. The translation comes to nothing because at this point the dog grows restive. He will not listen even to Faust's most potent demon-soothing magic. For he comes from Hell and is a devil.

Easter Sunday and a magician; *Logos* into Word, Word into Deed, dog into devil—the scene is set for the hazard of modern poetry.

But perhaps we ought to be more scholarly. Let us therefore turn to the *History of the Royal Society, its Institution, Design and Progress in the Advancement of Experimental Philosophy*. It was written in the second half of the seventeenth century by Thomas Sprat, Bishop of Rochester. The poet Cowley prefaced it poetically, stating the book's polemical and apologetic themes with that greater verve and vigour which, in mundane matters, the poet can more easily afford than the bishop. The poem celebrates Philosophy or Reason, referred to as He, for—so we are told—it is a 'Male Virtue'. Even before the foundation of the Royal Society he was a promising youngster:

> But, oh! the Guardians and the Tutors then,
>   (Some negligent, and some ambitious Men)
>   Would ne'er consent to set him free,
>   Or his own natural Powers to let him see,
> Lest that should put an end to their Authoritie.
> That his own Business he might quite forget,
> They amus'd him with the sports of wanton Wit,
> With the Desserts of Poetry they fed him,
> Instead of solid Meats t'encrease his Force . . .

Luckily, the importer of solid meats was close at hand:

> Bacon at last, a mighty Man, arose,
>   Whom a wise King and Nature chose
>   Lord Chancellor of both their Laws,
> And boldly undertook the injur'd Pupil's Cause.

And how, according to this vision of an early scientific enthusiast, did the Lord Chancellor set about his bold business? Thus:

> From Words, which are but Pictures of the Thought,
> (Though we our Thoughts from them perversely
>   drew)
> To Things, the Mind's right Object, he it brought:
> Like foolish Birds to painted Grapes we flew;
> He sought and gather'd for our Use the true;
> And when on Heaps the chosen Bunches lay,
> He pressed them wisely the mechanic Way,
> Till all their Juice did in one Vessel join,
> Ferment into a Nourishment Divine,
>   The thirsty Soul's refreshing Wine.

Maybe this is the first significantly ludicrous poem ever written. It not only reads like an anticipated parody of Faust's 'Word into Deed', but also states with naive earnestness a theme that for three centuries to come was to pursue the lives and works of poets and artists with a persistent curse, whispering into their ears now the sinister threats of unreality, and now again the subtle temptation of transcendent glory. Can we trace the flight of the foolish birds back to the nest where they were fledged; where on the wings of words, which are but pictures of the thought, they left behind the things, the mind's right object? The bird's-eye view of an immensely complex landscape of time may choose for closer inspection a scene in Marburg. There a theological dispute is in progress. The disputants are two powerful theologian-reformers of the sixteenth century: Martin Luther and Ulrich Zwingli. To the modern lay-mind their debate may seem like mere scholastic hair-splitting, but history would suggest that it was more like Samson's hair-cut. Its consequences most certainly unsteadied the pillars upon which a great house stood.

The dispute is about the nature of the eucharist, the sacrament of the Lord's Supper. The bread and the wine —are they the body and blood of Christ, or are they 'mere symbols'? Luther, with all his deviations from the traditional dogma, is the man of the Middle Ages. The word and the sign are for him not merely 'pictures of the thought', but the thing itself. Yet for Zwingli, steeped in the enlightened thought of the Italian Renaissance, this is a barbarous absurdity. The sacrament is 'merely' a symbol, that is, it symbolically represents what in itself it is not.

This is indeed a very particular occasion. It is a unique and uniquely sacred symbol that is being discussed. The issue is clearly defined and specified. It is not even new. There are precedents for it throughout the history of Christian theology. All this should warn us against facile generalizations. Yet there remains the fact that never before had this question raised so much dust and generated so much heat. For now it is merely the theological climax of a deep revolution in the thoughts and feelings with which men respond to the world they inhabit; the Miltonian opportunity for a 'Truth who, when she gets a free and willing hand, opens herself faster than the pace of method and discourse can overtake her'. It is now that thirty years of war lie ahead, and the slow emergence of an age in which not only the sacraments but the holiness of all that is holy will cease to be 'literally true'. There will be a world which must find it more and more difficult even to grasp, let alone accept, what was in Luther's mind when he fought Zwingli's 'demythologising' (an activity as hazardous as the word that expresses it, tongue-twister for angels and be-devilling the minds of men.) Lost will be that unity of word and deed, of picture and thing, of the bread and the glorified body. Body will become merely body, and symbol merely symbol. And as for the refreshing wine, it will be drunk by thirsty souls only when in the very depths of their thirst they are quite sure that it was pressed from real grapes in the mechanic way.

What, then, is the nature of the revolution signalled by a theological dispute that seems concerned merely with degrees of symbolic 'literalness'? And what, above all, has it to do with our subject, which is the fortunes of modern poetry? Perhaps we can answer both questions at once by saying that Zwingli's argument did to the status of religion, poetry, and art what some time later Copernicus did to the status of the earth. As the earth was to become merely a planet in the company of planets, so now the spirit of poetry became merely a spirit in the society of spirits. Of course, I do not confuse a theological controversy with an exercise in aesthetic theory. But I do suggest that at the end of a period that we rather vaguely call the Middle Ages there occurred a radical change in man s idea of reality, in that complex fabric of unconsciously held convictions about what is real and what is not. This was a revolution comparable to that earlier one which Nietzsche called the victory of the Socratic mind over the spirit of Dionysian tragedy. And indeed both victories saddled us with the unending bother of aesthetic philosophy. Plato was the first great man of Greece who charged poetry with the offence of confounding man's soberly useful notions about reality, an indictment that led to Aristotle's theory about the 'use' of tragedy. And ever since Zwingli the most common response to the reality of symbols has been a shrugging of shoulders, or an edified raising of eyes and brows, or an apologia for poetry, or an aesthetic theory.

It would, of course, be absurd to believe that before the triumph of that reason which Cowley celebrated, men were less able than we are (and are we really so able?) to distinguish between illusion and reality, between lunacy and common sense. This would be putting the question in terms that do not apply, because these are the terms of modernity. It is even possible that on

T

the level of an *élite* the ability to discriminate was more assured than is ours. For only when the spiritual is known and felt to be real, can there be realistic discrimination between things that claim to be things of the spirit. These men held in their hands, touching and weighing it, the reality of the infinite; we have merely its taste. And it is wiser, or so they say, not to judge in a conflict of tastes—*de gustibus non disputandum*. They knew the symbol when they saw it; we only see it, and are left in the dark. For it is merely a symbol, and may mean this or that or nothing on earth.

One way of speaking of the revolution I have in mind is to say that it reduced the stature of the symbol to the *merely* symbolic. Thus it deprived the language of religion as well as of art of an essential degree of reality. At the beginning the separation proved most beneficial to both partners. Reality, freed from its commitments to the symbol, became more really real than before. The hand of man, reaching out for his reality, was no longer unsteadied by the awe and fear of the symbolic mystery. He acquired the surgeon's hygienic dexterity. And reality, pressed the mechanic way, yielded ample nourishment, real if not divine. As reality became more real, so the symbol became more symbolic and art more artistic. The artist ceased to be a humble craftsman, supplying goods for the common trade between Heaven and earth. He set himself up as a dealer in very special specialties, with a Heaven all to himself and an earth to look down upon.

But there were also signs of uneasiness. They mounted to a climax of tension in the seventeenth century. What was first felt to be a liberation appeared more and more as a robbery. Robbed of its real significance, what did the symbol signify? Robbed of its symbolic meaning, what did reality mean? What was the State on earth? A Leviathan. What was God? More and more a *deus absconditus*, an infinitely remote and impenetrably veiled God. This was not only the century of Newton, the century of cosmic tidiness and calculable pulls and pushes. This it was indeed in the sphere of 'reality', that obedient patient under the fingers of man's mind. But in the sphere of the soul, disobedient sufferer of God's anger and grace, it was the century of Pascal and Hobbes, of the desperate and once more triumphant convolutions of the baroque, and of the metaphysical poets. Commerce between the separated spheres, felt to be urgent again, moved uneasily, intensely, and anxiously along disrupted lines of communication. Strategical points had to be gained by cunning, break-throughs to be dared with the passion of spiritual violence. The baroque was the architectural style of such manoeuvres of the soul. And as for spiritual cunning, it was in the conceits of metaphysical poetry, in the self-conscious ambiguities of poetical language (there are, we are told, as many types of it as deadly sins), and in the paradoxes of Pascal's religious thought. For ambiguity and paradox are the manner of speaking when reality and symbol, man's mind and his soul, are at cross-purposes.

The estrangement was to continue. The symbol was made homeless in the real world, and the real world made itself a stranger to the symbol. Architecture, the most 'real' of all the arts, steadily declined. After the seventeenth century Europe no longer dwelt or worshipped or ruled in buildings created in the image of authentic spiritual vision. For all that was real was an encumbrance to the spirit who, in his turn, only occasionally called on the real, and even then with the embarrassment of an uninvited guest. He was most at home where there was least 'reality'—in music. The music of modern Europe is the one and only art in which it surpassed the achievement of former ages. This is no accident of history: it is the speechless triumph of the spirit in a world of words without deeds and deeds without words.

The great revolutions in human history do not change

the face of the earth. They change the face of man, the image in which he beholds himself and the world around him. The earth merely follows suit. It is the truly pathetic fallacy of empiricism that it offers as safe harbour what is the ocean itself, the storms, the waves and the ship-wrecks, namely man's experience of himself and the 'objective' world. The history of human kind is a re-pository of scuttled objective truths, and a museum of irrefutable facts—refuted not by empirical discoveries, but by man's mysterious decisions to experience differ-ently from time to time. All relevant objective truths are born and die as absurdities. They come into being as the monstrous claim of an inspired rebel and pass away with the eccentricity of a superstitious crank. Only between these extremities of the mind is 'objective truth' truly true, alive at the centre of everything. Then this truth inspires the deeds of men and helps them to form the images of faith. Thus 'objective truth' is equally at work in the totems and taboos of savages, the pyramids of Egypt, the gods and centaurs of the Olympian friezes, the cosmology of Dante and the theory of the expanding universe. And who, I wonder, could journey from Delphi to the Byzantine monastery of Hosios Lucas, leaving the Charioteer in the morning, and in the evening gazing at the mosaic Madonna in the apse of the monastery's church, without being followed into his dreams by echoes from the abyss that divides throughout the ages truth from truth, and the image of man from the image of man?

The ostrich is said to bury his head in the sand at the approach of inescapable danger. Experience is to the empiricist what the sand is to the ostrich's head. Truth, however, does not reside in that which is both blinding and shifting. Only the inescapable danger that there may be no Truth is inescapably true. Hence it is not empirical knowledge that is the organ of Truth. What is empirically true and real now is largely what has escaped the atten-tion of the past, and will escape from the future as a boring anachronism. Uncertainty alone is ineluctably real. It is through despair that man escapes from even this inescapable reality. But he meets it in faith, recognizing it without losing hope and suffering it not without love.

The elusiveness of this faith and the persistent closeness of that despair make modern poetry the hazardous enterprise that it is. True, the poet is at all times more easily afflicted than others by despair and the waning of faith. But these are more than individual perils in our age, for at its very centre is an amorphous indecision. The physicists, always busy empirically to vindicate metaphysical notions about the nature of the world, seem today more directly preoccupied with the metaphysical beliefs insensibly accepted by the community. With the precision of mathematical reasoning they explore the terrible imprecision of our faith. For both our faith and our physics are fascinated by the vast voids inside and outside everything that exists, by empty fields of tension, and by the indeterminate motion of particles senselessly speeding around one another in order to hide from themselves the nothingness at the core of all things.

This, it seems, is the consummation of that revolution of which I have spoken. Before it began, the world, with its bread and its wine, was in all its sinfulness the centre of divine attention. From this obstinate supervision man struggled into a new freedom. He exercised it gloriously within the vast symbolic space that lies between divine presence and divine remoteness. He learned to speak his own language. But the more freely he spoke, the less the word counted. For it became the sport of wanton wit. And thought's more reliable objects were therefore things, the true outcome of the deed that was at the beginning. At the end there may be neither words nor deeds, but merely, for all we know, a slight disease, a rash of matter that matters little to so robust a body of nothingness.

Against this background I invite you to ponder the problems of modern poetry—problems that poetry shares with all the other arts. Therefore, in speaking about poetry we always mean more than poetry, just as poetry always means more than itself. What is it, then, that poetry means? Its meaning is the vindication of the worth and value of the world, of life and of human experience. At heart all poetry is praise and celebration. Its joy is not mere pleasure, its lamentation not mere weeping, and its despair not mere despondency. Whatever it does, it cannot but confirm the existence of a meaningful world —even when it denounces its meaninglessness. Poetry means order, even with the indictment of chaos; it means hope, even with the outcry of despair. It is concerned with the true stature of things. And being concerned with the true stature of things, all great poetry is realistic.

But what is to happen if doubt about the true stature of things invades the very sphere of experience and intuitive insight in which poetry is formed? If suspicion attacks the value of the real world? Then the poetic impulse will seek refuge in a sphere all its own, a little cosmos of inwardness salvaged from the devaluation of the world. 'The Discovery and Colonisation of Inwardness'—this might be a fitting title for the story of poetry from the Renaissance to our day. It begins with the vitality of adventurers, driven from their homeland by the impoverishment of its soil, and culminates in the display of unexpected treasures. Will it end with the homesickness of a defeated race? Or with the father's return to the prodigal son?

2

I said that all great poetry is concerned with the true stature of things; also that it is the vindication of a valuable and meaningful world. Saying this, I implied that the true stature of things lies in their having a meaningful place in a valuable world. Clearly, this was a pronouncement of faith, or, in terms more in keeping with the prevalent manner of speaking, the begging of a question—in fact, of the very question which the mind of the age seems bent on answering in the negative. The perpetual threat of this negative answer is, I suggested, one of the embarrassments of modern poetry.

Reason, as we have come to understand and exercise it, that is, reason as it dominates most of our rational activities, must, in the course of its own progress, lead to this negative answer. In a sense it is even true to say that it *is* this negative answer. For its chosen virtue is 'objectivity'. And what is its objectivity if not the determination to let 'things' have their own way in their dealings with the mind, and not to allow the human affections to interfere with the advance or direction of discovery—in other words, to follow the argument wherever it will take us? This virtue of rational objectivity is indeed both a trusting and a heroic virtue, and only self-seeking rogues or eccentric simpletons will wish to dispense with it lightheartedly. On the other hand, only simpletons with no self to seek and no centre to leave can for ever remain unaware of the problem raised by the very trust and heroism of objectivity. What is its trust? The conviction that the argument will lead to something that is not only of use, but of true value. What is its heroism? The readiness not to flinch if it does not. And what is its fallacy? The assumption that the values, banned from the method of enquiry, will yet make their way into the answers; that means, indifferent to values, can yield an end justified not merely by its 'correctness' or its usefulness, but by its intrinsic value. For things lose their value for man if he is set on withholding it from them.

The human affections are the only instruments of recognizing and responding to values. By treating the affections as the rascals in the school of reason, and as the peace-breakers in the truth-bound community, Reason—the rationalist's reason—has set up a kind of truth which leaves the human affections as idle as do, by general consent, the 'objective' methods that lead to its discovery. The workshops in which our truths are manufactured are surrounded by swarms of unemployed affections. Unemployment leads to riots, and riots there were and are. The most powerful among them in the recent history of thought was romanticism. The war between rationalism and romanticism has left modern poetry with its hazardous legacy.

Nietzsche, who lived and thought at the very centre of the turmoil, knew that in this situation the most urgent business of philosophy was the problem of values—a business uneasily shirked by philosophy to this very day. To him this problem was more fundamental than all the problems of knowledge. These, he said, are serious only if the question of values is answered; and without this answer the pursuit of knowledge may cease to be serious, becoming desperate instead, 'a handsome tool for man's self-destruction', as he called it.

If it is not in the rationalistic pursuits of objective knowledge but only through the exercise of human affections that the question of values can be answered, can it then be answered at all? Is knowledge, gained in this way, not necessarily as elusive and as fickle, as deceptive and as unreliable, as are the human affections themselves? And if poetry is what we believe it to be, namely the affections' appeal to the affections, what sort of truth or value can there be in poetry? There is, it seems, an odd disparity between the seriousness with which poets view their profession, and the use to which it is put. They toil in the exacting service of the spirit in order to please the spirit's more frivolous moods. This has been the quixotic predicament of poetry—and not only of poetry—throughout the modern age. It came to a climax when rationalism and romanticism between them contrived to destroy the last remnants of a rational order of values.

The recovery of a rational order of values was, in this

period, a task to which some of the greatest thinkers and
poets dedicated themselves. Among thinkers the truest
and most passionate was Pascal. The inventor of the cal-
culating machine—of an embryonic mechanical brain—
also knew that the heart had reasons of which reason
knew nothing. And Pascal meant *reasons* of the heart,
not that unreason of the emotions with which the romantic mind so often vented its exasperation at the
rationality of mechanical brains. The *esprit de finesse*
which he, the mathematician, opposed to the *esprit de
géométrie* had nothing to do with the emotional whims
of the irrational. Mind it was, if ever there was mind—
mind, intelligence, reason, an instrument of rational
knowledge, of rationally knowing *logos*, sense and value.
Pascal's *coeur* is the organ of recognizing what is at the
heart of things. His reasoning of the heart is the method
of discourse when the subject of the discourse is not the
logic of propositions but the logic of values. Here is the
source of that strange fascination that this most passionately Christian thinker of the seventeenth century had
for the most passionately anti-Christian mind of the
nineteenth—Nietzsche.

Both these men's minds were focused on the problem
of values, and it is not by accident but by reason of history that for Nietzsche this preoccupation so often took
the form of a seemingly aesthetic problem—the problem
of the relationship between poetry and truth. This was,
he said at the end of his conscious life, the first serious
concern of his youth and the 'holy terror' of his later years.
And to him it was identical with the question of the truth
or untruth of values. For in the period between Pascal
and Nietzsche it was above all in poets and artists that
this essentially religious problem retained its vexing
vigour. And if it inspired their most sublime thoughts, it
also was a constant strain on their poetic resources.

To support this by examples would amount to making
a dictionary of celebrated names—Blake, Wordsworth,

Coleridge, Keats; in France almost every poet between
Baudelaire and Valéry; in Germany above all Goethe,
Hölderlin, and Rilke—not to mention the theoretical writings of Schiller and the Romantics. And if we search for
the most precise words in order to define the hazards of
modern poetry, I doubt whether we need go on after
finding Hölderlin's great poem *Bread and Wine*:

> . . . *und wozu Dichter in dürftiger Zeit?*

> . . . in such spiritless times, why to be poet at all?

What was this *dürftige Zeit*, this time poor in spirit but
further than any from the Kingdom of Heaven, that made
Hölderlin question the justification of being a poet; this
meagre but forceful time that pushed poetry to the very
edge of silence, of that 'abyss' that Baudelaire too sensed
at the feet of poetry; this hostile time that yet inspired
in Hölderlin, and in Baudelaire, and in Rimbaud, poetry
truly unheard of before? For in their poetry speechlessness itself seemed to burst into speech without breaking
the silence. It was poetry separated from madness by the
mere margin of the miracle that reveals in one moment
the lucid depths of mystery at the price of darkness for
what afterwards remains of life. What indeed was the
dürftige Zeit?

It was a time in which bread and wine were mere com-
modities; a time in which reality meant nothing and
meaning was unreal; and if its sense of reality was to be
the measure of that 'real' which the poet, following Aristotle's precept, was to 'imitate', then poetry had to cease
to be poetry. It was a time of which Hegel, Hölderlin's
contemporary, said that 'art . . . is and will remain a
thing of the past' because 'the mode of prose has absorbed all the concepts of the mind and impressed them
with its prosaic stamp'. And in his awkward philosophical language he yet described exactly the hazards that

lay ahead for poetry. 'Poetry', he said, 'will have to take on the business of so thorough a recasting and remodelling of reality that, faced with the unyielding mass of the prosaic, it will find itself involved everywhere in manifold difficulties'.

Hegel was proved wrong—by poetry, not by reality. But at what a cost! One is almost tempted to say: at the cost of Hölderlin's sanity and the survival of Rimbaud's genius. And certainly at the cost of poetry's simplicity, of that profound simplicity which is the most precious fruit of peace prevailing between the poet's thought and the thought of his age. This peace is in the Homeric battles, in Aeschylus' tragedies, and even in Dante's descent into Hell. But it is nowhere in Hölderlin's poetry, not even in its sublime moments of utter tranquillity. For these come to pass when the exile finds a home with exiles, when the rootless poet is received into the company of rootless gods:

Aber wo sind sie? . . . über dem Haupt droben in anderer Welt.

Where, though, where are they? . . . far above ourselves, away in a different world.

The belief that the poet seeks inspiration in being beside himself is, even in its most 'classical' forms, a romantic fallacy. This fallacy has, ever since Schopenhauer, informed many of our most widely accepted aesthetic theories: for instance, the theory of the 'impersonal' character of poetry, of the poet as a neutral agent bringing about the fusion and crystallisation of nameless experience. These theories merely express, and express significantly, the spiritual depreciation of the real lives that real selves lead in the real world. It is neither in 'depersonalisation' nor in intoxication that the great poet finds his poetic self, but in that sobriety of vision which sees what really is. Hölderlin called it *heilige Nüchtern-heit*, 'holy sobriety', and Valéry once said, paradoxically: 'If I were to write, I would infinitely rather write something weak, in full consciousness and in complete lucidity, than give birth to a masterpiece in a state of trance'.

'Where sobriety leaves you', wrote Hölderlin, 'there is also the limit of your inspiration. The great poet is never beside himself'. To ponder this sentence, and then go to Hölderlin's greatest poetry, and then remember his fate—these are three acts of realising a tragedy. It is not only Hölderlin's tragedy, but the tragedy of a world that has set up its own sober reality on the far side of the poet's sobriety, and has pushed the poet to a place where he, who is never beside himself, is beside the world. And when Hölderlin defines poetic sobriety as the intellectual power to discover for every particular thing its rightful place within the whole, adding that there can be no excellence in either art or life 'without reason or thoroughly organised feelings', then the most lucidly true vision of poetry and life throws into relief the falsity of a thoroughly disorganised reality in which life has no poetry and poetry no life. And in such a homeless world the poet's home-coming is an adventure beset by incomprehensible dangers. For where there is neither holiness nor spirit, there the holy sobriety of the spirit is like addiction to intoxicants. And when reason insists on the sole validity of its reasons, then the heart, Pascal's heart, is broken by the very force of its own rationality.

What really is appears at such a time like the vision of a visionary, and the realism of great poetry becomes 'metaphysical'; not, however, by wilfully deserting the physical world, but by being left outside through a peculiar contraction of the circumference of the real.

Yet we must not lose sight of a fact that we have so far deliberately neglected in order to bring out more clearly a distinctive quality of modern poetry. Poetry, at all times, is not merely descriptive and imitative in the Aristotelian sense. It is always also creative; creative indeed in the sense of making things that were not there before —and the derivation of the word 'poetry' points to just this kind of 'making'. But it is creative also in a profounder and more elusive sense. Poetry heightens and cultivates the creative element that is in experience itself. For experience is not in the impressions we receive; it is in *making* sense. And poetry is the foremost sense-maker of experience. It renders *actual* ever new sectors of the apparently inexhaustible field of *potential* experience. This is why the poet is, as I said in my first talk, an easier prey to doubt and despair than people content to live with the sense made by others.

Every civilized society lives and thrives on a silent but profound agreement as to what is to be accepted as the valid mould of experience. Civilization is a complex system of dams, dykes, and canals warding off, directing, and articulating the influx of the surrounding fluid element; a fertile fenland, elaborately drained and protected from the high tides of chaotic, unexercised, and inarticulate experience. In such a culture, stable and sure of itself within the frontiers of 'naturalised' experience, the arts wield their creative power not so much in width as in depth. They do not create new experience, but deepen and purify the old. Their works do not differ from one another like a new horizon from a new horizon, but like a madonna from a madonna.

The periods of art which are most vigorous in creative passion seem to occur when the established pattern of experience loosens its rigidity without as yet losing its force. Such a period was the Renaissance, and Shakespeare its poetic consummation. Then it was as though the discipline of the old order gave depth to the excitement of the breaking away, the depth of joy and tragedy, of incomparable conquests and irredeemable losses. Adventurers of experience set out as though in lifeboats to rescue and bring back to the shore treasures of knowing and feeling which the old order had left floating on the high seas. The works of the early Renaissance and the poetry of Shakespeare vibrate with the compassion for live experience in danger of dying from exposure and neglect. In this compassion was the creative genius of the age. Yet it was a genius of courage, not of desperate audacity. For, however elusively, it still knew of harbours and anchors, of homes to which to return, and of barns in which to store the harvest. The exploring spirit of art was in the depths of its consciousness still aware of a scheme of things into which to fit its exploits and creations.

But the more this scheme of things loses its stability, the more boundless and uncharted appears the ocean of potential exploration. In the blank confusion of infinite potentialities flotsam of significance gets attached to jetsam of experience; for everything is sea, everything is at sea—

> . . . the sea is all about us;
> The sea is the land's edge also, the granite
> Into which it reaches, the beaches where it tosses
> Its hints of earlier and other creation . . .

—and Rilke tells a story in which, as in Mr. T. S. Eliot's poem, it is again the sea and the distance of 'other creation' that becomes the image of the poet's reality. A rowing boat sets out on a difficult passage. The oarsmen labour in exact rhythm. There is no sign yet of the destination. Suddenly a man, seemingly idle, breaks out into song. And if the labour of the oarsmen meaninglessly defeats the real resistance of the real waves, it is the idle singer who magically conquers the despair of apparent aimlessness. While the people next to him try to come to grips with the element that is next to them, his voice seems to bind the boat to the farthest distance so that the farthest distance draws it towards itself. 'I don't know why and how', is Rilke's conclusion, 'but suddenly I understood the situation of the poet, his place and function in this age. It does not matter if one denies him every place—except this one. There one must tolerate him'.

It is the farthest distance to which the poet is bound. What is next to him does not matter. Yet at any moment anything that is next to him may be illumined by sparks struck from the invisible wire that binds his boat to its mysteriously distant destination. The humblest object or the tiniest shred of experience may unexpectedly become a conductor of infinity, charged with a force that was once distributed over a whole comprehensive order holding in their right places the great and little things. This order is no more. Who knows our place, or the place of anything? Where are the links that join the creation with the creator, and creature with creature? This is the theme of Rilke's first *Duino Elegy*. Everything is separate; dissociation is the order of the world:

> . . . *Ach, wen vermögen*
> *wir denn zu brauchen? Engel nicht, Menschen nicht,*
> *und die findigen Tiere merken es schon,*
> *dass wir nicht sehr verlässlich zu Haus sind*
> *in der gedeuteten Welt* . . .

> . . . Alas, who is there
> we can make use of? Not angels, not men;
> and already the knowing brutes are aware
> that we don't feel very securely at home
> within our interpreted world . . .

Yet here or there, out of place and out of order, a strangely arbitrary object seems to mean everything to us:

. . . Es bleibt uns vielleicht
irgend ein Baum an dem Abhang, dass wir ihn täglich
wiedersähen; es bleibt uns die Strasse von gestern
und das verzogene Treusein einer Gewohnheit,
der es bei uns gefiel, und so blieb sie und ging nicht.

. . . There remains, perhaps,
some tree on a slope, to be looked at day after day;
there remains for us yesterday's road and the cup-
    board-love loyalty
of a habit that liked us and stayed and never gave
    notice.

The portraitist of this situation is Van Gogh. He
painted the tree of Rilke's elegy, the sunflower, the chair
and the boots that are the chance receptacles of all the
homeless energy of the spirit which had once its lawful
house with Giotto's angels and madonnas—once a king
of kingdoms, now a squatter in boots. Look at this bough
of almond blossom, look at this chair—indeed, they get
much more than their due of the spirit, almost bursting
with its superfluity. It is a mere moment of explosion that
separates Van Gogh's objects from the distorted fragments of surrealism.

The notorious obscurity of modern poetry is due to
the absence from our lives of commonly accepted symbols to represent and house our deepest feelings. And so
these invade the empty shells of fragmentary memories,
hermit-crabs in a sea of uncertain meaning. We may yet
reach the moon. Interplanetary traffic will soon prove
easier than communication between countless private
universes. For the following lines of Mr. T. S. Eliot are
not only true of words before the ultimate mystery; they
also apply to words caught in the penultimate muddle:

. . . Words strain,
Crack and sometimes break, under the burden,

Under the tension, slip, slide, perish,
Decay with imprecision . . .

3

Goethe, in his autobiography, complains angrily about the contempt with which occasional poetry has come to be regarded. Occasional poetry, poetry prompted by real occasions, is, he says, 'the first and most genuine of all types of poetry'. And in a conversation with Eckermann he made it quite clear that he did not mean merely rhymed toasts. 'All my poems', he said, 'are occasional poems; they are inspired by reality and founded on it. I think nothing of poetry that has no roots in the real'. Of course, this was aimed at the Romantics, a warning sounded into what he called the 'epoch of forced talents'.

What were these forced talents? To Goethe they were hot-house plants out of season, poets who left 'life' out in the cold and flowered in the heat of a purely reflective imagination. Goethe's irritation with them was so intense because he himself already knew the temptation. His Tasso is conceived half-way between the real Tasso and Baudelaire, and his Werther, had he survived a century or so, might have become Rimbaud. And if Goethe had completed the fragmentary masterpiece, *Pandora*, his Epimetheus might indeed have left the real wholly to Prometheus, choosing himself to rise, with Pandora in his arms, to a sphere where Mallarmé's *rêve dans sa nudité idéale* is realised. Did Goethe not, on two solemn poetic occasions, define the poet's distinctive gift from the gods as the power to say what he suffered—suffered at the hands of the real world? Indeed, Goethe's realism was already on the defensive. The peace in which he lived with the real world—his proudest possession, the most precious show-piece of the collector—was maintained only by endless diplomatic manoeuvres and compromises with the innate tendencies of his genius.

U

Occasional poetry, indeed! But the occasion was not always the real. More often it was the war between reality and poetry. How would Goethe have reacted to Nietzsche's belief that world and existence are justified only as an aesthetic phenomenon?—a declaration that contains the complete programme of that kind of poetry which, one-sidedly and ignoring many a poet of great merit, we have chosen to see as distinctively modern. No doubt, Goethe would have reacted with horror, but with a horror the greater for its intimate knowledge of the horrifying. For although Nietzsche had not yet arrived, Goethe knew and undecidedly opposed the philosophy of Immanuel Kant. And between Kant and Nietzsche there is a connection which does not lack in historical logic, and certainly not in that logic by which so much of modern poetry has come into being.

To cut a long and complicated story short: Kant brought to a dramatic halt the triumphal procession of rationalism. If Descartes was sure that rational thought was the firm anchor of existence—*cogito ergo sum*—then Kant was equally sure that thinking merely sailed through existence like a ship on the surface of the sea, exploring much, but always hemmed in by its own horizon. However far-away a distance the voyager may reach, there will always be horizon, the horizon of space and time, and for ever out of sight the ultimate ground and harbour—the Absolute. Therefore it was not in pure reason, in the rationalist's reason, that man could hope to find that final certainty the continual quest for which seems to be the flaw and crux and glory of his nature. Indeed, Kant did not deny the legitimacy of its claims; they had to be satisfied—not, however, through man's rational consciousness, but through his moral conscience. The moral law was the tool of the Absolute.

This came as a shock to poets who had begun to believe that, more than priests, they were in touch with the Absolute. Kleist was in despair. Schiller's aesthetic philosophy was an endless bargaining with Kant: give me a share, and be it a modest one, in the great Inaccessible; I shall pay in good moral currency for the sublime aesthetic pass. The Romantics, of course, went further. Taking Kant's constitutional monarchy of Reason for its abdication, they rushed Feeling to the empty throne. Nor was the disturbance confined to Germany. The Germans, willing executioners to the court of history, merely carried out a vague but commanding European order. Coleridge, too, received and accepted it. It reached Baudelaire by way of Schopenhauer and Richard Wagner. And even Goethe, who rarely allowed himself to be worried by philosophical upheavals, once frowningly resigned himself to Kant's dictate of 'absolute' ignorance without, however, trusting in the reliability of the Kantian moral guidance. 'Therefore', he noted at the end of a reflection about Kant's philosophy, 'we shall escape into poetry where we may hope to find some satisfaction'.

Goethe's urbane resignation was soon to turn into a manifesto of 'absolute' poetry. Prefigured in Schelling and Schopenhauer, the promotion of the aesthetic faculty to the minister of the Absolute was accomplished in Nietzsche's early philosophy. The world is at heart an aesthetic phenomenon. No knowledge and no moral law can comprehend its meaning. It is music that sounds its very depths, and poetry that circles around the central mystery—poetry illuminated, like the moon, by a distant sun, and illuminating, like the moon, the obscurity of the night. 'Only as an aesthetic phenomenon are world and existence for ever justified'. Nietzsche called this the artist's gospel—and again and again he returned to the belief that it was the only gospel of truth to be had on earth. Whenever he doubted its validity, he was left with Nothing, with that nihilism of which he was the grand, desperate, and despairingly hopeful explorer. For he was a late-comer in the succession that leads from Kant to Schopenhauer, and from Schopenhauer to Richard Wagner and Baudelaire. Nietzsche, in his time, went even further than Mallarmé. '*Après avoir trouvé le Néant, j'ai trouvé le Beau*', said Mallarmé. Nietzsche discovered an ever profounder Nothing each time he suspected that the Beautiful was mere illusion.

One year before his death Goethe published a message to young poets. He asked them to remember that poetry may well accompany life, but does not know how to guide it. However ambitious the artist may be, he added, in the end he will find that he has expressed merely his own individuality; for 'what is in a poem is essentially the same as that which is in one's own life'. It seems that poetry travelled an immeasurable distance in the forty years between Goethe's message and Nietzsche's *Birth of Tragedy*. A pleasant companion became a tyrannical master. What Goethe took to be the expression of the poet's personality was suddenly felt to be a suicidal weapon, killing the person in order to set free the absolute soul. This was not only the epoch of forced talents, as Goethe feared; it was the epoch of poetical martyrdom. Its heroes were selfless commissioners of the Absolute, fasting their lives out to produce the heavenly food, drugging and deranging their senses to catch a glimpse of the invisible. 'I am incompetent at everything except the Absolute', said Mallarmé, and Baudelaire felt he had buried, 'all my heart, all my tenderness, all my religion, all my hatred' under the Flowers of Evil. For it is through poetry, he said, that 'the soul sees glories beyond the grave'.

In the beginning was Kant, putting in order the world of reason and senses by shutting out the great Unknown; in the end was Rimbaud, letting in the great Unknown by 'slowly and deliberately confusing all his senses, drugging himself with every conceivable poison' and reaching the Holy of Holies as 'the great invalid and criminal', 'supreme scholar' of the Mystery and 'damned citizen' of the real world. For it is only as an aesthetic phenomenon that the world is justified.

To the devaluation of everything that is in the world —and, therefore, as Goethe still believed, also in poetry and art—that is, to the cheapening of all content corresponds the artist's heightened consciousness of the value and significance of pure form. And if all the meanings that are in words have become as worn and shabby as the cheap wares of traders in second-hand utilities, then the poet will trust pure sound to yield the vibrating intimations of the Absolute. Of course, art is at all times concerned with form, and poetry at all times not indifferent to sound. What matters here is the degree of emphasis and awareness, the distribution of significance and the scope of cultivation. Who, I wonder, could have said, before a Romantic poet, Novalis, said it, that there ought to be poems of mere beautiful sounds and beautiful words, disconnected and without sense? And who before Baudelaire could even have felt what Nietzsche saw and knew—that the artist experiences that which all non-artists call form as the content and the thing itself? For what Nietzsche had in mind was not what Goethe meant by form—*geprägte Form, die lebend sich entwickelt*—but an extreme which he himself denounced as perverse; an obsession with form *as* content, turning all real contents into 'mere formalities', including, as he added, our own lives. He meant, in fact, *le goût immodéré de la forme*, of which Baudelaire knew only too well that it led to 'disorders, monstrous and unheard-of'.

If Goethe still believed that 'life' was the inspiration of his 'occasional poetry', then in the nineteenth century a kind of poetry emerged that found its occasion in life's loss of inspiration. Valéry called it 'absolute' poetry. It was the confounding climax of the history of self-conscious artistic creativeness as it began at the time of the Renaissance. Hand in hand with it went a steady devaluation of the created world. At that climax nothing real seemed of value any more. Value was the contraband of unreality smuggled into the real world by cunning poets. Poetic creativeness became the illicit traffic in smuggled goods. The inflation of the real was both cause and effect of desperate investments in unreal property. Real contents were worthless; pure form was what mattered. The meaning of words meant nothing; their sound was the thing. Everything that was not created by the artist himself was felt to be dead and deadening matter; its mere touch threatened to paralyse the hand of the creator. Mallarmé cried out for 'immaculate words', esoteric hieroglyphs unsoiled by common meaning, and envied music—music again!—its ethereal medium. It was as though a creative furore without parallel in the history of the arts had been let loose in order to undo the done-for world and start afresh from chaos, this time working on a pattern more promising than that of the seven days which had led to so dismal a failure. Fishes swam through the air, the water teemed with birds, and from a rib of Eve's, Adam created God. For 'true anarchy', Novalis had predicted, 'is the creative element of true religion. It rises from total destruction as the creator of a new world'.

Its rising, however, met with considerable difficulties. The Symbolist and Surrealist impulse soon spent itself. Baudelaire already knew that this frenzied passion of art was a canker. No lasting universe of beauty was built from the fragments of creation. In the end they remained fragments shored against the poet's ruins. He was back in the waste land. The real world went to war. A seventeenth-century vision seemed to come true once more: 'No arts; no letters; no society; and which is worst of all, continual fear and danger of violent death; and the life of man, solitary, poor, nasty, brutish, and short'. Poetry lost confidence in its power magically to illuminate its self-created magical world. It woke up to a new concern for reality. I do not mean the vigorous yet short-lived political intermezzo of poetry between the two wars, but its slow, gradual realization of traditional poetic virtues. On devious routes and with varying success some poets returned to a new realism. Although there are even signs of a new simplicity, it is not this that I have in mind; and perhaps simplicity is not yet to be had without poets forcing the pace and losing depth. For in the deeper regions of consciousness Mr. T. S. Eliot's diagnosis is still, I think, true:

Because one has only learnt to get the better of words
For the thing one no longer has to say, or the way in
   which
One is no longer disposed to say it. And so each
   venture
Is a new beginning, a raid on the inarticulate
With shabby equipment always deteriorating
In the general mess of imprecision of feeling,
Undisciplined squads of emotion . . .

This is more than a description of the traditional predicament of poetry: it is also more than a statement of one particular poet's difficulties. It is said about poetry 'under conditions that seem unpropitious', about poetry in our world. Poetry is not always a raid on the inarticulate with shabby equipment. There are times when the raid is less violent, the inarticulate less obstinate, and equipment less shabby. It is at such times that poetry can be both simple and profound. It is then that the poet gets the better of words for the thing he has to say, because things then are not the nameless products of 'imageless deeds' (as Rilke called them) and words therefore not without object. Nor has the poet then to hunt up from the furthest recesses of soul and mind the thing that is worth saying, for the thing worth saying never ventures so far afield from the city of man.

It is not simplicity that I mean when I speak of a new poetic realism. What I do mean is the poet's concern for the place and stature of man in the real world. Compared with the Symbolists' chase after cosmic substances of insubstantial beauty, compared also with the pure enchantments of Valéry's intellectual imagination, Hofmannsthal, even Stefan George with all his insufferable poses and second-nature affectations, and even the later Rilke are, in this sense, realistic. Rilke's case is certainly the most puzzling of all. True, his 'realism' is forced and always uncertain of itself. Never before have words like 'perhaps' or 'maybe' played so large a part in poetic language. But his *Duino Elegies* do set out to search for man, not for the life-devouring beauty. Beauty is no longer the ultimate and absolute end. On the contrâry,

. . . *Denn das Schöne ist nichts*
als des Schrecklichen Anfang, den wir noch grade
  ertragen,
und wir bewundern es so, weil es gelassen verschmäht,
uns zu zerstören . . .

. . . Beauty is nothing
but the beginning of Terror we're still just able to
  bear,
and why we adore it so is because it serenely
disdains to destroy us. . . .

The Terror which begins with Beauty is in the wholeness and integrity of being; and it terrifies us because we have betrayed it. In betraying it we have corrupted not only ourselves, but all things around us. They fall apart and away, and their place is taken by *ein Tun ohne Bild*, deeds without words or images. It is the end of meaning and sense and thus the end of poetry. That poetry can only be recovered with the recovery of meaning and sense is, paradoxically, the starting-point of the poetry of

Rilke's final phase. Its conclusion is in the paradox of its beginning. The poet, confirmed by his own achievement in his power of song and praise, offers himself, his song and praise, as evidence for meaning and sense. Yet as he was a poet at the outset, this proof proves nothing; and Rilke's search for man's reality ends, once again, with the discovery of a reality that is the poet's own creation.

'The poetry does not matter'. These words from Mr. T. S. Eliot's *Four Quartets* acquire an all but revolutionary significance if we understand them not only in their particular context but also in the context of a period of poetry in which nothing mattered except poetry. Against this background the *Four Quartets* themselves appear, in all their complexity, as the poetry of simple civic virtue—the poetry of a poet trying to read the writing of the law that has become all but illegible. This, you may say, has nothing to do with poetry. On the contrary, it is one of the few truly hopeful signs that this civic virtue could once more be realised poetically. For in speaking of the hazard of modern poetry I did not wish to suggest that the end had come for singers and skylarks. There will always be skylarks; perhaps even a few nightingales. But poetry is not only the human equivalent of the song of singing birds. It is also Virgil, Dante, and Hölderlin. It is also, in its own terms, the definition of the state of man.

4   POSTSCRIPT

Listener

You are a reactionary and an obscurantist. You deplore 'the absence from our lives of commonly accepted symbols to represent and house our deepest feelings'. I suspect this to be a plea for religious *clichés*. Have you no faith in literary exploration, in poetic diversity and creativity, indeed in man?

Speaker

'Faith' strikes me as a misnomer. Faith is an attitude
of the soul towards the unknown. No faith is required
where there is knowledge. The results of centuries of
literary exploration and poetic creativity are known to
us. They mean as much to me as they mean to you. I
cannot imagine myself without them. They have formed
my idea of poetry—and are therefore responsible for
everything I have said in these talks. Do you really think
I have advocated religious *clichés?* I am unaware of
having advocated anything. My sole concern is to understand our situation.

Listener

Your situation.

Speaker

Our situation; yours too. If I had offered you, as you
suspect, a dogmatic 'solution', you would be right; but
your suspicion is wrong. 'Uncertainty alone is ineluctably real'—does this sound like the offer of a dogma?
Although I do not know what you mean by calling me a
reactionary, the 'obscurantist' strikes home. I believe we
are in the dark. Or does your faith in literary exploration, in poetic diversity and creativity, indeed in man,
provide you with a light that I cannot see?

Listener

These big words! Not much light is needed to discern
in your reactionary darkness the unique literary achievement of the European novel. It makes nonsense of your
contention that after the seventeenth century only music
flourished in Europe.

Speaker

My words are apparently not big enough to be noticed
by you. I did not say that only music flourished among
the arts of modern Europe. I said it was her *distinctive*
artistic achievement. It has yet to be seen whether the

novel will live as long as Homer, Virgil and Dante have done. Still, there is no doubt that Stendhal, Tolstoy, Dostoevsky, Henry James have made distinctive contributions to the genre 'literature', and contributions of a kind that I could have quoted in support of what I said. In their own way they raise all my questions—above all, by the fact that their works are written in prose. But be this as it may, I had no intention of belittling any literary achievement of modern Europe, but merely believe the achievement of music to be more distinctive in kind. Besides, compared with the assured artistic form of music the formal aspects of the novel are tentative and experimental.

Listener
For us, there is only the trying.

Speaker
True. And I shall not stop you. Is this what you mean by 'faith in man'?

Listener
Yes.

Speaker
To me it seems more like the faith in what is to be tried. And the faith in poetic creativity has been tried— and by no one, I believe, with as much intensity and poetic success as by Rilke:

*Wir stehn und stemmen uns an unsre Grenzen
und reissen ein Unkenntliches herein.*

When, I ask you, have poets ever felt they were doing this? Standing on their own frontiers, pressing against them, and tearing the unknowable into the confines of poetry? And within the setting of modern poetry Rilke is by no means an eccentric. Where prose is the mode of knowledge, there only the unknowable has a chance of being poetic. Do you know Rilke's poem *Taube, die draussen blieb?* He wrote it a few months before his death:

Taube, die draussen blieb, ausser dem Taubenschlag,
wieder in Kreis und Haus, einig der Nacht, dem Tag,
weiss sie die Heimlichkeit, wenn sich der Einbezug
fremdester Schrecken schmiegt in den gefühlten Flug.

Unter den Tauben, die allergeschonteste,
niemals gefährdetste, kennt nicht die Zärtlichkeit;
wiedererholtes Herz ist das bewohnteste:
freier durch Widerruf freut sich die Fähigkeit.

Über dem Nirgendssein spannt sich das Überall!
Ach der geworfene, ach der gewagte Ball,
füllt er die Hände nicht anders mit Wiederkehr:
rein um sein Heimgewicht ist er mehr.

The poem was written for 'the feast of praise', and the praise is for the precise tenets of your faith—exploration and poetic creativity. Its first stanza speaks of a dove that stayed outside the dovecot, an adventurous and 'creative' dove; but now the dove is back in the dovecot, united with the rest of its fellows in the routine of day and night, and only now, after all its exploits, has it come to know what it means to be at home, for only now is the movement of its wings truly felt and realized, enriched as it is by the assimilation of strangest terrors. Among doves, the second stanza continues, the most protected creature, never exposed to terrible dangers, knows not what gentleness is—as it is the recovered heart that is richest in feeling, and as power rejoices at its greater freedom won through renunciation. Above Being Nowhere, says the third stanza, extends the Everywhere (and the German word 'Überall'—everywhere—also carries the associations of 'above everything'). The ball, jeopardized in the most daring throw,—does it not fill your hands with a new sensation of return? Has it not increased by the pure weight of its home-coming? The time may have come.

Listener
The time for what?

Speaker
The time for the dovecot, for the home-coming, for the realization that we have assimilated as many terrors as we can without being destroyed. There is a point beyond which there is no recovery for the exposed heart. Too many terrors dull the mind, too many riches impoverish the imagination. Can poetry for much longer continue to be everywhere and above everything? On the far side of poetry's everywhere may be yet another nowhere. For the range that 'everywhere' offers to literary exploration is surprisingly limited. Its offer of illimitable freedom is deceptive. It is soon exhausted. Perhaps the fair has come to an end. The big showman has packed all the targets into boxes. The last ball dared hits an empty wall of canvas, canvas gives, and the ball is not returned.

Listener
How do you know?

Speaker
I was there.

Listener
Where?

Speaker
Where the big showman packed the targets into boxes. Where the canvas gave. Where the ball was not returned. Where children wept. Where, having spent their last exploratory sixpence, they cast creativity to the winds and followed another showman who promised them targets and hits.

Listener
I thought we were talking about poetry.

Speaker
So we were. And I am still talking about poetry and literary exploration.

Listener
To me it sounds like politics.

Speaker
And like morality, and like religion.

Listener
Certainly not like aesthetics. Yet are we not, in talking about poetry, concerned only with aesthetics?

Speaker
In talking about poetry we are concerned with aesthetics, and with politics, and with morality, and with religion. I envy you your tidy mind. Yet I suspect that this sort of tidiness can be achieved only in trivial matters. Truth is likely to be untidy, the *enfant terrible* in the systematic household. For the last three centuries the intellectual life of Europe has been dominated by a passion for rational tidiness, critical analysis and constructed systems. The results seem often little more than the logical guise of a constant hankering after trivialities. That which is systematic in a system is merely the trivial aspect of true order.

Listener
You have an irritating predilection for 'merely' and 'only'. Paradoxes too have their trivial aspects.

Speaker
No doubt—particularly when they confound the system for the sake of confusion. They are perhaps less trivial when they explode systematic trivialities for the love of true order.

Listener
And 'true order' can only be grasped 'symbolically'?

Speaker
By no means. True order can only be grasped symbolically.

Listener
I am sorry, but the inverted commas were due to your own obscurity. What is this true order?

Speaker
An order that is true to experience.

Listener
Empiricism? But as you do not mean empiricism, this means nothing to me. Everything is 'experience'—for instance, the experience that there is no true order.

Speaker
And the experience that even this experience has to be fitted into an order. Without *this* experience there would be no art and no poetry; in fact, nothing for us to explore or to talk about. Will you admit that the desire for meaningful order has been so persistent throughout recorded history that it is tempting to regard it as the characteristic stamp of man's nature? It certainly tempted Schopenhauer to call man *animal metaphysicum*. Will you allow me also to accept it as self-evidently true?

Listener
Not without the proviso that it may be nothing more than a persistent symptom of the partial maladjustment of the race. It may be the price paid for physical survival secured against heavy odds by the sheer exercise of intelligence. In realizing her whims Nature is profuse and wasteful. She may have endowed us with more intelligence than was necessary for the struggle of life. Perhaps it is by virtue of this unemployed surplus of intelligence that we ask superfluous questions.

Speaker

Who is paradoxical now? It is by virtue of sheer intelligence that we ask foolish questions. But I grant you your proviso. What follows?

Listener

What I said: that our desire for meaningful order may be meaningless, like letters written to a non-existent address. It is madness to wait for an answer.

Speaker

So Nietzsche may have been right. The *animal metaphysicum* is the diseased animal. It must die out. Let us create the Superman. Precisely that is the meaning of Zarathustra's message.

Listener

Nietzsche became hysterical because he believed God was dead. Funerals often promote hysteria, but there exist more proper ways of mourning.

Speaker

Indeed, and not to mourn at all may be the safest way of avoiding impropriety. Another way would be not to accept the notice of death. This leaves us with three possibilities. One is the belief that we are deluded in asking for meaningful order; the other is the faith that our demand corresponds to a real order of things; the third, I am afraid, is useless for the purpose of our discussion. I mean indifference, and I doubt whether one can be indifferent to this question and yet care for poetry. In fact, I doubt, even without this qualification, whether one can consistently and seriously maintain an attitude of indifference. I suspect it would be mere pose.

Listener

Granted that Nietzsche was most consistent, madly consistent, in exploring one of your two possibilities. What are the implications of the other?

Speaker
That I am right. That the great experiment of separating meaning from reality, and symbol from fact, has ended in failure. That our passion for 'reality' has rendered absurd our desire for meaning. That our insistence on 'fact' has given the lie to truth. That our love of 'truth' has begotten an unlovable world. We have become prisoners of our intellectual freedom, an amorphous mass of victims to our sense of rational order. We are the chaos inhabiting the tidiest of all worlds. We calculate splendidly, but our calculations show that we have not enough to live by; we predict infallibly—even unpredictability is merely a factor within high statistical probability—but what we predict is not worth living for. More often than not it is an eclipse of the sun. What I mean by true order? An order that embodies the incalculable and unpredictable, transcending our rational grasp precisely where it meets the reasons of the heart. The symbol is the body of that which transcends, the measure of the immeasurable and the visible logic of the heart's reasoning. And perhaps the reasoning heart is more single-minded than your faith in permanent exploration and creativity assumes. Perhaps symbols are in truth less promiscuous than some poetic practitioners suggest.

Listener
Stop. Poetry is not dead.

Speaker
Nor is true order. But all signs, and above all the signs of poetry, point towards a grave disturbance.

Listener
We cannot go back to your single-minded symbolic order of the Middle Ages.

Speaker
Clearly not. But from this it does not follow that we

X

must rush forward. The order is neither behind us nor before us. It is, or it is not. The sensible movement is in another dimension.

Listener
I wonder.

Speaker
So do I. Maybe we differ only in degrees of wonder.

Except for quotations from Goethe and Nietzsche, all references are to individually specified works. Where no translator is mentioned, the translations are my own.

In the case of Nietzsche all references are to the *Musarion-Ausgabe* of his works, twenty-three volumes, Munich, 1922, abbreviated M.A.

With so many editions of Goethe in existence, I have tried to enable the reader to look up the context of the quoted passages in any edition available to him, by giving chapter, act, scene or numbered verse of the individual work. Where this method has proved impossible, references are to the *Jubiläums-Ausgabe* of Goethe's works, forty volumes, Stuttgart and Berlin, abbreviated J.A., or the large *Grossherzogin Sophie von Sachsen-Ausgabe*, four sections, Weimar, 1887, abbreviated W.A. Poems are quoted from Goethe's *Gedichte in zeitlicher*

Folge, two volumes, Leipzig, 1920, abbreviated P. For the sake of the particular accuracy demanded by the context 1 have avoided English verse renderings of Goethe's poetry. Letters and conversations are specified, either in the text itself or in the following notes, only by their dates. The same applies to letters of Nietzsche and Burckhardt, and to letters or diary notes of Franz Kafka.

The biographical and critical literature on the subjects of these essays is so vast that even a selective bibliography would almost fill a volume of its own. Apologies are offered for the unavoidable omission.

GOETHE AND THE IDEA OF SCIENTIFIC TRUTH

[1] J.A., XXX, 18–31, 388–92.
[2] J.A., XXVI, 314–15.
[3] J.A., XXVII, 5.
[4] P., II, 224.
[5] *Goethes Schriften zur Naturwissenschaft*, Berlin, 1926, I, xxxviii–ix (Introduction by Richard Müller-Freienfeld).
[6] J.A., XXXIX, 294–5.
[7] *Goethes Schriften zur Naturwissenschaft*, I, xl.
[8] J.A., XXXIX, 312–13.
[9] Ibid., 251.
[10] Ibid., 249–50.
[11] Ibid., 131.
[12] Conversation with Kielmayer, September, 1797.
[13] P., II, 56.
[14] Ibid., 381.
[15] J.A., XXXIX, 374.
[16] Ibid., 81.
[17] Ibid., 64.
[18] Ibid., 64.
[19] J.A., XL, 61.
[20] Ibid., 63.
[21] J.A., XXXIX, 72.
[22] J.A., XL, 200.
[23] Ibid., 202.
[24] W.A., 3, VI, 59.
[25] J.A., XXXIX, 106.

[26] Ibid., 34.
[27] J.A., IV, 242.
[28] J.A., XXXIX, 58.
[29] Ibid., 72.
[30] Ibid., 72.
[31] J.A., XL, 71.
[32] J.A., XXXIX, 70.
[33] J.A., XXXIV, 325.
[34] J.A., IV, 229.
[35] J.A., XXXIX, 35.
[36] Ibid., 68.
[37] Ibid., 76.
[38] *Wandlungen in den Grundlagen der Naturwissenschaft*, Zürich, 1947, 65.
[39] J.A., XXXIX, 374.
[40] J.A., XXXV, 305.

GOETHE AND THE AVOIDANCE OF TRAGEDY

[1] Karl Jaspers, *Unsere Zukunft und Goethe*, Zürich, 1948, 22.
[2] Letter to Schiller, December 9th, 1797.
[3] Act IV, scene 5.
[4] March 17th, 1832.
[5] *Sämtliche Werke*, in six volumes, Berlin, 1923, IV, 124. Translation, with a slight modification of my own in the last line, by J. B. Leishman, *Selected Poems of Friedrich Hölderlin*, London, 1944, 98.
[6] J.A., XXVIII, 251.
[7] Book II, chapter 2, J.A., XIX, 191, 192.
[8] *Faust II*, verses—in the numbering including both parts—11300–3.
[9] *Faust I*, verse 3217.
[10] Ibid., verses 1745–6.
[11] Ibid., verse 1700.
[12] Ibid., verses 3249–50.
[13] Ibid., verse 324.
[14] *Faust II*, verse 11585.
[15] Ibid., verse 11586.
[16] Ibid., verses 11936–7.
[17] To Karl Ernst Schubarth, November 3rd, 1820.

18 *Faust II*, verses 11404–07.
19 To Frau von Stein, March 8th, 1808.

BURCKHARDT AND NIETZSCHE

1 *Jakob Burckhardt-Gesamtausgabe*, Stuttgart, Berlin und Leipzig, 1930, V, 21, 22.
2 Burckhardt's letter to Riggenbach, August 28th, 1838.
3 *Gesamtausgabe*, VIII, 3.
4 Ibid., V, 215.
5 Ibid., VII, 14.
6 Ibid., VII, 15, 16.
7 Ibid., VII, 15.
8 *Maximen und Reflexionen*, J.A., XXXVIII, 261.
9 Burckhardt's letter to Willibald Beyschlag, June 14th, 1842.
10 *Gesamtausgabe*, VIII, 5.
11 Ibid., VII, 52.
12 Ibid., VII, 2.
13 Ibid., VII, 1.
14 Ibid.
15 Ibid., VII, 2.
16 Nietzsche's letter to Gersdorff, November 7th, 1870.
17 Schopenhauer, *Sämmtliche Werke*, Grossherzog Wilhelm Ernst Ausgabe, Leipzig, II, 1217–19.
18 *Gesamtausgabe*, VII, 3.
19 Ibid.
20 M.A., III, 138.
21 Nietzsche's letter to Gersdorff, November 7th, 1870.
22 Burckhardt's letter to Schauenburg, March 5th, 1846.
23 *Gesamtausgabe*, VII, 28.
24 M.A., VII, 369.
25 M.A., XV, 245, 246.
26 Nietzsche's letter to Burckhardt, January 6th, 1889, first published in Edgar Salin, *Jakob Burckhardt und Nietzsche*, Basle, 1938, 227.
27 Ibid., 226.
28 *Gesamtausgabe*, VII, 6, 7.
29 Ibid., 202.
30 Burckhardt's letter to Preen, June 16th, 1888.
31 Burckhardt's letter to Alioth, November 19th, 1881.

[32] Burckhardt's letter to Riggenbach, December 12th, 1838.
[33] Burckhardt's letter to Brenner, March 16th, 1856.
[34] *Gesamtausgabe*, VII, 126.
[35] H. Gelzer, *Ausgewählte kleine Schriften*, Leipzig, 1907, 325.

NIETZSCHE AND GOETHE

[1] J.A., XXXVII, 102–05.
[2] M.A., VII, 204.
[3] M.A., XVII, 364.
[4] *Wilhelm Meisters Wanderjahre*, Book I, chapter 6, J.A., XIX, 72.
[5] Ibid., chapter 10, J.A., XIX, 132.
[6] Ibid., 146.
[7] *Faust II*, verses 11127–42.
[8] March 17th, 1832.
[9] J.A., XXXVII, 104.
[10] J.A., V, 247, 248.
[11] M.A., XIX, 85.
[12] *Wilhelm Meisters Wanderjahre*, Book I, chapter 10, J.A., XIX, 138, 139.
[13] M.A., XVI, 235.
[14] M.A., XVII, 149, 150.
[15] J.A., XXXVIII, 266.
[16] Ibid.
[17] J.A., IV, 219.
[18] *Wilhelm Meisters Wanderjahre*, Book III, chapter 13, J.A., XX, 187.
[19] M.A., XVII, 48.
[20] M.A., VII, 207.
[21] Ibid., 349.
[22] J.A., XXVII, 175.
[23] P., II, 20.
[24] Ibid., 39.
[25] M.A., III, 365.
[26] M.A., XVI, 8.
[27] M.A., XVII, 150.
[28] *Faust II*, verses 11600–03.
[29] Ibid., verses 7438–9.
[30] Ibid., verses 11404–7.

[31] P., II, 66.
[32] M.A., XVII, 344.
[33] M.A., IX, 174, 175.
[34] M.A., XIV, 109.
[35] M.A., XXI, 73.
[36] M.A., IX, 55, 56.
[37] Ibid., 245.
[38] M.A., III, 247.
[39] M.A., IX, 448.
[40] Ibid., 252.
[41] M.A., XXI, 81.
[42] Ibid.
[43] M.A., XVIII, 65.
[44] M.A., XIV, 11.
[45] *Faust II*, verses 6222–7, 6246–8.
[46] M.A., XVII, 346.
[47] M.A., XIX, 352.

RILKE AND NIETZSCHE
WITH A DISCOURSE ON THOUGHT,
BELIEF AND POETRY

[1] T. S. Eliot, *Selected Essays* (1917–32), London, 1948, 141.
[2] Ibid., 135.
[3] Ibid., 13.
[4] Ibid., 137.
[5] Ibid., 138.
[6] First published in a Berlin literary journal and reprinted in *Erzählungen und Skizzen aus der Frühzeit*, Leipzig, 1930, 347–56.
[7] *Ewald Tragy*, Munich, 1929–30.
[8] Unpublished, but partly quoted in Ruth Mövius, *Rainer Maria Rilkes Stundenbuch*, Entstehung und Gehalt, Leipzig, 1937, and in M. Sievers, *Die biblischen Motive in der Dichtung Rainer Maria Rilkes*, Berlin, 1938.
[9] Lou Andreas-Salomé, *Friedrich Nietzsche in seinen Werken*, Wien, 1894.
[10] *Das Florenzer Tagebuch*, published together with other diaries in *Tagebücher aus der Frühzeit*, Leipzig, 1942.

[11] *Ausgewählte Werke*, Leipzig, 1938, I, 14.

[12] Ibid., 17.

[13] M.A., XX, 158.

[14] Letter to Malwida von Meysenbug, January 14th, 1880.

[15] *Tagebücher aus der Frühzeit*, 92.

[16] M.A., XXI, 248.

[17] M.A., XIX, 359–365. Cf. also Nietzsche on the Dionysian Goethe, M.A., XVII, 149, 150.

[18] Letter to Ellen Key, quoted in Paul Zech, *Rainer Maria Rilke: Der Mensch und das Werk*, Dresden, 1930, 118, 119.

[19] *Tagebücher aus der Frühzeit*, 38.

[20] Cf. Rilke, *Sonnets to Orpheus*, 1, III, and Nietzsche, M.A., XII, 156, 157; XIX, 228.

[21] M.A., XIII, 237.

[22] *Tagebücher aus der Frühzeit*, 89.

[23] M.A., XX, 248.

[24] *Ausgewählte Werke*, I, 176.

[25] M.A., XX, 152.

[26] *Ausgewählte Werke*, I, 143.

[27] M.A., XXI, 251.

[28] *Briefe*, Wiesbaden, 1950, II, 308–11.

[29] Ibid., 382, 407.

[30] *Selected Essays*, 135.

[31] Ibid., 134.

[32] Ibid., 135 (my italics).

[33] Hegel, *Werke*, Berlin, 1835, X_3, 243, and X_1, 16.

[34] *Rainer Maria Rilke*, Cambridge, 1952.

[35] *Briefe*, II, 395.

[36] *Ausgewählte Werke*, II, 297.

[37] M.A., XIV, 80.

[38] M.A., XII, 157.

[39] *Briefe*, II, 480.

[40] M.A., XIV, 234.

[41] *Briefe*, II, 405.

[42] *Tagebücher aus der Frühzeit*, 71.

[43] M.A., XIV, 121, 125.

[44] M.A., XIV, 187.

[45] Ibid., 191, 180.

[46] Cf. J. F. Angelloz, *Rainer Maria Rilke*, Paris, 1936, 3.

[47] M.A., XIII, 97, 101.

48 *Ausgewählte Werke*, I, 364, 365.
49 *Briefwechsel in Gedichten mit Erika Mitterer*, Wiesbaden, 1950, 56.
50 M.A., XIV, 119.
51 *Briefe*, II, 481–3.
52 M.A., XIV, 121.
53 M.A., XI, 79.
54 *Ideen* 13, Athenäum III, Berlin, 1800.
55 *Werke*, ed. Kluckhohn, III, 357.
56 M.A., XIII, 166.
57 M.A., XX, 190.
58 M.A., XIV, 326, 327.
59 M.A.,XIX, 229.
60 Ibid., 228.
61 M.A., III, 10.

OSWALD SPENGLER AND THE PREDICAMENT OF THE HISTORICAL IMAGINATION

1 First volume: *Der Untergang des Abendlandes—Gestalt und Wirklichkeit*, Munich, 1918. Second volume: *Der Untergang des Abendlandes—Welthistorische Perspektiven*, Munich, 1922. Authorized English translation by Charles Francis Atkinson: *The Decline of the West*, London, first volume: *Form and Actuality*; second volume: *Perspectives of World-History*. My references are to the English edition to which I am also indebted for the—sometimes modified—translations.
2 I, 37.
3 I, 44.
4 I, 293.
5 I, 41.
6 I, 25.
7 Arnold Toynbee, *Civilization on Trial*, Oxford, 1948, 10.
8 I, 8–10.
9 *Civilization on Trial*, 9–10.
10 I, 29.
11 E. H. Carr, *The New Society*, London, 1951, 19.
12 I, 35.
13 I, 47.
14 Cf. I, 23.

THE WORLD OF FRANZ KAFKA

[1] Franz Kafka, *Gesammelte Schriften*, edited by Max Brod, Prague, 1937, VI, 108. The definitive edition of Kafka's works (S. Fischer Verlag, Frankfurt am Main) is now available in English translation. However, the confused state of Kafka editions prevailing at the time of the original publication of my book is still reflected in my references. Even when I refer to English translations, I frequently have had to modify the English text, partly for the sake of greater accuracy and partly for the sake of the particular emphasis required in the context of my discussion. Where my references are to the original, the translations are my own.

[2] *The Great Wall of China*, translated by Willa and Edwin Muir, London, 1946, 151.

[3] Ibid., 140.

[4] *Gesammelte Schriften*, VI, 237.

[5] *The Great Wall of China*, 145.

[6] *The Castle*, translated by Willa and Edwin Muir, London, 1947, 6.

[7] *Gesammelte Schriften*, VI, 231.

[8] M.A., XIV, 179.

[9] Ibid., XIV, 187.

[10] Ibid., XVIII, 45.

[11] *Gesammelte Schriften*, VI, 108.

[12] *The Great Wall of China*, 129.

[13] M.A., XIV, 80.

[14] J.A., XXXVIII, 266.

[15] Ibid., 132.

[16] *The Castle*, 79.

[17] Ibid., 38.

[18] Ibid., 95.

[19] Ibid., 150.

[20] *The Great Wall of China*, 136.

[21] Ibid., 133.

[22] Ibid., 145.

[23] Ibid., 135.

[24] *The Castle*, 98.

[25] Ibid., 316, in Max Brod's 'Additional Note'.

[26] Ibid., 317.

[27] *Gesammelte Schriften*, IV, 380, 381.
[28] *The Castle*, 269.
[29] Ibid., 21.
[30] Ibid., 317.
[31] Ibid., 15.
[32] Ibid., 132, 133.
[33] Quoted by Max Brod as motto to *Franz Kafka*, A Biography, translated by G. Humphreys Roberts, London, 1947.
[34] *The Great Wall of China*, 157.
[35] Ibid., 149.
[36] *Gesammelte Schriften*, IV, 353.
[37] Ibid., 355.
[38] Ibid., 300.
[39] Ibid., 308, 309.
[40] *The Great Wall of China*, 146.
[41] *Gesammelte Schriften*, IV, 428.
[42] M.A., XV, 393.